PRENTICE-HALL

Foundations of Economic Geography Series
NORTON GINSBURG, Editor

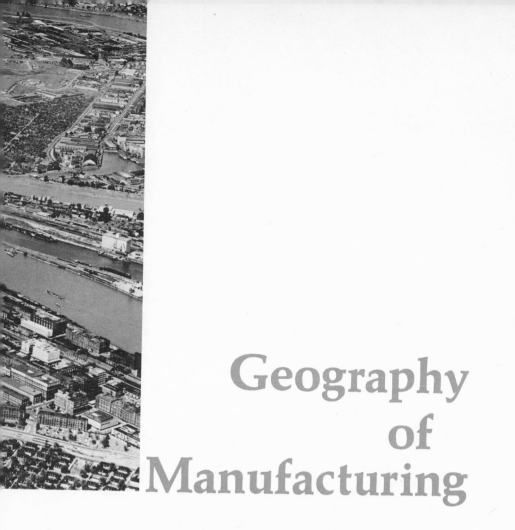

Geography
of
Manufacturing

GUNNAR ALEXANDERSSON

Professor of International Economic Geography

The Stockholm School of Economics

PRENTICE-HALL, INC., Englewood Cliffs, N.J.

Library of Congress Catalog Card No.: 67-13356
Maps and diagrams drawn by Birgit Nordqvist.

Frontispiece: Main plant of BASF in Ludwigshafen. In its 1,500 units, more than 47,000 people work, 8,800 of them in research, exclusively.

Current printing (last number):
10 9 8 7 6 5 4 3 2 1

PRENTICE-HALL INTERNATIONAL, INC., London
PRENTICE-HALL OF AUSTRALIA, PTY. LTD., Sydney
PRENTICE-HALL OF CANADA, LTD., Toronto
PRENTICE-HALL OF INDIA PRIVATE LTD., New Delhi
PRENTICE-HALL OF JAPAN, INC., Tokyo

Foundations of Economic Geography Series

Among the various fields of geography, economic geography, perhaps more than any other, has experienced remarkable changes within the past twenty years—so many that it is almost impossible for one scholar to command all aspects of it. The result has been increasing specialization on the one hand and, on the other, a fundamental need for bringing the fruits of that specialization to students of economic geography.

The *Foundations of Economic Geography Series* consists of several volumes, each focusing on a major problem in economic geography. It is designed to bring the student, whether novice or more experienced, to the frontiers of knowledge in economic geography, and in so doing, forcefully to demonstrate the methodological implications of current research —but at a level comprehensible even to those just becoming aware of the fascinating problems in the field as it is developing today.

Each volume stands as a contribution to understanding in its own right, but the series as a whole is intended to provide a broad cross-section of on-going research in economic geography, stemming from concern with a variety of problems. On the other hand, the series should not be regarded as a complete synthesis of work in economic geography, although the volumes explore in depth certain major issues of keenest interest to economic geographers and others in related fields to a degree impossible in textbooks that attempt to cover the entire field. At the same time, the student is brought face-to-face with the kinds of intellectual and conceptual problems that characterize economic geography in a way that no over-all survey can accomplish. Each volume thus provides a basis for an intensive exploration of issues that constitute the cutting edge of research in this most dynamic and demanding field of knowledge.

As time goes on and new volumes appear in the series, the original volumes will be modified in keeping with new developments and orientations, not only in economic geography, but in the field of geography as a whole. The first volume to appear in the series, Wilbur Zelinsky's *A Prologue to Population Geography,* acts as a bridge between economic and cultural geography and as a means for exploring ideas and methods concerning a problem of increasing interest to geographers and social scientists alike: the growth, diffusion, and distribution of populations throughout the world. Other volumes in the series, whether concerned with trade, retail activities, manufacturing, transportation, or water resources, have similar "bridging" qualities that transcend the narrow limitations of ordinary descriptive handbooks. All are concerned with the new and the fresh, and with the transformation of a traditional field of scholarly interest to one that is highly innovative and pioneering.

NORTON GINSBURG

Contents

introduction

The geography of manufacturing may become one of the most controversial topics on the international scene in the next few decades. Standards of living among the 3.3 billion people on earth vary strikingly. The 10 per cent with the highest income—Anglo-America, northwestern Europe, Australia, and New Zealand—account for some three-fifths of the factory capacity of the world. If the rich group is widened to include such countries as Japan, the Soviet Union, and Italy, it can be estimated that one-fourth of the people on earth account for some 90 per cent of the world's manufacturing capacity.

Such imbalances are politically impossible within a country, and are probably also impossible in the world community. Obviously the poor countries cannot raise their standards of living just by producing agricultural and mineral products for export to the rich nations. They must also undergo the Industrial Revolution which has changed so profoundly conditions of life in the wealthier nations.

Sören Kierkegaard once said that life can only be understood backwards, but it must be lived forwards. The geographer as a scientist can best describe, analyze, and interpret the present distributions and their roots and changes in the past; he must leave to the politician and the businessman the job of finding the course ahead. But a thorough understanding of the past and the present, as interpreted by the social scientist, will provide a basis for educated guesses, predictions, or projections about the future.

The problems connected with the vast changes that can now be foreseen in manufacturing distributions on the global and national scenes are a matter of importance not only for the small group of people classified as professional economists, geographers, businessmen, or politicians; they are of direct concern to the man in the street. A factory worker in a wealthy nation may be retrained for new jobs several times in his active life span, and move from a stagnating town to one with rapid growth industries; as a citizen he may have to face the demand from less fortunate countries that the tariff behind which his factory works be lowered to allow industries in the poor countries to enter the market.

Global economic thinking will be required as modern technology shrinks all distances. The poorer nations will study carefully the organization and distribution patterns of manufacturing industries in the rich nations before embarking on their own industrialization. And the student in the fortunate nation will study the manufacturing industries because more than any other single factor they have changed conditions of life in the last century and a half. Manufacturing is chiefly responsible for the urbanization which has become a hallmark of the industrialized nation.

A detailed treatment in this book of some general problems, some manufacturing industries, and some manufacturing regions to the exclusion of others is intentional; within the compass of a small volume only representative samples can be served. The American Geographical Society's *Current Geographical Publications* and other bibliographies will help orient the interested student to the many publications on the geography of manufacturing.

CHAPTER 1   *world manufacturing*
and economic geography

The Nature of Manufacturing

When man in early Pleistocene, some 1.8 million years ago, constructed a simple cutting tool by chipping a stone, it was a momentous
event; anthropologists were provided with a basis for defining man, and
the first simple form of manufacturing had taken place.[1] After that, man
devoted much of his time to the manufacturing of tools, clothing, food,
and shelter, but chiefly within the framework of family or village, *usufacture*. The Industrial Revolution, starting in England in the second half
of the eighteenth century, made possible a large-scale division of labor.
It was no longer necessary for more than 80 per cent of the population
in an area to devote its main attention to farming. The Industrial Revolution, which soon had secondary centers in the Low Countries, France,
West Germany, Bohemia, and New England, was also a scientific revolution, with its roots in the Enlightenment. The last two centuries, a short
span of human history, have seen an ever-increasing accumulation of
knowledge.[2] The long step from early man's chipping of a simple cutting
tool to the first steam engine was accomplished in 18,000 centuries. The
other long step, from the first steam engine to the first space missile, was
taken in two centuries.[3] In these 200 years the word manufacturing has
lost its original meaning—to transform material into useful things by
hand—and now implies that this process is effected by machinery.

In some of the most economically advanced countries less than 10 per
cent of the gainfully employed population is now engaged in farming and
ancillary industries, and still these countries may produce farm surpluses,
a great change from the beginning of the Industrial Revolution. But only

---

[1] L. B. S. Leakey, *Olduvai Gorge* (London: Cambridge Univ., 1965).

[2] They have also seen an ever-increasing accumulation of people on earth, from
approximately 660 million in 1750 to 3,000 million in 1960. Population is growing at
an increasing rate and is projected at more than 6 billion by the year 2000.

[3] The expansion of science is often illustrated by the statement that an estimated
90 per cent of the scientists that have lived on earth are still alive.

a few nations qualify as economically advanced. Ranked by percentage engaged in agriculture, the nations arrange themselves in a continuum from the "preindustrial" more than 80 per cent to the present less than 10 per cent in the United States and Great Britain.

Mechanization and new sources of power were the chief characteristics of the Industrial Revolution, but mechanization does not set manufacturing apart from other industries in the modern world. A modern farmer, fisherman, or lumberman is just as much a machine-operator as any factory worker. On a dairy farm, cows move freely in the barn, feed is transported to them mechanically, and the manure flows under the floor to large containers. At milking time the farmer attaches the cow to a pumping system which pumps the milk to a tank, later emptied by a tank-truck from the dairy. The main job of the farmer is to supervise the smooth functioning of the physical plant; one man can now do the job performed by a dozen 50 years ago.

A major geographic difference between farming and manufacturing lies in their different distribution patterns. Farming is a surface-demanding economic system and farmers are scattered over the land, on farmsteads or in villages, whereas manufacturing requires much less land per employee and tends to concentrate in towns and cities.[4] The shift from farming to manufacturing and other urban industries—now almost completed in the economically advanced countries—has meant relocation of people from rural to urban residence. Farm hands have sought employment in town, some perhaps in a factory manufacturing farm machinery, in which substantial work is devoted to the elaboration of systems for simplifying work on the farm. The dairy farmer does not buy a given number of feet of plastic tubes, but rather a system for transporting milk from cow to tank and eventually to the dairy, a system for carrying feed to his cows, and a system for collecting manure. Employees of the farm machine factory engaged in devising systems to solve the farmer's problems are not really employed by manufacturing in the old sense. They produce ideas, but they do not transform substances into useful things. To an even larger degree this holds true of people engaged in a space program. The ultimate goal of their efforts is hardware that can be sent into space, but only a fraction of total time and cost is spent on manufacturing this hardware.

The complex manufacturing industry of today is quite different from the infant industry of one hundred years ago. There are now international corporations more global in interests than either the Catholic Church or the British Empire at the height of their influence. The range of products is enormous, and designs change rapidly. Many products are ephemeral visitors on the market; others, which have existed for 50 or 100 years, may have only the name and general principles in common with their predecessors. Most pre-World War I industry used much more raw material per ton of product, and the products themselves were bulky. A

---

[4] The amount of space required per employee varies from industry to industry, from country to country, and from time to time. In Lyon, France, chemistry requires most (165 m²), printing and clothing least (18 and 13 m²). Factories vary from anonymous buildings or apartments within buildings to the complex technical landscape of a large oil refinery or petrochemical plant. See M. Laferrère, *Lyon, ville industrielle* (Paris: Presses Univ., 1960).

ship, a railroad car, or a truck weighed much more in relation to its ton-mile per hour transport capacity. The infant industry was served by a transportation system which, by present standards, had low efficiency and high costs.[5]

Increased efficiency in transportation has been striking in the period after World War II. Mammoth tankers, bulk carriers, containers that simplify transfer among sea, road, and rail transport, diesel-electric trains, larger and more economic trucks, faster roads, and air freight are some key words in this development. Transport costs are now a small percentage of the price paid by the consumer for most products. In recent years Japanese steelworks, importing iron ore from Brazil and other distant sources, and coking coal and scrap from the American east coast, have successfully competed on the European and American markets for certain types of steel, epitomizing a situation drastically different from the interwar period. But transportation costs have not lost their importance completely. Small differences may, in some industries, spell the difference between success and failure.

In many industries the uninterrupted, smooth flow of raw materials to the parts and component factories and of parts and components to the assembly plants may be a more important consideration than small freight-cost differences. Producers of automobiles and other consumer durables have cut inventory costs substantially since the 1920's and 1930's. Assembly plants operate with only a few hours supply of parts and components. Construction firms that build apartment houses with prefabricated concrete elements (walls and floor slabs) have no inventories at all at the construction site, but hoist the heavy elements directly from the truck to the designated places in the building. In such cases, interruptions in the flow of parts may lead to heavy losses if production comes to a standstill. This organization of production has geographic implications on the regional scale. In metropolitan areas lacking circumferential freeways, it is essential that the component or element factory is located in the right direction from the suburban assembly plant or construction site to avoid downtown traffic jams and other unpredictable situations.

Manufacturing Geography

Modern manufacturing is the creation of scientific man, and science in its various forms is the basis for industrial progress. Two scientific disciplines have made the manufacturing industry their object of study:

[5] Much early theoretical work on industrial location was based on these premises. Transport costs were emphasized, although the vital distinction between terminal costs and line-haul costs was not always made. These works now have an indirect, though significant, interest. They help us understand how industrial regions which are now obsolete first developed. They would not have developed in a new continent settled by people with our present knowledge and techniques. Such regions may now be economically depressed areas, or they may have successfully adapted themselves to changed circumstances; historic geography provides a key to a deeper understanding of their existence.

For a critical discussion of pioneer works in the theory of industrial location (by Alfred Weber, Bertil Ohlin, Tord Palander, August Lösch, and others), see Edgar M. Hoover, *The Location of Economic Activity* (New York: McGraw-Hill, 1948), Melvin L. Greenhut, *Plant Location in Theory and Practice* (Chapel Hill: Univ. of North Carolina, 1956), Walter Isard, *Location and Space-Economy* (New York: Wiley, 1956), and W. Isard, *Methods of Regional Analysis* (New York: Wiley, 1960).

descriptive or empirical economics, and economic geography. The former describes and analyzes the economic characteristics of manufacturing,[6] while the latter describes and interprets its geographic distribution. To understand economic characteristics, the economist cannot neglect distribution patterns, and the geographer must take economic characteristics into account when interpreting his maps of industrial locations. The difference between the two approaches is in part a matter of emphasis.[7]

Geography of manufacturing is concerned with the interpretation of present distribution patterns, global, continental, national, regional, or urban. Interest is focused on recent and planned changes since they reveal present location tendencies. The geographic approach, using the map as the chief tool of analysis, is eminently suited to this type of study. The mapmaker can manipulate any amount of data, and present them in a way that allows a trained observer to draw important conclusions. The map will also reveal insufficiencies in the data that are not so readily found when they are presented in tables or in mathematical formulas.

For the interpretation of an industry map, the student should know *a*) essentials about the technique of the industry under study, *b*) its economic characteristics (cost structure, marketing situation, labor requirements), and *c*) the historic development of the industry's distribution pattern.

Background knowledge of the last type is provided by economic history and historic geography, and is of paramount importance. A large part of any distribution pattern remains unexplained if reference is made only to present location tendencies. Steel mills oriented to coal fields or iron ore deposits are a case in point. If a new continent were to be settled now by people with a Western market economy, such locations as the Ruhr, the Lorraine, greater Pittsburgh, or Youngstown would hardly be considered. But such obsolete locations account for most of the world's steel capacity. In the past they attracted not only a large industrial capacity, but also a tremendous population, since the original base industries also lured a host of manufacturing and service industries. They formed an *industrial complex*. As a result, these steel mills, originally raw material oriented, are now to a large extent market oriented, thus having a new *raison d'être* in the present distribution of population and manufacturing industry.

[6] See, e.g., E. B. Alderfer and H. E. Michl, *Economics of American Industry*, 3rd ed. (New York: McGraw-Hill, 1957); Walter Adams, *The Structure of American Industry* (New York: Macmillan, 1950); J. G. Glover and W. B. Cornell, *The Development of American Industry*, 3rd ed. (Englewood Cliffs, N.J.: Prentice-Hall, 1951); G. C. Allen, *British Industries and Their Organization* (London: Longmans, Green, 1959); R. C. Estall and R. Ogilvie Buchanan, *Industrial Activity and Economic Geography* (London: Hutchinson, 1961); E. Willard Miller, *A Geography of Manufacturing* (Englewood Cliffs, N.J.: Prentice-Hall, 1962); and Pierre George, *Géographie industrielle du monde*, 6th ed. (Paris: Presses Univ., 1962).

[7] Compare, e.g., studies on manufacturing industries in New York and Pittsburgh made by teams of economists (New York Metropolitan Region Study, Raymond Vernon, Director, nine volumes, Cambridge, 1959, and Economic Study of the Pittsburgh Region, Pittsburgh Regional Planning Association, four volumes, Pittsburgh, 1963) with studies on London by geographer P. G. Hall, *The Industries of London since 1861* (London: Hutchinson, 1962), and *London 2000* (London: Faber, 1963).

This *industrial inertia* is promoted by the economy, in many industries, of adding capacity rather than building new factories. For instance, on the coal and iron ore fields in Western Europe, very few new steel mills have been built since 1914, and in Pittsburgh and Youngstown not one has been built since 1911, but in both regions a considerable expansion of steel capacity has occurred.

Writers who approach locational problems with a Weberian emphasis on transportation costs often refer to those industries for which transfer costs are of little significance as *footloose industries*.[8] The term may sometimes be misleading. A comparison of detailed geographic distribution patterns for so-called footloose industries in different parts of the world will often reveal that locational factors other than transfer costs are at work. A certain pattern may be repeated in many regions. Very few, if any, industries are footloose in the sense that they have a haphazard distribution pattern arrived at by pure chance.

Just as history is about what happened and not what could have happened, geography is primarily concerned with where it happened and not where it might have happened. In the history of inventions it is often found that many people in various parts of the world were simultaneously toying with the same idea when suddenly one of them obtained a patent for his invention ahead of the others. In economic geography we are interested in those inventions that influenced the distribution of man and his economic activities on earth. A student of the history of science will look at this differently. He will be primarily interested in giving credit where it is due, regardless of the practical consequences of the invention.

General Location Factors

Manufacturing industry comprises two main elements, *processing* of raw materials and *assembly* of produced parts. To these may be added a third element, *repair* of manufactured products. Some kinds of repair work, carried out in assembly shops (such as ships and railroad equipment), are generally accepted as manufacturing; others, combined with sales establishments (automobiles, bicycles), are often seen as service production.[9]

An inventory of general location factors will help to illuminate some of the broad principles that influence industrial location decisions. As shown elsewhere, existing distribution patterns are not necessarily the most favorable in terms of present location strategy. Most location theories

---

[8] Alfred Weber, *Über den Standort der Industrien, Erster Teil, Reine Theorie des Standorts* (Tübingen: Mohr, 1909). English translation, *Theory of the Location of Industries* (Chicago: Univ. of Chicago, 1929), with important introduction and notes by Carl J. Friedrich. For more detailed discussion of footloose industries, see Edgar M. Hoover, *The Location of Economic Activity*. For a discussion of *industrial complexes*, see Jean Chardonnet, *Les grands types de complexes industriels* (Paris: Armand Colin, 1953).

[9] The United Nations recommends that all kinds of repair be considered as manufacturing. Many countries, including the United States and Japan, have not accepted this view and do not include automobile repair shops in their manufacturing statistics.

deal with the hypothetical settlement of a new continent by people with our own knowledge and technology, but all actual location decisions must take their departure from existing, centuries-old patterns. In reality, many decisions are made with an eye to moves expected from competing firms, which further complicates the situation.

Assembly costs for raw materials and energy, as well as *labor costs, depreciation,* and *administrative overhead costs,* the chief elements of the *value added by manufacturing,* rank high in most industries. The *economies of scale* are usually substantial, but in industries based on agriculture or forestry they are counteracted by growing assembly costs for raw materials which, as factory size increases, must be hauled longer distances.[10] In all industries the economies of scale are counteracted by increasing *distribution costs,* since there are hardly any industries in which the world market is supplied from one factory. Economies of scale, or internal economies, are directly reflected in the costs of a firm; *external economies,* economies derived from an advantageous milieu, are more subtle, but they govern the location of some manufacturing industries. For instance, the external economies enjoyed by the apparel industry of New York have led to a larger concentration of manufacturing employment than the internal economies enjoyed by the automobile factories of Detroit.

Raw materials exert a decreasing pull on modern industrial plants. The greatest strides in transportation efficiency have been made in the movement of bulk cargo, especially by water. In transportation terms, integrated steel mills and some other heavy industries (such as grain mills or sugar refineries) use bulk-transported raw materials and produce general cargo items. Such industries seek tidewater locations near the market, and many of the large port cities in industrialized areas have made heavy investments to meet the demands of the new trend. Rotterdam, Hamburg, and Dunkerque have become increasingly important centers of heavy manufacturing industry. More and more of the cargo turnover of these ports is accounted for by port industries, and decreasing percentages by transit trade.

If the raw material loses much bulk or weight in the manufacturing process, the factory location may still be tied to the sources of raw materials (sawmills, pulp mills, brickyards, and packing plants). This principle is stressed if the product can be sent in bulk (as, for example, cement). Additional manufacturing processes may be tied to the site of the weight-losing industry by the economies of a *continuous process:* pulp mill—newsprint mill, blast furnace—steel furnace—rolling mill, packing plant—meat canning department, etc. Perishable raw materials, such as sugar beets and sugar cane, vegetables, fruit, milk, and seafood, must be processed near their sources. Many ores (copper ore, bauxite, and, increasingly, iron ore) are beneficiated [11] to stand the cost of shipment

---

[10] In reality, the establishment of a canning factory or a pulp mill will lead to a more intense land use, which helps to keep down the increase in average haul of raw materials. This modifies but does not change the general proposition.

[11] *Beneficiation* means any treatment by which raw materials, ore, coke, and limestone are rendered more effective for use in the blast furnace or smelter, and includes improvement in physical form and properties as well as enrichment.

to market-oriented smelters or refineries. This involves some processing near the mine. Iron ore of some 35 per cent iron content is now mined in Labrador for European steelworks; the ore is beneficiated to over 60 per cent iron content at the mines.

Conversely, if a product gains in bulk or weight, production will be located near the market. The soft drink bottling plant is the classical example; assembly plants fall within the same category. It is cheaper to send automobiles, for example, in knocked-down form to be assembled in the market area if the sales volume warrants an assembly plant.

Energy was almost immovable in the early phase of the Industrial Revolution, so plants had to be built where water power, charcoal, or coal was available. More than any other single factor the availability of energy moulded the urban population distribution of our time by creating urban nuclei, the crystallization points of so many present-day towns. When direct water power was used, factories were strung along rivers and creeks. If they used charcoal, they were scattered along streams in the forests. With the perfection of the steam engine, new factories were built on or near the coal fields, or in port cities where water-transported coal was available. The advent of electricity gradually freed manufacturing from these bonds, but the story was repeated in the early days of hydroelectric power generation before World War I. Power could not be transmitted long distances, and the first electro-metallurgical or electro-chemical plants were built right at the power stations, even if these happened to be in the interior of a Norwegian fiord or mountain valley (Odda, Rjukan). The factories may still operate, supporting a small and isolated town, and epitomizing the difficulties a modern industrial firm finds in leaving a community built at a time when this was the most rational location for a factory.[12] The premises for industrial location may change rapidly, but investment inertia acts as a conserving factor.

Energy is becoming almost universally accessible in industrial nations; cost differentials are shrinking as electricity is transmitted at higher voltages and electric power grids are hooked on to each other on a continental scale. Price differences for petroleum products and natural gas in the ports are small, and the cost of transport inland is relatively low. Coal is losing most of its markets, with the exception of thermoelectric power stations and metallurgical uses. In most manufacturing industries, regional differences in energy cost are now of little importance as a locational factor. But a few heavy consumers of energy, like aluminum refining, find a location near the source of supply still advantageous, as a substantial part of the delivered price of energy in the large market areas is made up of transport cost.

Labor has always been mobile as compared with raw materials and energy. From the beginning of the Industrial Revolution people have been lured off the land by better job opportunities in town. The starting date of the Industrial Revolution in an area can often be fixed at the point where the population curves of local towns start upward. These

[12] Jens Christian Hansen, "Notodden," *Norsk Geografisk Tidsskrift*, Vol. 19 (1963-1964), 273-90.

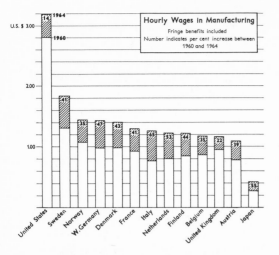

Total wages per working hour, including fringe benefits, for workers in manufacturing, mining, and construction in selected countries, 1960 and 1964. (From Swedish Employers' Confederation, Bureau of Statistics, Direct and Total Wage Costs for Workers: International Survey 1957-1964, Stockholm, 1964.)

migrations have taken millions of people to other continents, across continents, to neighboring countries or states, to metropolitan cities, but most often to one of the nearest towns. The large postwar migration of industrial workers from Mediterranean Europe to Switzerland, France, West Germany, Benelux, Britain, and Sweden is just one example of international labor migrations.

The skills, traditions, and external economies developed in an industrial region are a major factor behind the *industrial inertia* that keeps an industry in an area long after the locational premises have changed. Some of the originally coal field-oriented industrial regions have retained a reasonably favorable growth rate, but now with a large labor pool and local entrepreneurs as their chief locational asset. Many manufacturing towns have changed their industrial structure completely in the process.

Wage differences between nations and regions and between metropolitan cities and small towns are a major locational factor, especially in the production of some labor-intensive products or products in which labor cost makes up a large part of the value added.[13] It should be noted that low wages are by no means synonymous with low labor costs. Low efficiency often counteracts low wages and makes labor costs high. The cotton and furniture industries of the Southern Piedmont region had to concentrate on coarser and cheaper products to overcome the disadvantage of an unskilled labor force in competition with established industries of the North. Both industries, after some decades, produced a full range of products; they offer the best examples of a wholesale migration of an industry from a high-wage to a low-wage region. New industries in underdeveloped countries often hire foremen and skilled workers from the industrial nations to train local workers. In the initial

[13] Some labor-intensive industries are tied to metropolitan cities in spite of their high wages. Examples are ancillary branches of the printing and publishing industry (bookbinding, typesetting, engraving, electrotyping) and luxury industries (processing of fur goods, jewelry, *haute couture,* pharmaceutical preparations). Allan Pred, "The Concentration of High-value-added Manufacturing," *Economic Geography,* Vol. 41 (April 1965), 108-32.

period these firms will have high labor costs. The postwar expansion of labor-intensive production in Japan, Hong Kong, Taiwan, and Singapore represents an international migration of industry to low-wage countries.[14]

Generally, wages are lower in small towns than in metropolitan cities. But land is cheaper in the small town, which means lower housing costs, recreation may be more accessible and less costly, air pollution is a less serious problem, journey-to-work costs are lower, and retail trade prices are usually somewhat lower. Many manufacturing employees find life in a small town more satisfactory in spite of the wage differential, which is only one factor to consider. Metropolitan *diseconomies*, reflected in high money wages, land values, rents, and training costs,[15] prevent all manufacturing firms from being concentrated in one enormous city.

Countries with a *full employment* policy encourage the transfer of employees from low-wage industries to high-wage industries to achieve a higher growth rate. The transfer, often involving a change in residence, is facilitated by an efficient labor exchange, retraining courses, and subsidized movement. But older citizens often hesitate to move from a region with low and declining real estate values to one with high and rising values. A fresh start may mean a lowering of their standard of living, in spite of much higher wage levels. In addition, it means a break of social ties which they are not willing to accept. Many large manufacturing firms have found it easier to recruit labor by establishing a branch plant in such regions.

Capital has a greater influence on location decisions than is generally realized. It can be discussed under two headings, *money capital* and *physical capital*, or the forms under which capital appears before and after implementation of the investment decision.

Physical capital, such as factories, machinery, and homes, is not easily movable. Factories evacuated by declining industries or by temporary war-time establishments have often attracted new industrial firms, which benefit not only from cheap factory space but also from a local labor pool tied primarily by investment in homes. Among numerous examples are Japanese raw silk factories, which after the war were taken over by camera factories and other industries.

Physical capital is a major factor of *industrial inertia*. Seldom are steel mills or chemical plants closed simply because it has become obvious that another location would be better; as a rule, the facilities in which heavy investments already have been made are modernized and expanded in the old location. A multi-mill firm may adjust itself to changed circumstances by expanding the favorably located mills more than the others, but

[14] Migration in this sense does not imply a physical movement of plants from high-wage countries to low-wage countries but simply a more rapid expansion in the latter areas and changed trade patterns. The migration of the cotton industry from Lancashire to Egypt and India simply means that Egypt and India gradually built their own industry and made themselves independent of cotton goods from Lancashire. The migration of the cotton industry from New England to the Southern Piedmont was to a large extent of the same kind, although some firms actually transferred their operations from the former to the latter area.

[15] Metropolitan employees are more mobile than small-town employees; more people have to be accepted for expensive on-the-job training in the big city to provide a given number of new employees.

it usually does not close any mills except in times when a changed technology requires a concentration to fewer plants. As long as some depreciation can be made on the fixed capital of a mill the firm is better off in not closing; scrap value may be negative or at least very low.

Money capital is quite mobile, but the history of manufacturing shows local bankers and investors to have played an important role in the first critical period of new firms. Money made in one industry has often been invested in another; shipping in New England and coffee in São Paulo provided much of the early capital invested in the cotton industry of the two regions. The industrial growth climate, difficult to define and measure, has varied considerably from town to town in the same country, indicating a far from perfect mobility of money capital.

Investments abroad may involve greater risks, especially in underdeveloped countries with unstable political conditions, but they may also be quite attractive, as evidenced by heavy investments in European branch plants by American manufacturing corporations in recent years. Foreign affiliates of U.S. manufacturing concerns reported sales of $42 billion in 1965, of which 44 per cent was in Europe and 32 per cent in Canada. The postwar creation of large market areas in Western Europe is shaping large "domestic markets" for European manufacturing firms similar to those enjoyed by American corporations. Many American, European, and Japanese manufacturing firms are following the example of the big oil companies and putting their eggs into many baskets; business recession in the United States may see normal business in Europe or Japan, and vice versa. Most of the foreign investments made by private capital of developed countries are made in other developed countries; only a trickle goes to the underdeveloped world. Such investments have made an important contribution to the economic growth on both sides of the Atlantic and in Japan; they are an efficient vehicle for the spread of scientific and technical innovations.

The developed countries normally save enough to maintain an adequate rate of investment and economic growth, but the level of saving in the poor countries is, by definition, low. Some 50 to 80 per cent of the population barely eke out a living in subsistence farming and ancillary activities.

Manufacturing and the City Region

The typical factories in the early stages of the Industrial Revolution were multistoried structures near the center of town. Multistoried buildings were rational when the machines received power from a central power source, first from direct water-power and later from a steam engine. Manufacturing, the chief city-forming industry, created a multitude of mill towns and helped other urban centers inflate their population. Workers at first lived within walking distance; later, trains and streetcars extended the possible residential areas. Public transport converged on the center of the city and made it even more advantageous as a location for factories.

The early mill towns were strung along rivers. Small waterfalls could be harnessed directly, but larger falls, like those at Paterson (1790's) on the Passaic River, and Lowell (1823), Manchester (1838), and Lawrence (1848) on the Merrimack River (dates indicate the first large-scale power developments) required ingenious engineering works. At Paterson, now a manufacturing suburb of New York and a leading cotton center of the United States in the 1830's, a series of cotton mills received power through three raceways providing a total of 2,400 horsepower. The multistoried brick buildings at the Great Falls, the old industrial area of Paterson, are still being used; silk followed cotton from 1860 to 1930, and since then the buildings have been used by a multitude of manufacturing firms. The raceways can still be seen outside the factory buildings. One of them, the Bull Mill, was built in the late eighteenth century in anticipation of the raceway, and for some time oxen working a treadmill were used as a source of power.[16]

The towns that grew around the waterfalls on the Merrimack, the Connecticut, the Susquehanna, the Miami, the Fox, the Rock, and many other rivers in the American Manufacturing Belt fill an important place in the present urban pattern. When seen from a plane, huge, multistoried factories, now often used for purposes other than those of a century ago, line the river adjacent to the downtown area in the nucleus of the present sprawling city.

Gradually, direct water power got more competition from steam engines, and coal fields, rivers touching on coal fields, and seaports became favored locations. But only electricity made the manufacturing industry "footloose" in a wider sense. Electricity also helped make most manufacturing industries "footloose" within the city itself. Wide acceptance of the private car and the rapid decline in public transport in American cities helped push this development.

The general switch to the electric motor in factories after World War I gave each machine, each tool, its own source of power. Multistoried buildings on a waterfall or over a steam engine were no longer necessary. Single storied buildings permitted a more rational plant layout; horizontal transport of raw materials and parts by cranes and rails at ceiling level and by conveyor belts and fork-lift trucks on the floor is more economic than vertical transport. The new trend was clearly seen in the United States in the new cotton factories built in the South in the 1920's and 1930's. The migration of the cotton industry was not only a movement away from a high labor-cost area to a low labor-cost area, but also from crowded, multistoried buildings with old machinery to efficient one-story buildings and new machinery.

The new trend has been in evidence in the postwar period even in the old manufacturing regions. Smoke, grime, ugly buildings, and other nuisances associated with industrial districts in the early decades of the Industrial Revolution are no longer part of manufacturing areas housing engineering works, textile mills, and other light manufacturing industries, which employ most of the labor force engaged in manufacturing. At-

[16] William Goodwin, "The Middle Passaic Valley" (unpublished Ph.D. thesis, Columbia Univ., 1957); William H. Wallace, "Merrimack Valley Manufacturing: Past and Present," *Economic Geography*, Vol. 37, (October 1961), 283-308.

tractive, single story buildings located some hundred yards from the road, surrounded by landscaped lawns and parking areas, are characteristic of the new trend. This extensive use of land, compared to the older system with multistoried buildings, has caused much of the postwar manufacturing expansion in Anglo-America, Western Europe, Australia, and New Zealand to take place in suburbs, where land is cheaper, largely in industrial parks or other organized industrial districts.[17] Industrial parks are especially advantageous for small or medium-sized firms, since the developer [18] will provide a comprehensive *infrastructure,* including railroad sidings, streets and parking, water, gas, electricity, sewage, and drainage systems. The manufacturing firm is spared the involved process of acquiring raw farm land and turning it into a suitable manufacturing site. The park usually assures compatible neighbors, and the central management attempts, through zoning laws, to maintain the appearance of the park area. The zoning laws often restrict expansion on existing lots, but if buildings are of standardized design a firm that outgrows its premises usually will find a ready market for its plant. In a carefully planned industrial park many firms—not all of them manufacturing plants —do business with each other, just as in the downtown manufacturing area of most metropolitan cities. Machine shops, tool-and-die makers, job printers, packaging plants, and warehouses can sell part of their output, or services, to other companies within the industrial park. Restaurants and cafeterias and, in exceptional cases, data-processing plants with computers provide the small and medium-sized firms of the park with external economies usually associated with the downtown district.

The industrial parks are, as a rule, located close to major transportation facilities and especially to the new expressway systems.[19] A factory site that can be seen from a four or six lane expressway has a high advertising value, and such locations are not at a premium for residential use. The land under the approaches to airport runways also has low

[17] There were some 1,000 industrial parks in the United States in 1964. A survey of industrial parks in the United States and Canada has been published annually since 1960 by Conway Research, Inc., Atlanta, in *Industrial Development Manufacturers Record: Industrial Parks.* The survey for 1964 listed 755 parks that had replied to a questionnaire. The seven leading states were California (88), Texas (54), Illinois (50), Ohio (37), Pennsylvania (36), Iowa (29) and Missouri (26).

Britain was also a pioneer in industrial parks. The Trafford Park Industrial Estate, close to the terminal docks of the Manchester Ship Canal, was developed after 1896 and is still the largest in Britain, with 300 firms and 50,000 employees. The French *Commissariat au Plan* in 1962 decided to build a pilot industrial park with six factories.

[18] Many industrial parks in Anglo-America have been developed by public industrial development corporations or by local Chambers of Commerce, but the majority seem to have been developed by private groups, including railroad companies.

[19] The situation in the United States before the rapid postwar expansion of industrial parks is summarized in Robert L. Wrigley, "Organized Industrial Districts," *Journal of Land and Public Utility Economics,* Vol. 23 (May 1947), 180-98. For an extensive bibliography of recent studies, see *Highways, Trucks and New Industry: A Study of Changing Patterns in Plant Location,* American Trucking Associations, Inc., Washington, D.C. (1963). For a study of a new industrial park in Chicago, see Harold M. Mayer, "Centex Industrial Park: An Organized Industrial District," in R. S. Thoman and D. J. Patton, eds., *Focus on Geographic Activity* (New York: McGraw-Hill, 1964).

value for residential use but is well-suited for industrial parks. Easy access to a large airport is a major asset for any park; executives travel by plane, spare parts are sent as air freight, and increasing quantities of high value manufactured products are shipped by air. Sites near major airports are especially attractive for branch plants of large corporations.

In a few remarkable cases in Anglo-America, corporate headquarters of large firms have moved to suburbs where a "campus-like atmosphere" can be created. For industries employing a high ratio of university-trained personnel, such as electronics, aerospace, or book publishing, the suburbs are thought to have attractions other than cheap land and low taxes. But gains for the suburbs are usually losses for the downtown area. The stagnation of the downtown area as a viable unit in the urban complex in most metropolitan cities in the United States as a result of inadequate, unattractive, and obsolete public transportation may have acted as a pushing force. In Europe, Canada, and Japan, where more care has been taken to provide modern public transport, corporate headquarters seem to be very reluctant to move from downtown, the focus of business, finance, and culture. But everywhere, with the expansion of office space in the central business district, small and medium-sized manufacturing firms that have existed on the back streets find it increasingly difficult to compete for space; they move to a suburb and just leave a shop downtown for contacts with customers who are either in the central business district or converge on it from outside.

The spread of new manufacturing plants to industrial areas on the periphery of cities and to independent towns on the approaches to the big cities seems to be a universal phenomenon of the early 1960's. It has been reported from Chicago, Toronto, Boston, London, Paris, Cologne, Stockholm, Tokyo, and other cities. But outward migration of manufacturing plants is nothing new; such moves occurred during the last century. Ironworks on the Chicago River, locomotive works near the heart of Philadelphia, and sugar mills on Manhattan had to move when the cities grew and the central business district expanded.[20] What is new is the stagnation and decline of the downtown area as a center of manufacturing employment. Even industries which traditionally have been associated with the central business district, job printers, lithographic shops, clothing shops, and others, are now moving out.

A study of the suburbanization of manufacturing industry in Toronto in the 1950's revealed that manufacturing employment dropped 25,000 in the city between 1950 and 1955, and increased by 40,000 in the suburban municipalities; a net loss of 514 plants was recorded in the city and a net gain of 815 in the 12 suburban municipalities. An analysis of plant migration within the metropolis showed that industries, with few exceptions, moved to suburbs located in the general direction of their old sites in the city. Labor orientation was the most important reason, especially when highly skilled workers were involved, but earlier estab-

[20] Charles C. Colby, "Centrifugal and Centripetal Forces in Urban Geography," *Annals,* Association of American Geographers, Vol. 23 (March 1933), 1-20.

Rapid postwar expansion of manufacturing in the suburbs of metropolitan Toronto, as a result of the migration of firms from the city and the establishment of branch plants by Canadian and foreign companies, has been concentrated along the high-speed roads of the area. New, single-story plants line the Queen Elizabeth Way, a six-lane, limited access highway connecting Toronto (center, horizon) with Hamilton and Buffalo. Frontage on this highway does not provide better access than locations a few blocks away, but it carries a high advertising value. Highway 27 in the foreground, part of the bypass around central Toronto, has also attracted manufacturing plants. (Hunting Survey Corporation, Ltd.)

lished business associations and the owner's residence also influenced the decisions.[21]

Similar observations were made in an economic impact study of Massachusetts' Route 128. In seven years 137 million dollars were invested in plants and equipment along this circumferential highway at Boston, and 27,500 new jobs were created. Seven major reasons for location near Highway 128 were listed: 1) Land needed for expansion and operating efficiency, 2) Accessibility for commercial purposes, 3) Attractiveness of site, 4) Labor market considerations, 5) Accessibility for employees, 6) Advertising value of site, 7) Employee parking facilities. Employees of the new plants were found to be moving outward

[21] Donald Kerr and Jacob Spelt, "Manufacturing in Suburban Toronto," *Canadian Geographer,* No. 12 (1958), 11-19, and *The Changing Face of Toronto,* Memoir 11, Department of Mines and Technical Surveys, Geographical Branch (Ottawa: Queen's Printer, 1965).

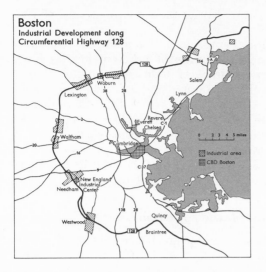

In the Boston area, Route 128 attracts large manufacturing plants and industrial parks that are made up of small and medium-sized units. Many of the industries are research-oriented, and they use the facilities of nearby universities, such as Harvard and MIT.

The six-lane divided highway is in the foreground. Railroad sidings, fanning out from the upper center on the lower side of the river, provide most plants with direct rail access. (Eastern Aerial Surveys, Boston, and Cabot, Cabot & Forbes, Boston.)

to new homes, 35 per cent of them driving their own cars and 65 per cent participating in car pools.[22]

The relative decline in agricultural employment (in many countries also an absolute decline) and the rapid increase of urban industries have radically changed the settlement pattern of industrial nations. Urban sprawl, and its concomitant problems (water and air pollution, traffic congestion, inadequate recreation areas), is universal. In most countries, but especially those with a high population density, like Germany and Japan, the impact of the settlement pattern has been somewhat cushioned by commuting habits. The children of farmers in villages commute to a factory job in a nearby town. The village is still there, but its functions have changed; it has become a commuter suburb of the town.

Manufacturing and the Distribution of Urban Places

Manufacturing industries have made a greater impact on the economic and social geography of any country than is indicated by employment figures, contribution to Gross National Product (GNP), or similar evidence. Among the urban industries, service production employs more people and accounts for larger values added to the GNP, but these industries characteristically have ubiquitous distribution patterns; they occur in all urban places. Examples are grocery stores, barbers, and grade schools. Manufacturing industries, on the other hand, characteristically have sporadic patterns: they occur in some towns, but do not occur at all in others. Watch factories, steel mills, and automobile plants are examples.

The only general theory for the distribution of urban places, the central-place theory, originally assumed an evenly distributed rural population served by an urban population employed in retail trade and a few other service industries.[23] However, the pattern provided by this theory, in all its geometric beauty and simplicity, often does not fit in with observed patterns in the real world, particularly insofar as industrial places are concerned. 1) Farmers make up a small and dwindling part of the gainfully employed population in economically advanced countries. The percentage, asymptotically approaching a value near zero, is already be-

[22] A. J. Bone, Economic Impact Study of Massachusetts Route 128, Massachusetts Institute of Technology (December 1958).

[23] Walter Christaller, Die zentralen Orte in Süddeutschland: Eine ökonomisch-geographische Untersuchung über die Gesetzmässigkeit der Verbreitung und Entwicklung der Siedlungen mit städtischen Funktionen (Jena: Fischer, 1933), trans. Carlisle W. Baskin, Central Places in Southern Germany (Englewood Cliffs, N.J.: Prentice-Hall, 1966).

Christaller's study, which stimulated a lively discussion, was introduced to the American public by Edward L. Ullman ("A Theory of Location for Cities," American Journal of Sociology, Vol. 46 [May 1941], 853-64). In the introduction to a recent bibliography (Brian J. L. Berry and Allan Pred, Central Place Studies: A Bibliography of Theory and Applications. Philadelphia: Regional Science Research Institute, 1961), Christaller's general theory for the distribution and development of towns and cities is reduced to a theory of location of tertiary activity (p. 6). As shown below, even the reduced claim may be too ambitious, but the theory provides a useful device for analyzing the distribution and hierarchical relations among some service activities.

low seven in the United States.[24] 2) Manufacturing is a more important city-forming industry than all the service industries combined,[25] and although such manufacturing branches as apparel and steel have quite different location demands, they have at least one characteristic in common: their patterns are different from that of retail trade. 3) Several service industries, for example, state capitals and universities in the United States, military establishments, and the tourist industry, have location patterns that deviate considerably from those assumed in central-place theory. These deviating industries may account for more than half of the city-forming service employment.

Expressed in other words, almost any industry or combination of industries may, in theory, be the basic activity which starts a multiplier-accelerator process of urban growth, but empirical American material indicates that manufacturing and mining are more important than the service industries combined. The credo of many early geographers—accepted as the basis of central-place theory—that retail trade and ancillary activities, serving a surrounding rural population, is the main function of urban places, cannot be accepted as a general principle.

In the real world, the "central place" often seems to have an eccentric location within its region, which would suggest that the gateway concept, never developed into a general theory, should merit reconsideration and further development and refinement.[26]

The only general theory available provides a poor fit to observed urban distribution patterns in the manufacturing belts of the world, and thus has a low explanatory value. It is doubtful if a general theory for the location of cities that will reasonably explain such complex patterns can ever be formulated. But a combined historic and geographic analysis goes a long way to illuminate the present patterns.

Changing Distribution Patterns

The continual changes in the distribution pattern of any manufacturing industry, as revealed by two consecutive censuses, are aggregate net effects of a multitude of changes in individual establishments, based

[24] Gradmann's statement that "the main function of a town is to be the center of its rural Umland," which was based on observations in southern Germany before World War I and later was made the point of departure for Christaller, may have been correct for the time and area where it was made, but cannot be accepted as a general principle.

[25] For a discussion of the concepts "city serving" and "city forming" industries, see G. Alexandersson, *The Industrial Structure of American Cities* (Lincoln: Univ. of Nebraska, 1956).

In 1950, manufacturing, including construction and mining, employed 33.7 per cent of the gainfully engaged American population, and the service industries employed 52.4 per cent. But in cities of 10 to 25 thousand inhabitants an estimated 38 per cent (more in larger cities) of the gainfully employed population were engaged in city-serving activities and six-sevenths of these were found in the service industries. When the city-serving element is deducted from the two groups, manufacturing turns out to be more important as a city-forming industry (even if construction and mining are excluded) than the combined service industries.

[26] R. D. McKenzie, *The Metropolitan Community* (New York: McGraw-Hill, 1933).

largely on rational decisions. It may therefore be of interest to focus attention on the decision-making units in the study of manufacturing distributions. Manufacturing cannot be treated as a homogeneous industry. Extremes like oil refineries, automobile factories, and shipyards, in which all decisions are made within a few firms, and the apparel industry, in which decisions are made within thousands of small enterprises, must be taken into account. The central part of this book contains a series of case studies by industry.

The individual plant is part, not only of the world pattern of its industry, but also of the regional and national economy. The Philadelphia oil refinery, the Göteborg shipyard, the Paris automobile factory, the Hong Kong clothing manufacturer, and the Jamshedpur steelworks have

Phillips Petroleum Company's 19-story headquarters, with research and development units, are at Bartlesville, Oklahoma. Two adjacent buildings have additional office space. A mining-manufacturing center of 28,000 people, Bartlesville—even more than New York—is dominated by executives and white-collar workers. When Phillips was incorporated in 1917, it was a small-town firm that aimed at the southwestern market around U.S. Highway 66, which runs from Chicago to Los Angeles. Becoming nationally known as Phillips 66, it entered the international market in the 1950's, a leader among the American independents. Today it has about 25,000 employees, numerous refineries and petrochemical plants at various locations including Sweeny, Houston, and Phillips, all three in Texas.

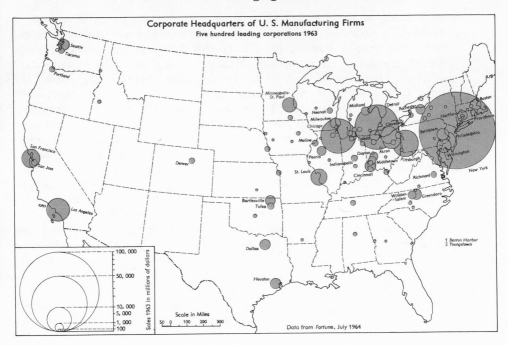

Corporate Headquarters of U. S. Manufacturing Firms
Five hundred leading corporations 1963

Data from *Fortune*, July 1964

Although large corporations with global activities can be directed from small cities, New York continues to be the economic capital of the United States and the center of corporate headquarters for manufacturing firms. Detroit's automobile industry is the main exception to New York's dominance.

one eye on regional and national economic development, and the other on national and international competition. For a well-organized and efficient manufacturing firm in a poor country, the misbehavior of the national economy (inflation, bureaucracy, and so on) may be a greater hurdle to further expansion than foreign competition.

The changes made by decision-making units may be better understood if they are grouped systematically. Two types of positive changes may be distinguished.[27]

EXPANSION OF EXISTING ESTABLISHMENTS. For most industries and most periods, this is probably the most important type of change. It is often cheaper to add capacity to existing facilities than to build a new branch plant somewhere else, but this means that a plant built at an optimum location may continue to grow, although its location is now obsolete. Many coal field-oriented steelworks serve as examples. If frank appraisal

[27] Leonard C. Yaseen, *Plant Location* (New York: Business Reports, Inc., 1952). Thomas R. Smith, "Locational Analysis of New Manufacturing Plants in the United States," *Tijdschrift voor Econ. en Sociale Geografie*, Vol. 45 (January 1954), 46-50. Glenn E. McLaughlin and Stefan Robock, *Why Industry Moves South: A Study of Factors Influencing Recent Location of Manufacturing Plants in the South* (National Planning Association, 1949). John D. Garwood, "An Analysis of Postwar Industrial Migration to Utah and Colorado," *Economic Geography*, Vol. 29 (January 1953), 79-88. G. J. R. Linge, "The Concentration and Dispersion of Manufacturing in New Zealand," *Economic Geography*, Vol. 36 (October 1960), 326-43.

were made of the location of existing manufacturing establishments, it might be found that few had both an efficient location and an efficient site.[28] The cost of moving is so large that few establishments will take this step; when a move occurs, often in connection with expansion, it is usually between two sites within the same location, e.g., from the inner part of a city to the suburbs.

NEW ESTABLISHMENTS.   These may be divided into three groups.

New firms.   In this case, the choice of location is largely predetermined by personal reasons. The problems of starting operations preclude much attention to locational considerations. The place where the entrepreneur lives and has manufacturing experience is usually the only one where he has personal contacts with banks, key workers, and market outlets. The propensity to establish manufacturing firms seems to have an interesting geographic distribution pattern of its own. Some areas, e.g., Bergslagen, Sweden, are dominated by "company towns" in which one company used to be not only the chief employer but also the owner of homes, local stores, and local transportation. The company looked after all needs of the inhabitants in a patriarchal way, and the desire to establish new manufacturing firms was low. In other regions, e.g., Jönköping's län, Sweden, small manufacturing firms dominate. Everyone can watch at close range the success story of several firms; the propensity to start new firms is high.

Branch plants.   Personal reasons play almost no part. More study is given to the locational problem, and it may be assumed that large parent firms analyze it thoroughly. The strategists of a large corporation watch the moves of competing firms; several large corporations may decide almost simultaneously to establish branch plants in a given market. Often they will pick the same location for their branch plants. The growth of Los Angeles since World War I provides many examples of this mechanism. The West Coast, a market larger than France or Norden, was singled out as the logical area for a new branch factory. Los Angeles, the largest and fastest growing population center, was the logical location for a West Coast plant. The South, another regional market, had no such dominating focus, and branch plants were scattered among several cities.

The relocated firm.   Its decision is based on dissatisfaction with a previous location. Locational considerations are more important than they are to the new firm, but the problems are probably less thoroughly studied than they would be for the branch plant, as the relocated firm is not part of a larger organization.

CHANGING PATTERNS REFLECTED IN OFFICIAL STATISTICS.   The only official data which help to pinpoint changes in manufacturing patterns are inventories made at regular intervals, censuses of manufacturing and population. But a comparison of two inventories will not reveal what has happened; it will only show the net effects of the changes as residuals. The seemingly simple pattern obtained by comparing two inventories may, in reality, be complex. Some firms have expanded employment,

---

[28] *Location* refers to the general situation of the establishment in the country or region; *site* refers to its specific situation within a smaller geographic unit, a town or a county.

Anderstorp, in the province of Småland, Sweden, is a rapidly growing area. Its small-scale manufacturing has been, and still is, characteristic of several parts of Europe. Most of the firms in this town of 3,600 inhabitants were developed by workers starting on their own, as is shown in this "pedigree" for the period 1877-1945. Plants range in size from a small, fully automated factory, run by the owner, to a plastic factory that today employs over 400 workers (opened in 1941; fourth from bottom of chart). The firms skillfully make use of external economies by placing mutual full-page ads in a large Stockholm newspaper and sharing an exhibition building on the main highway through Sweden. Principally, they are subcontractors to large engineering companies, but they also produce consumer goods. (From W. William-Olsson and Per Fries, Halmstad Nässjö Järnvägar och näringslivet i deras trafikområde, Halmstad: Halmstad Nässjö Järnvägar, Memorial Volume, 1950.)

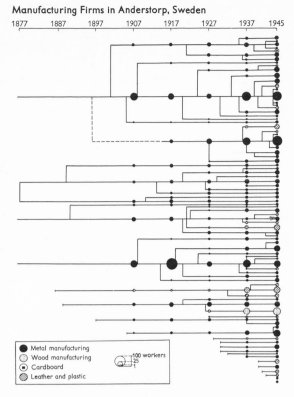

Manufacturing Firms in Anderstorp, Sweden

● Metal manufacturing
◉ Wood manufacturing
◉ Cardboard
▨ Leather and plastic

100 workers
25
1

others have contracted; new firms have been established and old ones have discontinued operations; a few firms moved in from other areas and others moved out; some branch plants were established and others were discontinued.

It is technically quite possible for a mapmaker to present the data of two inventories in such a form that the reader can see where small cities have gained and big cities have lost manufacturing jobs, where there has been a rapid decline in the countryside and where there has been a slow increase. This presentation is simplified if color can be used. But maps of this type, quite common in agricultural geography, have seldom been made for manufacturing industries.

Most studies on changes in manufacturing distribution have been made by economists with no training in the use of maps as analytical tools. They often use crude reference regions, countries in Europe, Africa, or Latin America and states or provinces in Anglo-America. But a state boundary in the United States often separates that which functionally belongs together (the steel district in Chicago straddling the Illinois-Indiana state line, the oil refineries of Philadelphia in Pennsylvania and New Jersey) and brings together that which is separate (Illinois steel mills in parts of Chicago and suburban St. Louis, New Jersey oil refineries in suburban Philadelphia and New York).

For some general observations a crude state map may be sufficient. It will show that American manufacturing employment in the last quarter

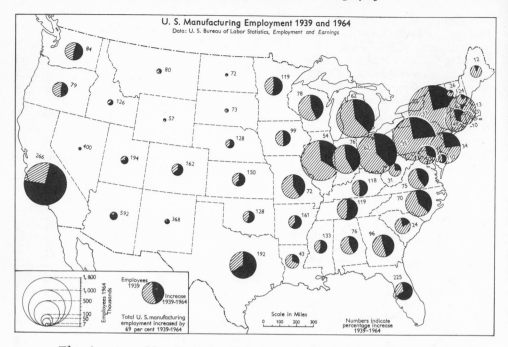

U. S. Manufacturing Employment 1939 and 1964
Data: U. S. Bureau of Labor Statistics, *Employment and Earnings*

Employees 1964 Thousands
1,800
1,000
500
100
50
7

Employees 1939

Increase 1939-1964

Total U. S. manufacturing employment increased by 69 per cent 1939-1964

Scale in Miles
0   100   200   300

Numbers indicate percentage increase 1939–1964

The American Manufacturing Belt is gradually losing its dominant position. New growth industries (aerospace, electronics, petrochemicals, paper) are influenced by locational factors other than iron and steel and the metal manufacturing industries, backbone of the Manufacturing Belt. Favorable climate and other amenities attract industry to a southerly tier of states from California and Arizona to Florida.

century has expanded much above the national average in the southwestern quadrant of the United States, from California to Kansas-Texas and in Florida, suggesting that climatic amenities have become a major factor in the location of industry.[29] The map also reveals that New England and the Middle Atlantic states have had a low expansion rate, the western states of the Manufacturing Belt have expanded close to the national average,[30] and two states in the South (South Carolina and Louisiana) have had an unfavorable rate. A time sequence of maps would show the general observations to be a continuation of a trend; since

[29] Edward L. Ullman, "Amenities as a Factor in Regional Growth," *Geographical Review,* Vol. 44 (January 1954), 119-32; Tom L. McKnight, *Manufacturing in Arizona* (Berkeley: Univ. of California, 1962).

[30] A theoretical model by Chauncy D. Harris ("The Market as a Factor in the Localization of Industry in the United States," *Annals,* Association of American Geographers, Vol. 44 [December 1954], 315-48), suggests that manufacturing plants serving the national market should seek a location in Greater New York. Experience shows (see James M. Hund, "Electronics," in *Made in New York,* Max Hall, ed. [Cambridge: Harvard Univ., 1959], p. 271, and Maurice Fulton and L. Clinton Hoch, "Transportation Factors Affecting Locational Decisions," *Economic Geography,* Vol. 35 [January, 1959], 51-59) that such plants have a clearcut preference for locations in the Midwest, which goes a long way to explain the favorable manufacturing development in that part of the United States. Are the premises of Harris' model unrealistic, or are the decision-makers poorly informed?

the latter part of last century there has been a slower growth rate of manufacturing in New England and the Middle Atlantic states than in the rest of the country.

Maps for individual industries will help explain the composite manufacturing map. The rapid growth in California and Texas is associated with such fast-growing industries as aerospace, electronics, and chemicals. In the southeast, from Virginia to Mississippi, the migration of the clothing industry from the New York region and the expansion of the manmade fiber industry has not been sufficient to counteract the slow growth in cotton textiles.

A more detailed geographic picture of manufacturing changes in the United States can be drawn on the basis of the 501 State Economic Areas (SEA).[31] But only maps based on the smallest administrative units, counties, individual urbanized areas, and urban places will show the changes in satisfactory detail for geographic studies.

Statistics on Manufacturing

A reader who turns to economic geography for a quantitative description of manufacturing industries in the world may be disappointed. The plethora of studies on manufacturing in individual cities or small areas has no counterpart in continental or global survey studies.[32] Textbook authors, with spotty and unsatisfactory primary reports, are not in a position to write well-informed global surveys. Detailed maps with pertinent comments found in chapters on agriculture and mining are lacking in chapters on manufacturing. Limitations imposed by unavailable statistics seem to be a chief reason why this important field of study has been so little cultivated by economic geographers.

Number of gainfully employed persons is widely accepted as the best measure for mapping manufacturing distributions. In anthropocentric studies it provides the direct approach: it tells how people make a living in an area. In economic studies it is also often the measure preferred by planners in government and business and by market researchers. Statistics on gainfully employed persons in many countries are found in two periodic series: the *census of population*, usually published every ten years, and the *census of manufacturing*. The former is based on information received from the household, and the individual will appear under his residential address; the latter obtains data from the business establishment, each person being listed at his place of work. In both series the individual may be grouped by *industry* and by *occupation*. The former means that a truck driver employed by a steelworks will appear

[31] See, e.g., Wilbur Zelinsky, "A Method for Measuring Change in the Distribution of Manufacturing Activity, the United States, 1939-1947," *Economic Geography*, Vol. 34 (April 1958), 95-126.

[32] Among the few exceptions are: Edgar M. Hoover, *Location Theory and the Shoe and Leather Industries* (Cambridge: Harvard Univ., 1937); William Glenn Cunningham, *The Aircraft Industry: A Study in Industrial Location* (Los Angeles: Morrison, 1951); N. J. G. Pounds and W. N. Parker, *Coal and Steel in Western Europe* (Bloomington: Indiana Univ., 1957); and Peter Odell, *An Economic Geography of Oil* (London: Bell, 1963).

under the steel industry; in thè latter grouping he will appear with other truck drivers, irrespective of the business of his employer.

The population census will publish data for as small a unit as one individual; the chief drawback of this source is the incomplete breakdown of industries. Textile, apparel, and primary metals are examples of the divisions it applies; cotton, women's clothing, and the steel industry are distinctions too fine for the population census. The manufacturing census has a finer breakdown of industries, but a disclosure rule prevents the U.S. Census of Manufactures from publishing data that would make it possible to calculate employment in any one plant. This rule makes the U.S. Census of Manufactures almost useless as a source for detailed mapping of manufacturing industries.

In the United States there is a third source of information on employment, *Employment and Earnings*, published by the Bureau of Labor Statistics. Here, data are first broken down into main industries, then further, into states and metropolitan areas.

All three U.S. sources on employment relate their industry groups to the Standard Industrial Classification (U.S. SIC). The difficult problem of achieving comparability among nations having various classifications of industries has been tackled by the United Nations. The *International Standard Industrial Classification of all Economic Activities* serves as a guide.[33] The acceptance of the principles and definitions of the ISIC will permit data collected by individual countries for their own purposes to be rearranged for international use. But much remains to be done before good comparability has been achieved, both on the national and on the international levels.[34]

Value added by manufacturing is theoretically another possible yardstick for measuring manufacturing distributions. Some geographers have expressed a preference for this measure as being more "economic" than employment. It is doubtful, however, if value added gives a more accurate measure than employment when studying economic impact on a city or region. Value added reflects the inputs of both labor and capital, but only labor is tied to the city or region; owners of manufacturing establishments usually live somewhere else. How important is value added as a yardstick for detailed geographic research in the United States? Data are published in the U.S. Census of Manufactures, but, because of the disclosure rule, are available only for states and other large administrative units. For global studies the measure has another shortcoming: information on it is collected in only a few countries.[35]

[33] *The International Standard Industrial Classification and the U.S. Standard Industrial Classification*, U.S. Department of Commerce, Bureau of the Census, Technical Paper No. 14 (Washington, D.C.: Government Printing Office, 1965).

[34] The United Nations defines manufacturing as the "mechanical or chemical transformation of inorganic or organic substances into new products, whether the work is performed by power driven machinery or by hand, whether it is done in a factory or in the worker's home, and whether the products are sold at wholesale or retail." The definition includes assembly and repair work.

[35] In a recent study based on 2146 areal units in the United States, a high correlation coefficient was established between several conventional yardsticks for measuring manufacturing distributions, including value added and number of employees.

For the analysis of a single, well-defined industry, the adequate measure may be obvious. If the trade uses metric tons per year or barrels per day (oil refineries), or gross register tons of tonnage launched (shipyards), the same measure should be used in analysis. Detailed statistical data for individual industries are often available in trade journals and similar sources, making it possible for a geographer to proceed with a detailed cartographic analysis.

National atlases are another source of detailed information on the economic geography of manufacturing industries in individual countries. They have often been made with access to unpublished official statistics, and are therefore more detailed than published tables. *The Atlas of Britain*, published in 1963, is outstanding in the scope and sophistication of its presentation of manufacturing industries. *The Economic Atlas of Japan* [36] is another good example.

For crude production statistics by countries, the U.N. statistical volumes are indispensable. The *Statistical Yearbook* gives more or less complete coverage, and the *Monthly Bulletin of Statistics* contains the latest available data in some of the major countries. Industrial production data by provinces is usually contained in the statistical yearbooks of individual countries.

Map Analysis of Manufacturing Distributions

King Henry IV of France once stated that Paris was well worth a Mass. In geographic analysis, not only Paris, London, and New York, but also Newton, Iowa, are well worth attention. If interest is focused both on Newton's uniqueness and its similarities with other urban places, it becomes essential to know the characteristics and associations, not only of Newton, but also of the other urban places in Iowa, the Middle West, the United States, or the world with which Newton is being compared. Maps, the most important and characteristic tools of analysis in the geographer's kit, are the logical solution to this problem.

Simple maps, indicating in a general way the location of a manufacturing industry, convey information not readily presented in text. If maps are made to show magnitude in addition to latitude and longitude (e.g., by showing industrial centers with symbols proportionate to employment, value added by manufacturing, production, production capacity, or some other meaningful measure), they become packed with easily assimilated information.

Maps can be made even more sophisticated tools of analysis by a careful selection of symbol scales and the introduction of a reference

---

This justifies the map maker's doing what he has always done: choosing the only available measure that provides sufficient detail. (John W. Alexander and James B. Lindberg, "Measurements of Manufacturing: Coefficients of Correlation," *Journal of Regional Science*, Vol. 3 [Summer 1961], 71-81.)

[36] Published in Tokyo, 1954, with Koichi Aki, Shigehito Tsuru, Shinzo Kiuchi, and Kaoru Tanaka as editors. A translation of the map legends has been made by Norton Ginsburg and John D. Eyre, *The Economic Atlas of Japan, Nihon Keizai Chizu* (Chicago: Univ. of Chicago, Dept. of Geography, 1959).

Newton, Iowa, 30 miles east of Des Moines, is a one-company town dominated by the Maytag Company, founded in 1893 to manufacture farm machinery. But since 1923 it has produced only home laundry equipment. In 1907, as a side-line to production of attachments for threshing machines, the company made a hand-powered, wooden-tub washing machine, to even out seasonal slumps in its main business. In 1922 a former mechanic, Howard Snyder, invented the gyrofoam process by which water is forced through the clothes, instead of the clothes through the water. Maytag discontinued the manufacture of all other products, and within two years had reached world leadership in washer production. In the lower right center is the headquarters building. (Maytag.)

pattern (here called "a hundred model").[37] Assume that a map of urban population is used as a reference pattern. Urban places over a certain limit are shown with two-dimensional symbols proportionate to the number of inhabitants. The map of a given industry, e.g., manufacturing, is then drawn on the same scale, with the same technique, and in such a

[37] John W. Alexander overlooks this possibility in his evaluation of the map as an analytical tool in economic geography. See John W. Alexander, *Economic Geography* (Englewood Cliffs, N.J.: Prentice-Hall, 1963), pp. 592 ff., and Alexander and Lindberg, *op. cit.*, p. 72. In his well-argued book, *Locational Analysis in Human Geography* (London: Arnold, 1965), Peter Haggett, referring to works by Schaefer and Bunge, touches rather lightly on the central geographical problem of the uniqueness of a place. He discusses two pieces of white chalk, which on closer inspection show many individual characteristics but which Haggett wants to treat as just two pieces of white chalk (p. 3). If Paris and London (or the United States and Cuba) are substituted for the two pieces of white chalk, the argument is less convincing. From a true cosmological point of view it would be reasonable to argue that a piece of chalk is a piece of chalk, a city is a city, and a country is a country. But since the earth is small, it is meaningful for the geographer to study cities, countries, and regions both as unique individuals and as members of systems of cities, countries, and regions.

In 1949 a second Maytag plant was completed on the outskirts of Newton. This plant and the adjoining Central Service warehouse, with its rail and truck shipping facilities, represent postwar American plant layout. Maytag is now the only major independent washer producer. Its prewar competitors have been absorbed by diversified industrial giants. (Maytag.)

way that the sum of symbol surfaces equals the corresponding sum on the population map.[38] The reader can now, if the maps are carefully drawn, easily judge which urban centers have more and which have less than the average amount of the given industry. It is also possible to see approximately how much more important X-ville is as, for example, a manufacturing center than as a town. This comparison is facilitated if an index number is inserted at each symbol on the manufacturing map. The number 100 means that X-ville is represented by symbols of the same size on both maps, 200 means that it is twice as important as a

[38] Technically this is a simple matter. The diameter scale (A) used for drawing the population map is extended to the point Σp, representing the total urban population shown on the map. The same vertical distance is marked off on scale B at point Σe, representing the total employment (or floor space, installed horsepower, or whichever yardstick is being used) of the given industry within the region. From point Σe scale B is then constructed backwards.

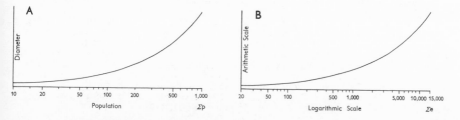

manufacturing center than as a town, and 50 means that it is only half as important as a manufacturing center than as a town.[39]

The hundred model does not represent an equilibrium towards which the investigated pattern is tending, nor does it represent an ideal pattern which politicians should try to attain. It is a conceptually and mathematically simple tool which simplifies the description and comparison of distribution patterns referable to a number of points on a map, e.g., the urban places. It is so simple that the hundred model (population map) can be left out if the index values are marked on the main map. However, the best visual impression will be attained if both hundred model and index numbers are used.[40]

Maps of the American Manufacturing Belt and the Gulf Coast area should be seen as parts of large maps for the whole of Anglo-America. A comparison of maps of the Manufacturing Belt (pp. 40-41) indicates that a population map may serve as a reasonable substitute for a map of manufacturing employment within the manufacturing belts of the world, but will not do for areas outside the manufacturing belts (Gulf Coast maps). For some areas (e.g., the Soviet Union), data on manufacturing employment are not available; in other areas (Western Europe), data were not available at the time of writing. The seven population maps in this book (the American Manufacturing Belt, the Gulf Coast area, parts of Brazil, Western Europe, parts of the European Soviet Union, and Japan) are comparable in symbols and map scales, the only exception being Japan's higher threshold value for inclusion and less detail for smaller cities. The maps should provide a visual impression of the

[39]

$$I = \frac{m_x/m_r \cdot 100}{P_x/P_r},$$

where I is the index number, m_x the manufacturing employment in X-ville, m_r the manufacturing employment in all urban places on the map, P_x the population of X-ville, and P_r the population of the urban places. For a highly urbanized and economically developed area, total data for the region can be used, which somewhat simplifies the construction of maps and indexes.

This is the formula of the location factor (location quotient) which has been widely used by economists since it was suggested by P. Sargant Florence in *The Statistical Method in Economics and Political Science* (London: Routledge, 1929), pp. 327-28.

[40] A conceptually more complicated and visually less satisfactory method is the mapping of positive and negative deviations from a hundred model or a regression line. This can be done in two ways. Least satisfactory is to show deviations in absolute terms. The map reader then has no way of knowing if a given symbol is a relatively insignificant deviation for a large city or a very large deviation for a small city. For examples of such maps, see Wilbur Zelinsky, "A Method for Measuring Change in the Distribution of Manufacturing Activity: the United States, 1939-1947," *Economic Geography*, Vol. 34 (April 1958), 95-126, or Peter R. Gould and Robert H. T. Smith, "Method in Commodity Flow Studies," *The Australian Geographer*, Vol. 8 (1961), 73-77 (Ghana map).

If the symbols on the map are made proportionate to total quantities, and relative deviations are indicated by hatchings, the smallest symbol must be fairly large to show the hatching adequately. Six types of hatchings can be used at the most; the method provides less detail than the use of individual index values at each symbol. If deviations are expressed as standard deviations from a regression line, the reader does not know what percentage a given symbol is off from the model. For example, see Gould and Smith, *op. cit.* (Sidney map). See also Robert H. T. Smith, "Transport Competition in Australian Border Areas: The Example of Southern New South Wales," *Economic Geography*, Vol. 39 (January 1963), 1-13.

general manufacturing distribution in some of the most important manufacturing regions of the world.

Modern Manufacturing Industry in Underdeveloped Countries

All countries undergoing the Industrial Revolution have witnessed a period of keen competition between the old handicraft and cottage industry, with its roots in the indigenous culture, and the modern manufacturing industry. The revolutionary elements were machinery, new sources of power, and a new social organization. The modern manufacturing industry has penetrated to all corners of the world, first with its products and its search for raw materials, and later as an innovation. But only Europe, Anglo-America, Japan, and the Soviet Union have so far experienced the full impact of the Industrial Revolution, the greatest cultural change in the history of mankind. These areas are now beginning a second industrial revolution, sometimes called the Information Revolution, which may speed up the rate of change even more. Meanwhile, a wide tier of countries, stretching from Latin America over Africa to South Asia, are still in the early stages of the first industrial revolution. Almost all of them are in the tropical zone or on its margin. All tropical countries are poor, although some are poorer than others; all economically advanced countries are in the temperate zones. China's long expected economic take-off [41] may make it possible in the future to reverse the first statement, and say that all countries in the temperate zones are economically advanced.

The slow acceptance of modern industry and science in poor countries cannot be explained by any single factor, such as physical milieu (climate, soils), population (age structure, growth rate, education), cultural pattern (religion, value systems), social organization (big estates or small farms, tribal system, extended families), economic system (market economy, or centrally planned economy), political organization (colony or independent nation), or the propinquity factor (proximity to or distance from the chief economic foci of the world). Most poor countries show a big list of negative factors: hot climate, leached and easily eroded soils, excessive population growth, malnutrition and poor health, high rates of illiteracy, and a society opposed to economic and social change. It is, however, becoming increasingly obvious that rapid population growth, resulting from high birth rates and decreasing death rates, is a key factor in tropical (and Chinese) poverty. Almost all of these countries now have higher birth rates than any recorded in Sweden, a country with a series of vital statistics detailed back to 1749. Most populations grow at higher rates than any ever known in European countries. Modern family planning offers the only hope of breaking this vicious circle, but even under the best of circumstances it will take a long time and tremendous investments to provide those already born with manufacturing jobs on a scale comparable with that of the North Atlantic world.

[41] W. W. Rostow, *The Stages of Economic Growth* (New York: Cambridge Univ., 1960). Pierre George, *Panorama du monde actuel* (Paris: Presses Univ., 1965).

CHAPTER 2 *selected* *industries*

Traditionally there are two approaches to the geography of manufacturing, by industry and by region. The former is analytical, the latter, synthetic. The analytical approach recognizes that geographical generalizations about manufacturing, to be meaningful, must be made for subgroups, since manufacturing is a heterogeneous group of industries ranging from newspapers to watch factories and brickyards. Most generalizations that can be made about the economic geography of the newspaper industry are irrelevant for the watch industry or the manufacturing of bricks, and vice versa.

The emphasis in this book is on the analytical approach. A fair sample of industries, discussed in some detail, includes such pillars of the industrial revolution as steel and cotton textiles, on the one hand, and modern growth industries like aerospace and electronics on the other; oligopolistic industries like the manufacturing of cars and ships and small-firm industries like apparel; raw-material oriented industries like pulp-and-paper or industries in a tug-of-war between raw materials and markets like petroleum refineries. This section ends with a discussion of the chemical industry, as heterogeneous in its economic geography as the entire group of manufacturing industries.

The Iron and Steel Industry

Iron and steel works produce the chief raw materials of a wide range of metal manufacturing industries, whose products include automobiles, ships, railroad equipment, household appliances, and machinery for farming and other industries. Other metals (aluminum and copper) and plastics are used in much smaller quantities. In addition, steel is a major construction material. Only a few products, such as rail, nails, wire, and construction beams move directly from steelworks to consumer without undergoing further manufacturing processes. The primary metal industry and the vast superstructure of metal manufacturing activities account for some two-fifths of American manufacturing employment, forming the largest manufacturing complex in any developed nation. The average per capita consumption of steel in the world was 133 kg in 1963, ranging from some 540 kg in Sweden and the United States to 16 kg in China and India.

The steel industry occupies a key position in modern industrial society; in the United States it has been customary to look at the steel production curve as a general indicator of business activity.[1]

The iron and steel industry also held a key position in the Industrial Revolution; machinery and transportation apparatus necessary for industrial development were increasingly made of iron or steel, after early attempts to use wood. "It did not take much more than a couple of decades to provide the country (Britain in the middle of last century) with a very adequate network of railways—that first and most typical enterprise of the Industrial Revolution—and once Britain was supplied, the enterprising railwaymen went abroad." [2] Western Europe, the United States, and Japan followed Britain.

The capital-intensive steel industry, most inflexible of the manufacturing industries in its geographic location, still reflects investment decisions made some two hundred years ago in the oldest manufacturing regions. Heavy engineering plants were geographically linked to the iron and steel industry on the coal and iron ore fields. The coal-steel-metal-manufacturing complex has had a fundamental influence on population redistribution in Western Europe, northeastern United States, and the European part of the Soviet Union, as evidenced by maps of urban places.

The war of 1914 brought to a sudden close a period of astonishing progress in the iron and steel industry; the period after the middle 1950's has again witnessed revolutionary changes in the industry, with great influences on its distribution pattern.

HISTORIC GEOGRAPHY OF IRON MAKING. Before the age of steel, iron-making was widely scattered in forested areas. The use of charcoal as a fuel prevented the concentration of blast furnaces and forges, since each ton of iron required several tons of charcoal corresponding to an even larger quantity of wood. The other basic requirements of the iron industry were also widespread: ores suited to the small furnaces, producing only a few tons per day; small rapids for direct water power needed both by furnace and forge; limestone; and the market, since people still lived predominantly on farms. Farmers bought cast-iron items (pots, pans, stove grates) and forged iron converted into steel (chain, nails, horseshoes, scythes, axes, cutlery) either directly from furnace or forge,

[1] The stagnation of U.S. steel production in the decade preceding 1965, when most other indices of manufacturing activity pointed upwards, may be an early indication of the less central role of steel in future industrial society. The rapid growth of substitutes (aluminum, plastics, glass, and concrete) and the miniaturization of products made of steel are major contributing factors. Such modern growth industries as electronics and petrochemicals are light steel consumers.

[2] Barbara Ward, *The West at Bay* (New York: Norton, 1948), p. 24.

Table 2.1. Production and Consumption of Steel

Selected countries	Production 1964 steel ingots million m.tons	Per capita consumption 1963 kilogram
United States	115.2	540
Canada	8.3	377
EEC	82.2	357
West Germany	37.3	473
France	19.8	326
Italy	9.8	277
Belgium	8.7	} 348
Luxembourg	4.6	
Netherlands	2.6	262
Britain	26.7	368
Sweden	4.5	545
Austria	3.2	236
Spain	2.4	100
Japan	39.8	258
India	6.0	16
Australia	5.1	389
South Africa	3.1	141
Mexico	2.2	56
Brazil	3.1	44
Argentina	1.3	62
U.S.S.R.	85.0	344
Poland	8.6	242
Czechoslovakia	8.4	487
East Germany	4.3	378
China	11	16
World	432	133

Sources: United Nations: *Statistical Yearbook, 1964; Monthly Bulletin of Statistics* (May 1965); *The European Steel Market in 1963* (New York, 1965), p. 12; *Quarterly Bulletin of Steel Statistics for Europe*, Vol. 15, No. 4 (1964). Statistisches Bundesamt, Düsseldorf, *Eisen und Stahl*, No. 2 (1965).

from the village blacksmith, or through distributors in the nearby town. Transport of finished products was a problem of secondary importance, except in the peripheral, forested regions of Europe (the Bergslagen District of Sweden, the Ural District of Russia), which produced bar-iron for the world market. The world market was the densely populated, deforested land around the North Sea, and especially Britain. The steels of Solingen, Styria, Ariège, and Dauphiné in Europe enjoyed a good reputation and were sold at high prices in distant places, but most parts of Europe and other continents were self-sufficient in the simple ironmongery required by an agricultural people. The per capita consumption of iron was extremely small compared to the present situation.[3]

COKE BLAST FURNACES. Coke was used successfully by Darby to smelt iron as early as 1709, but not until after 1750 did the use of coke

[3] Norman J. G. Pounds and William N. Parker, *Coal and Steel in Western Europe* (Bloomington: Indiana Univ., 1957). C. Prêcheur, *La sidérurgie française* (Paris: Armand Collin, 1963). Donald A. Fink, "Primary Metals," in *Region in Transition*, Vol. 1, Economic Study of the Pittsburgh Region (Pittsburgh: The Pittsburgh Regional Planning Association, 1963).

in the blast furnace spread rapidly in England. By 1788 four-fifths of British pig iron came from coke-fired blast furnaces, and by 1806 charcoal iron had diminished to a bare 3 per cent. On the Continent and in the United States, however, charcoal iron reigned supreme far into the nineteenth century. The Ruhr area, best endowed with coking coal in Europe, was late in using coke in its blast furnaces. Until 1849, iron ore was smelted on or near the Ruhr coal field with charcoal alone. In the United States, where wood for charcoal was more plentiful than in Western Europe, ironmakers continued to produce the superior and more versatile charcoal iron, so well suited to the needs of the village blacksmith. The coke-fired blast furnaces, larger than those fired by charcoal, were not introduced into the thriving iron-producing district of southwestern Pennsylvania, centered on Pittsburgh, until 1859. In Russia, charcoal iron made up 99 per cent of the pig iron in 1870. In other continents coke furnaces had to wait even longer; the first Japanese furnace was built at Kamaishi in 1874.

MASS PRODUCTION OF STEEL.   By the middle of the nineteenth century it had long been known that soft iron could be changed to steel by adding carbon. Crucible steel works were numerous but small, and the product far too expensive to be used in rails, ships, and bridges. The industrial world of Europe and the United States had a great need for a general purpose, low-cost metal.

A British metallurgist, Henry Bessemer, was first with a method to mass produce steel, protected by a series of patents taken out between 1855 and 1860. The first American Bessemer plant was erected in 1864 at Wyandotte, Michigan. The process involves blowing air through a bath of molten pig iron from the bottom of a vessel lined with acid (siliceous) refractories. The unwanted elements in the pig iron combine with the oxygen, and either leave the bath as gases or enter the slag. At the same time, the high carbon content of the pig iron is lowered to that of steel. The process thus represents a direct method of converting pig iron into steel, and the vessel is referred to as a converter. The Bessemer process had the advantage of speed and simplicity—the blow takes some 20 minutes. But it was impossible to control the final carbon content closely, and the method was limited to ores low in phosphorus, found in Bergslagen (Sweden), where the first Bessemer converter was successfully blown in 1858, Cumberland (England), Bilbao (Spain), Elba (Italy), and a few other areas in Europe and the United States. Bessemer built a steelwork at Sheffield, England, in 1860, and others were soon built in many countries.

Another British inventor, German-born Wilhelm Siemens, developed a rival process. He used a furnace in which gases were burned above a hearth on which pig iron and iron ore were melted on a bottom of sand. Siemens applied his regenerative principle, by which the gases were preheated before entering the furnace. The Martin brothers in France substituted scrap for ore in order to provide the extra oxygen necessary for oxidation of the impurities and reduction of the high carbon content of the pig iron. The process is referred to as the Siemens, the Martin, the

Siemens-Martin, or the open-hearth method. It represented another acid process and did not overcome the fundamental difficulty of the Bessemer method; it did not remove phosphorus and sulfur from the pig iron. But it was a slower process, and permitted closer control over the quality of the steel.

In 1879 an amateur London metallurgist, Sidney Gilchrist Thomas, collaborating with his cousin, Percy Gilchrist, proposed to replace the standard converter lining with one made of limestone and dolomite. This lining permitted the use of lime or limestone as a slag-making material, which made the process capable of removing phosphorus (and sulfur) from the pig iron. The process, known as the Thomas, the Thomas-Gilchrist, or the basic Bessemer method, was never adopted in the United States, but developed very rapidly on the Continent. The *minette* ores of Lorraine abruptly became a tremendous asset. The high-grade magnetite ores of Swedish Lapland and Bergslagen (Grängesberg), which also had a high phosphorus content, could be used as soon as railways and port facilities had been constructed. The basic Bessemer process requires a pig iron of 2.0 per cent or more phosphorus. The basic open-hearth method, developed simultaneously, permits the economical use of pig iron of any phosphorus content up to 1.0 per cent. This made available immense iron ore deposits in the United States with phosphorus contents too high for use in the acid processes and too low for the bottom-blown basic converter.

Electric current as the source of heat has been used in numerous types of steel furnaces.[4] The first commercially successful furnaces were introduced before World War I, and the increased demand for high-grade alloy and tool steels after the war led to a slowly increasing percentage of electric steel. In most industrialized countries this share is less than 10 per cent. Sweden is an exception; traditional concentration on high-grade steel combined with low cost hydroelectricity has made the electric furnace the leading steel process with some 50 per cent of Swedish steel production. Although inherently more expensive in operation than other steel making processes, the electric furnace is also used to make ordinary steels. Some small steel works produce construction steel from local scrap, protected by long distances from the full impact of the economies of scale in large steel centers (e.g., Jackson, Mississippi; Tampa, Florida; Edmonton, Alberta).

The open-hearth process was long predominant in almost every region of the world.[5] In 1955 it accounted for 78 per cent of world production, followed by converter steel (13 per cent), and electric steel (9 per cent). Only in Western Europe did converter steel, primarily Thomas, approach open-hearth steel in importance, with 37 and 52 per cent respectively. In North America, open-hearth accounted for 89 per cent, and in the

[4] Electric furnaces are also used for pig iron smelting, mainly in countries with cheap electricity. The largest electric smelting shops are at Mo-i-Rana, Norway, and at the new Orinoco steelworks in Venezuela (Ciudad Santo Tomé de Guayana).

[5] *Long-term Trends and Problems of the European Steel Industry* (Geneva: Economic Commission for Europe, 1959), is a well-documented and penetrating inventory of problems in the steel industry at the end of the 1950's.

Soviet Union 88 per cent. Bessemer converters declined in North America from 30 per cent in 1913 to 3 per cent in 1955. The acceptance in all parts of the world of the oxygen converters has brought about drastic changes in these relations.

The problem of lowering nitrogen content by adding oxygen in the airblast was tackled by Henry Bessemer, but not until the late 1920's were methods developed for producing pure oxygen cheaply. Gradually oxygen was used in all steel making processes, but the specially designed, top-blown oxygen converters developed in the 1950's justify talk of a new metallurgical breakthrough. The practicability of using oxygen in a Bessemer converter was proven (1937-1939) by C. V. Schwartz of Brassert Oxygen Technik, Zürich, who then led the German Steel Institute.

The LD-process, developed in Austria and first put into operation at Linz (1952) and Donawitz (1953), has proven to be very flexible and economical. By 1959 the annual capacity of existing LD-installations in the world was 12.5 million tons, and 14.1 million tons were under construction, which indicates the rapid acceptance of the new method. Brassert of Zürich own and control the basic patents; the Swedish Kaldo-process and the German Rotor-process account for smaller tonnages.

The ratio of steel to pig iron was roughly 1:1 in the United States before World War I,[6] but in 1964 the production of steel was 115 million tons, and of pig iron 78 million tons. The open-hearth furnace, long accounting for some 90 per cent of the U.S. capacity, and the electric furnace have encouraged the use of scrap. The electric furnace normally uses only scrap, and the open-hearth furnace often has a 50:50 charge of scrap and hot iron. The LD-process is most economical with an 80:20 ratio of hot metal and scrap. The rapid acceptance of the oxygen processes should lead to a world surplus of scrap and an increased demand for iron ore. In free-market nations, integrated in the world economy, steel mills located on the coast, able to receive ore carriers of 50 to 100 thousand tons, should have great advantages. In centrally planned, protectionist economies, like the Soviet Union, the locational pull of the iron ore fields should increase substantially.

Automation in the steel industry may, in the next ten years, create problems comparable with postwar experiences in the bituminous coal industry, where open-pit mining and other methods permitting advanced mechanization have made it possible for a drastically reduced labor force to produce a given volume. In addition to new steel processes, steelworks have recently acquired a fantastic array of mansaving methods: continuous casting, high frequency induction heaters, ultrasonic inspection devices with a number of computers linked on the production line, off-line computers for the office routines, and so on. More than ever, the iron and steel industry is a *capital-intensive industry.*

UNITED STATES AND CANADA. The primary metal and metal manufacturing of Anglo-America is highly concentrated in the Manufacturing

6 Norman J. G. Pounds, "World Production and Use of Steel Scrap," *Economic Geography,* Vol. 35 (July 1959), 247-58.

Belt.[7] One-eighth of the conterminous United States holds two-fifths of its population, but no less than four-fifths of production and employment in the metal manufacturing complex. The Canadian manufacturing districts are adjacent to the American.

The United States exceeded Britain as a steel producer in the 1880's, and by 1913 American production surpassed the combined output of Germany, Britain, and France. America's rapid rise to manufacturing eminence in the half century between the Civil War and World War I went rather unnoticed in Europe. The European powers were engaged in building their own manufacturing capacity close to the innovation center of the Industrial Revolution. They looked to each other, and especially to Britain, for new techniques and new industrial organization. America, immersed in the gigantic task of settling a continent and assimilating millions of immigrants, was not heavily engaged in the building of a colonial empire, the status symbol among nations at the time. When the Americans laid 1,000 miles of railroad for heavy traffic at home, it hardly received as much attention as the dramatic construction, under adverse conditions, of 100 miles of light traffic railway in Africa by British or French capital.

The United States' share of world output of steel reached a peak of three-fifths in the early 1920's, but has since been slipping, especially since the middle 1950's, and is now one-fourth. There are several reasons why increase in steel production should gradually level off in the most advanced countries—competition from substitutes, miniaturization of products—while maintaining a high growth rate in the less developed

---

[7] Delimited and described by Sten De Geer in a pioneer study, "The American Manufacturing Belt," *Geografiska Annaler,* Vol. 9 (1927), 235-359. Other criteria were used by subsequent writers: Richard Hartshorne, "A New Map of the Manufacturing Belt of North America," *Economic Geography,* Vol. 12 (January 1936), 45-53; Helen Strong, "Regions of Manufacturing Intensity in the United States," *Annals,* The Association of American Geographers, Vol. 27 (March 1937), 23-47; Alfred J. Wright, "Manufacturing Districts of the United States, *Economic Geography,* Vol. 14 (July 1938), 195-200; and Clarence F. Jones, "Areal Distribution of Manufacturing in the United States," *Economic Geography,* Vol. 14 (July 1938), 217-22. A recent delineation of the Manufacturing Belt, based on value-added data by county for 1958, shows a striking similarity with De Geer's map based on data from 1919: Allan Pred, "The Concentration of High-value-added Manufacturing," *Economic Geography,* Vol. 41 (April 1965), 108-32. An undated but recent outline of the Manufacturing Belt made with the regionalist's "feel" of the area is found in C. Langdon White, Edwin J. Foscue, and Tom L. McKnight, *Regional Geography of Anglo-America,* 3rd Ed. (Englewood Cliffs, N.J.: Prentice-Hall, 1964), p. 34.

The White-Foscue-McKnight map distinguishes 13 principal manufacturing districts within the Manufacturing Belt. These manufacturing core areas stand out by the pattern of manufacturing employment and manufacturing intensity on the map on p. 41 in this book. A delineation of the Manufacturing Belt in 1960 could easily be made by including cities with an index value of 100 or more on the map on p. 41. It would agree with the White-Foscue-McKnight map in the east, incorporating the Montreal region, and with Pred's map in the west. All maps seem to agree in the south and the north.

The 13 principal manufacturing districts are: southeastern New England, centered on Boston; southwestern New England, chiefly the Connecticut Valley; Metropolitan New York; the Philadelphia-Baltimore district; central New York state, along the former Erie Canal; the Niagara Frontier, centered on Buffalo-Hamilton-Toronto; the middle St. Lawrence district, centered on Montreal; the Pittsburgh-Cleveland district; the southern Michigan automotive district, centered on Detroit; the Chicago-Milwaukee district; the inland Ohio-Indiana district; the middle Ohio Valley; and the St. Louis district.

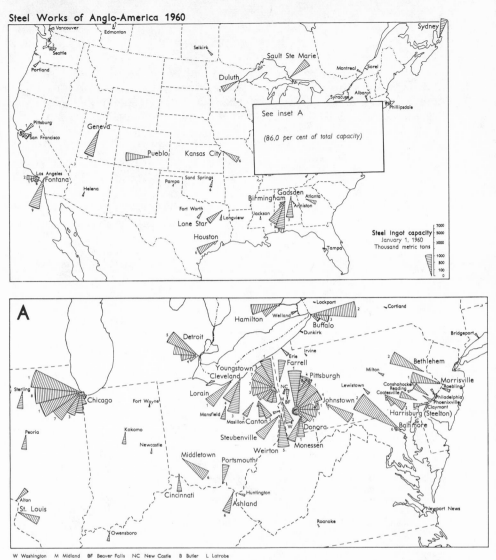

Numbers refer to 9 leading American steel companies in table below. (From Annual Capacities of Coke Ovens, Blast Furnaces, and Steelmaking Furnaces as of January 1, 1960, *New York: American Iron and Steel Institute, 1960.)*

| | Million Metric Tons | | |
Company	Production 1961	Capacity Jan. 1, 1960	Employment 1961
1 U.S. Steel	22.8	38.0	199,000
2 Bethlehem Steel	13.5	20.9	126,000
3 Republic Steel	6.5	11.5	48,000
4 Jones & Laughlin Steel	5.1	7.3	41,000
5 National Steel	5.5	6.4	26,000
6 Armco Steel	4.9	6.2	36,000
7 Youngstown	3.9	6.2	27,000
8 Inland Steel	4.7	5.9	29,000
9 Kaiser	2.0	2.6	11,000
U.S. Total	88.9	134.0	569,000

Cities of the Anglo-American Manufacturing Belt

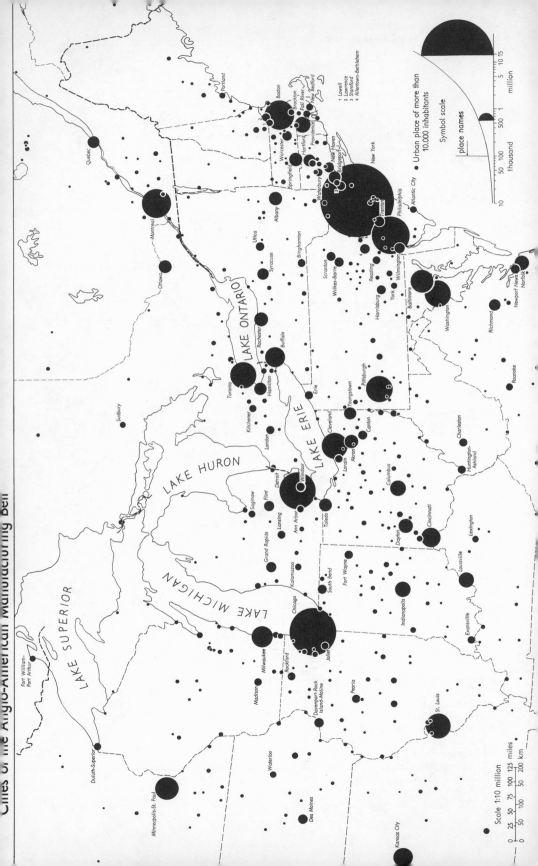

LAKE SUPERIOR

LAKE HURON

LAKE MICHIGAN

LAKE ONTARIO

LAKE ERIE

Fort William–Port Arthur

Duluth–Superior

Minneapolis–St. Paul

Des Moines

Waterloo

Kansas City

St. Louis

Peoria

Davenport–Rock Island–Moline

Rockford

Madison

Milwaukee

Chicago

Joliet

South Bend

Fort Wayne

Indianapolis

Evansville

Louisville

Lexington

Kalamazoo

Grand Rapids

Lansing

Flint

Saginaw

Ann Arbor

Detroit

Windsor

Toledo

Dayton

Cincinnati

Columbus

London

Kitchener

Hamilton

Toronto

Cleveland

Lorain

Akron

Canton

Youngstown

Erie

Pittsburgh

Charleston

Huntington–Ashland

Roanoke

Richmond

Buffalo

Rochester

Sudbury

Ottawa

Montreal

Quebec

Portland

Boston

Brockton

Fall River

New Bedford

Providence

Hartford

Waterbury

New Haven

Bridgeport

Worcester

Springfield

Albany

Utica

Syracuse

Binghamton

Scranton

Wilkes-Barre

Reading

Harrisburg

York

Wilmington

New York

Trenton

Philadelphia

Atlantic City

Baltimore

Washington

Newport News

Norfolk

1 Lowell
2 Lawrence
3 Stamford
4 Allentown–Bethlehem

● Urban place of more than 10,000 inhabitants

Symbol scale

place names

million

thousand

10 50 100 500 1 5 10 15

10 50 100 125 miles

0 25 50 75 100 125 miles

0 25 50 75 100 200 km

Scale 1:10 million

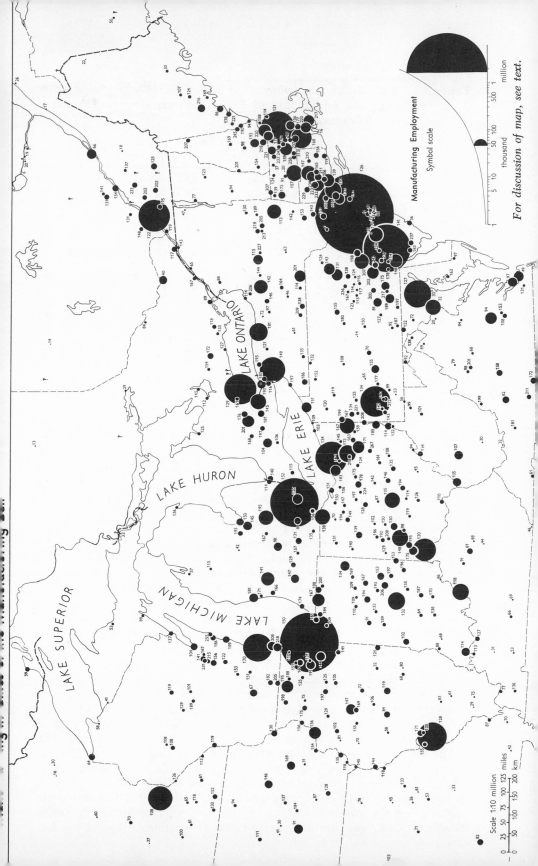

Manufacturing Employment

Symbol scale

For discussion of map, see text.

LAKE SUPERIOR

LAKE HURON

LAKE MICHIGAN

LAKE ONTARIO

LAKE ERIE

Scale 1:10 million

0   25   50   75   100   125   miles
0   50   100   150   200   km

Table 2.2. **Cumulative Percentages of Total U.S. Industrial Market for Steel, by Amount of Freight Absorption from Principal Steel Production Centers**

| | (*Freight absorption, cents per hundred pounds*) | | | | | | | | | | |
	0	10	20	30	40	50	60	70	80	90	100
Chicago	19	24	29	35	54	63	74	83	85	93	93
Pittsburgh	5	8	13	29	41	68	86	88	90	91	91
Youngstown	3	5	21	31	51	78	86	87	90	91	91
Baltimore	3	4	18	18	21	29	46	59	78	89	91
Cleveland	5	10	24	48	59	74	82	89	91	91	91
Detroit	18	20	27	43	64	72	77	83	91	92	92
Buffalo	4	5	8	26	54	64	76	87	88	91	91
Wheeling-Weirton-Steubenville	1	7	14	29	41	68	85	87	89	91	92
Birmingham	3	4	5	6	7	17	28	41	79	92	94
Fontana	5	6	6	6	6	6	6	6	6	6	6
Bethlehem	3	16	17	20	20	29	38	55	76	88	91
Middletown	9	10	17	30	70	78	83	91	91	91	92
Morrisville	12	14	17	19	20	22	37	49	76	88	91
Johnstown	0	2	11	20	47	65	74	87	88	91	92
Geneva	1	1	1	1	1	1	2	2	4	4	7
St. Louis	4	7	12	20	38	41	57	68	78	88	94
Houston	3	4	4	4	5	5	6	8	12	17	18

Source: Donald A. Fink and Pittsburgh Regional Planning Association, *op. cit.*

countries and also in the underdeveloped world, where the first steel works may not even yet exist. The American share of global steel production should thus continue to decline slowly. Domestically, steel's prominent position among manufacturing industries should continue to weaken; aerospace, electronics and petrochemicals, rather than such heavy steel consumers as railroads (U.S. 1880's), ships (U.K. before World War I, postwar Japan) and automobiles (U.S. 1920's, postwar Europe), are the modern growth industries.

The American metal manufacturing complex, concentrated primarily in the western half of the Manufacturing Belt, took shape under the influence of three basic geographic factors: *a*) the enormous Appalachian coal field stretching from western Pennsylvania to Alabama, containing excellent coking coal at Connelsville near Pittsburgh and at Pocahontas in West Virginia; *b*) the iron ore ranges near Lake Superior, mined for their high-grade ore for a hundred years, and now also yielding beneficiated taconite ore from tremendous deposits; and *c*) the Great Lakes, connecting the iron ore and coal deposits by a cheap waterway. The metal manufacturing industries, including steel, are major city-forming activities, not only in such metropolitan cities as Detroit and Pittsburgh, but also in Chicago, Milwaukee, Cleveland, Buffalo, and a multitude of smaller cities in the trans-Appalachian part of the Manufacturing Belt.

The steel mills in this region are oriented to coal fields (Pittsburgh, Youngstown, Johnstown), to iron-ore fields (Duluth), or to intermediate lakeside locations (Chicago, Cleveland, Detroit, Buffalo, Hamilton). As in Europe, the pull of the coal fields was strong at the end of the nineteenth century, but the iron mines never exerted any great influence in Anglo-America, chiefly because of their peripheral location. All steel produc-

Table 2.2. *(cont.)*

(see text for further explanation)

110	120	130	140	150	160	170	180	190	200	210	220	230	240	250
94	94	94	94	97	97	97	97	100	—	—	—	—	—	—
91	93	93	94	94	94	97	97	97	97	97	100	—	—	—
91	93	93	94	94	94	97	97	97	97	97	100	—	—	—
92	92	92	93	94	94	94	94	94	97	97	97	97	100	—
92	93	94	94	94	94	97	97	97	97	97	100	—	—	—
93	93	94	94	94	97	97	97	97	100	—	—	—	—	—
92	92	93	93	94	94	97	97	97	97	97	100	—	—	—
92	93	93	94	94	94	97	97	97	97	97	100	—	—	—
94	94	94	94	94	97	97	97	97	100	—	—	—	—	—
6	7	8	8	11	12	15	21	32	49	69	86	92	97	100
91	92	92	93	94	94	94	94	94	97	97	97	97	100	—
92	94	94	94	94	94	96	97	97	97	100	—	—	—	—
91	92	92	93	93	94	94	94	94	97	97	97	97	100	—
92	92	93	94	94	94	94	97	97	97	97	100	—	—	—
7	8	8	9	11	12	15	21	32	49	69	86	92	97	100
94	94	94	97	97	97	97	100	—	—	—	—	—	—	—
24	40	54	62	93	97	100	—	—	—	—	—	—	—	—

tion centers attracted some steel users, but the lake cities (Chicago, Milwaukee, Detroit, Cleveland, Toronto) became outstanding centers of metal manufacturing and engineering. They were the dominating focal points in the transportation net; today they are leading markets for the steel industry. In contrast to Europe, the steel industry of the United States operates in a single free-trade area, and has not been exposed to war damage and lengthy reconstruction periods twice in half a century. The American steel pattern should be more rational than the European, although it has been exposed to the same influences of general industrial inertia.

In the 1950's the differences in assembly costs for raw materials had narrowed to insignificance among blast furnace sites on the coast, lake shores, or waterways of the Manufacturing Belt,[8] but with increasing size of ore carriers may again have widened in favor of tidewater sites. Nevertheless, the advantage of a location with good access to markets weighs heavier than small differentials in the cost of materials. Both steel production and steel consumption are concentrated in relatively few points on the map; 17 industrial areas accounted for 90 per cent of American steel production in a recent year, and 120 areas for 95 per cent of consumption.[9] It is essential for the steel mills to have a large percentage of steel consumption in their "home market," or the area in which they enjoy a freight cost advantage over mills of competing centers. Table 2.2 shows that steel mills in Chicago, Detroit, and Morrisville (New York and Philadelphia) have the largest American "home markets," and

[8] Marvin J. Barloon, "The Expansion of Blast Furnace Capacity, 1938-52," *Business History Review*, Vol. 28 (March 1954), 1-23.
[9] Donald Fink, *op. cit.*, 280 ff.

that western mills must absorb much freight to reach any sizeable percentage of the market. In Table 2.3, market access is seen in relation to capacity. The markets reached by selected amounts of freight absorption are expressed as multiples of the production capacity of principal production centers. The more freight a mill has to absorb to keep busy, the less profitable is its location.

Table 2.3. Cumulative Industrial Market for Steel (Expressed as a Multiple of the Production Center's Capacity), by Amount of Freight Absorption from Principal Steel Production Centers

	(Freight absorption, cents per hundred pounds)										
	0	10	20	30	40	50	60	70	80	90	100
Chicago	1.1	1.3	1.6	1.9	3.0	3.5	4.1	4.6	4.7	5.1	5.1
Pittsburgh	.3	.5	.9	1.9	2.7	4.5	5.7	5.8	5.9	6.0	6.0
Youngstown	.4	.6	2.6	3.8	6.2	9.3	10.3	10.5	10.8	11.0	11.0
Baltimore	.5	.6	3.0	3.1	3.6	4.9	7.7	9.9	13.0	14.9	15.2
Cleveland	.9	1.8	4.4	8.8	10.8	13.5	15.0	16.4	16.7	16.8	16.8
Detroit	3.4	3.8	5.0	7.9	11.9	13.5	14.4	15.6	17.0	17.1	17.1
Buffalo	.9	1.0	1.6	5.4	11.1	13.2	15.5	17.8	18.0	18.7	18.7
Wheeling-Weirton- Steubenville	.2	1.8	3.4	7.3	10.3	17.0	21.4	21.8	22.3	22.8	22.9
Birmingham	.9	1.1	1.4	1.7	1.8	4.6	7.6	11.2	21.7	25.1	25.7
Fontana	1.7	1.8	2.0	2.0	2.0	2.0	2.0	2.0	2.0	2.0	2.0
Bethlehem	1.0	6.2	6.6	7.4	7.8	10.9	14.5	21.1	29.2	33.5	34.6
Middletown	3.9	4.5	7.5	13.5	31.1	34.7	37.3	40.6	40.8	40.8	41.1
Morrisville	6.7	7.9	9.6	10.5	10.9	12.1	20.2	27.0	42.1	48.6	50.3
Johnstown	.1	1.1	7.0	12.5	29.0	40.0	45.4	53.2	54.0	55.8	56.1
Geneva	.6	.6	.6	.6	.6	.6	1.6	1.6	2.3	2.3	4.3
St. Louis	2.9	5.0	8.4	13.3	25.7	28.0	39.0	46.6	53.1	60.0	64.1
Houston	3.5	4.0	4.2	4.4	5.4	5.4	6.7	8.1	12.5	18.1	18.8

Source: Donald A. Fink and Pittsburgh Regional Planning Association, *op. cit.*

Pittsburgh was a major iron center from the early nineteenth century. Located where the Monongahela and the Allegheny join to form the Ohio River, the chief axis of penetration in early settlement of the present Middle West, Pittsburgh was the principal supply point for the rapidly developing interior. The iron produced in the forests near Pittsburgh, based on charcoal and local iron ore, was largely sold via distributors in the city to village blacksmiths in the form of bars; some was rolled and manufactured in the city.[10]

The all-purpose iron required by blacksmiths became too expensive for some factories, which could use the cheaper wrought iron made in coal-fired puddling furnaces. The rail manufacturers, who increased their share of American pig iron production from 5 per cent in 1849 to a peak of 55 per cent in 1865, were the most important in this category. It became economic to integrate puddling and rolling in Pittsburgh rather than puddling and charcoal smelting in the forest areas. By 1857, 80 per cent of the iron coming into Pittsburgh was pig iron; the refining function had been withdrawn from the countryside. The first coke-fired blast furnace in Pittsburgh was built in 1859, and in the following 20 years

[10] The section on Pittsburgh draws heavily on Donald Fink, *op. cit.*

the charcoal furnaces were driven out of business by new and large coke furnaces in the Pittsburgh area. Good coking coal was found at Connelsville. Despite its rapid growth, Pittsburgh declined from over 15 per cent of the national iron output in 1857 to less than 10 per cent by 1872. Chicago, Wheeling, and Youngstown were important rival centers in the Middle West. The railroads had reduced the importance of Pittsburgh's command of river routes to interior markets.

The period of relative decline came to an end with the opening of the first Bessemer plant in the region in 1875. Pittsburgh's rapid rise to dominance in steelmaking was a result of its proximity to the Connelsville coking coal, the finest metallurgical coals in the world. Coke was made in beehive ovens near the mines, and shipped to the furnaces by rail; by-product coke ovens were not introduced on a large scale in the United States until World War I. Virtually all metallurgical coke used in the country came from the Connelsville coal of southwestern Pennsylvania. Pig iron accounted for an estimated 60 per cent of the cost of a Bessemer steel rail in 1875; coke costs were the main determinant of regional differences in pig iron costs. The last of the 11 major steel works in the Pittsburgh area was built in 1911. Pittsburgh's peak share of national production and capacity for pig iron and steel was reached around the turn of the century. In the production of steel ingots it reached an alltime high of 43 per cent in 1894; its high in pig iron was 27 per cent in 1904.

The ingot capacity of the Pittsburgh region increased from 15 million short tons in 1916 to 24 million tons in 1960, but the total U.S. capacity in that time increased from 49 million tons to 147 million tons. The poor market location of Pittsburgh, compared with most other major producing centers in the United States, is evident from Table 2.3. The table is based on rail rates only, and Pittsburgh's position is significantly improved by its location on the Ohio-Mississippi River system. Pittsburgh's prominence in the production of oilfield equipment, which goes back to the early days of American petroleum and gas industries, is based not only on an early start but also on river transport. But this position is challenged by the growing steel industry of Texas and by foreign competitors that ship products directly to Galveston. Chicago has recently had its position vis-à-vis the oilfield market improved with the widening of the Calumet Sag Channel.

The iron and steel industry accounts for about one-third of manufacturing employment in the Pittsburgh region. The growth of office and research employment in recent years has benefited Pittsburgh, the main administrative and research capital of the American steel industry.

Only two or three of the 11 major steel works in the Pittsburgh region have room for expansion; the others are seriously hemmed in by the narrow river valleys and by competing claimants for space.

The *Youngstown* area has a background similar to Pittsburgh. The steel mills line the Mahoning and Shenango rivers, tributaries of the Ohio River.[11] A large expansion in the decade before 1870 was based on local

[11] Allan Rodgers, "The Iron and Steel Industry of the Mahoning and Shenango Valleys," *Economic Geography*, Vol. 28 (October 1952), 331-42.

block coal, which could be used directly in the blast furnace. After the introduction of modern steel mills, the industry used beehive coke hauled by rail from Connelsville. In this century the greatest change in assembly costs for raw materials was affected by the introduction of by-product coke ovens. Pittsburgh and steel works on the Ohio River obtained cheap coal by barge from coal mines on the Monongahela River, but Youngstown had to pay for additional rail haul from the Ohio. Like Pittsburgh, Youngstown has had a low expansion rate in recent decades. The district has long emphasized production of sheets and strips for the automobile industry. It has a more favorable market location than Pittsburgh, if measured by rail freight only.

Chicago has had steady growth from the middle of the last century to its present position as the world's leading steel center, surpassing the steel capacity of the Ruhr. Including a large number of metal manufacturing centers within easy trucking distance in Illinois, Indiana, Wisconsin, and Michigan, Chicago is also the largest market for steel in the United States, slightly exceeding Detroit (Table 2.2). The industry is concentrated to the southern part of the urbanized area, stretching along the southern shore of Lake Michigan, from Calumet River in Illinois to Indiana Harbor, Gary, and the proposed Burns Harbor in Indiana.[12]

The first major steel works in southern Chicago was built in the 1880's on the Calumet River by a company that, in 1901, merged with the Carnegie interests of Pittsburgh and other companies into the giant U.S. Steel Corporation. International Harvester, Republic Steel, and Acme Steel also have steel works on the Calumet River.

The first steel mill on the Indiana side of the state line was opened by U.S. Steel in 1906. It was named Gary in honor of the president of the corporation; for a long time it was the world's largest steel mill. The steel works and adjacent plants, which are subsidiaries of U.S. Steel (engineering plants and a large cement plant), are served by two private harbors within company property.

Between the Calumet River and Gary are two steel works on Indiana Harbor, a public port opened in 1916. The single plant of the large Inland Steel Company is second in size only to Gary. Youngstown Sheet and Tube Company concentrates its Chicago operations in its Indiana Harbor works; until recently, the company had a second plant at the entrance of the Calumet River. The two steel companies share the public port with other industries, including oil refineries and a gypsum plant.

Two steel companies, National Steel and Bethlehem Steel, have built finishing plants at the proposed Burns Harbor, with the intention of constructing fully integrated mills in the future. According to announced plans, the Bethlehem works may eventually be larger than Gary.

Shore sites provide many advantages for an integrated steel mill, always in need of elbow room: an unlimited supply of industrial water, dumping areas for slag and other wastes (the steel mill creates its own land for

[12] J. B. Appleton, "The Iron and Steel Industry of the Calumet District," *University of Illinois Studies in the Social Sciences*, Vol. 13, No. 2 (1927); Harold M. Mayer, "Politics and Land Use: the Indiana Shoreline of Lake Michigan," *Annals*, Association of American Geographers, Vol. 54 (December 1964), 508-23.

future expansion), and deep water quays for receipt of iron ore, limestone, and shipments of heavy products. When National Steel and Bethlehem Steel sought entrance to the Chicago market as steel producers, they looked to the Michigan shoreline to the east of Gary. The area between Gary and Chicago is almost completely industrialized, and the shoreline north of Chicago is a wave-cut bluff on which residential suburbs reach the Wisconsin state line.

The shoreline east of Gary is an ideal location for steel mills if deep water channels are provided, but it is also a recreation area for the seven million population of Greater Chicago, a remarkable sand-dune country with excellent bathing beaches. This conflict between heavy industry, with demands for industrial land, and the recreation interests and need for land of the urban population will become increasingly acute everywhere.[13] A third steel producer seeking entrance to the Chicago market, Jones & Laughlin, has announced plans for a large steelworks in an even more peripheric location, at Peoria on the Illinois Lakes-to-Gulf Waterway, where the large Caterpillar works will be a compatible neighbor and where the iron ore situation will be substantially improved with the new iron ore mines now being opened in Missouri.

MAJOR U.S. STEEL COMPANIES. The giant U.S. Steel was concentrated in the Pittsburgh and Chicago areas when formed in 1901, and three-fifths of the company's capacity is still in these two districts. In the financial panic of 1907, U.S. Steel acquired control of the largest steel company in the South. It had two steel works at Birmingham, built after 1886 on the basis of local iron ore, coal, and limestone, making for low pig iron costs. In 1915 a steel plant was completed at Duluth, after pressure from the ore-exporting state of Minnesota. During World War II, U.S. Steel built and operated a steel mill for the government at Geneva, Utah. This and other peripheral steel mills built with government support during the war to supply the tremendous shipbuilding industry, strategically deployed to all coastal areas, were acquired on favorable terms by private interests after the war; they would hardly have been built by private concerns under normal conditions.[14]

After the war, U.S. Steel built an integrated steel works on the Atlantic seaboard at Morrisville, located between the New York market, most of which is in northern New Jersey, and the Philadelphia region. This was the first steel works planned and constructed by the company on a green-field site, and without outside pressure, since the opening of the Gary works in 1906. The opening of a new steel works is indeed a rare event.

The second largest American steel corporation, Bethlehem Steel, organized in 1904, has its homeworks at Bethlehem, in the Lehigh Valley. This was a leading iron producing region before the Civil War, because

[13] For a detailed discussion of the Indiana shoreline case, see Mayer, *op. cit.* The speed of the urbanization process can be measured in two ways: by increase in the urban population, and by increased demand for urban land. Since the average urban dweller demands more private space for himself, more public space for his car, and more elbow room in his office or factory, the demand for urban land increases at a higher rate than urban population.

[14] Strategic considerations also influenced the selection of sites for steel mills; Kaiser's works at Los Angeles would normally have been constructed on the coast, and not inland at Fontana.

of anthracite coal and local ore deposits. During World War I the company acquired a steel works at Sparrows Point, Baltimore, originally built in the late 1880's. It has been expanded several times, and in 1960 had the world's largest ingot capacity, 7.5 million metric tons a year, and a work force of 30,000. Before the construction of U.S. Steel's Morrisville works, it was the only major steel mill on the Atlantic seaboard, favorably located to supply the East Coast market, the expanding West Coast market, and foreign markets. Tinplate, for the large local canning plants and for the California market, and ship plate are its specialties. The works is adjoined by a shipyard, and most American construction and repair yards are located on the East Coast. Both Sparrows Point and Morrisville have benefited from the opening of new deposits of high-grade iron ore in Latin America, Africa, and Labrador, and in the switch to huge ore carriers. The freight divide for Labrador ore moving inland from Cleveland or Baltimore/Philadelphia is at Youngstown rather than at Pittsburgh.[15]

In 1917 Bethlehem Steel acquired a steel works at Johnstown, Pennsylvania, and in 1922 added the Lackawanna works on the outskirts of Buffalo. The latter mill had been moved from Scranton, in anthracite country, to Buffalo at the turn of the century. This move took advantage of low freight costs for iron ore and the growing Great Lakes market while retaining a favorable location for supplying the New York market.

Bethlehem Steel has been concentrated in the eastern part of the Manufacturing Belt, while U.S. Steel and other major steel companies were in the western part. This pattern changed when U.S. Steel opened the Morrisville works in 1952; in 1963, Bethlehem Steel announced that the company was going to build a large integrated works at Chicago.

U.S. Steel, long the largest manufacturing company in the United States, is now surpassed by several companies. In sales it ranks sixth after General Motors, Ford, General Electric, and two oil companies, Jersey Standard and Socony Mobil Oil; in employment it ranks fourth. Its share of the national steel capacity has declined from a peak of more than half in 1907 to a little over one-fourth.

The seven steel companies next in rank after the two giants, almost all formed through mergers, are on a par with the largest European companies. Republic Steel, with most of its capacity in Ohio, is a leading producer of alloy steels, and has specialized in steel for the automotive industry. Republic Steel is represented in Chicago, in the South (Gadsden), and at Buffalo. Jones & Laughlin, an old Pittsburgh firm, also has steel capacity at Cleveland and Detroit. National Steel has works at Weirton on the Ohio and at Detroit. Like Bethlehem Steel, it has built finishing facilities at the proposed Burns Harbor at Chicago, with the intention of eventually building an integrated mill. Youngstown Sheet and Tube is producing steel at Youngstown and Chicago, and Inland Steel has works at Chicago only. Inland Steel is the largest one-plant corporation in the United States. Armco Steel has grown out of a sheet

[15] Cyrus J. Sharer, "The Philadelphia Iron and Steel District: Its Relation to the Seaways," *Economic Geography,* Vol. 39 (October 1963), 363-67.

rolling mill at Middletown, Ohio. This company pioneered the continuous rolling mill in the 1920's.[16]

CANADA. The Steel Company of Canada (Stelco), with almost half the national capacity, dominates Canadian production. Hamilton is by far the largest Canadian steel center. It has an excellent market location, within trucking distance of the large Toronto market and most other Ontario markets, and with rail or ship connections with the rest of the Canadian ecumene. Coastwise shipping as an alternative often means lower rail freight, and is therefore of greater importance than indicated by actual tonnages carried. With the large iron ore developments in Labrador, the Montreal area, the largest steel deficit region in Canada, has become a potential location for steel works, but so far no integrated steel mill has been completed on the St. Lawrence River.

WESTERN EUROPE. The rapid postwar expansion of the West European steel industry has again brought this continent on a par with Anglo-America among steel producing areas of the world. In 1964 it produced 122 million tons of steel ingots, equalling Anglo-America's 123 million, and followed by the Soviet Union (85 million), Japan (40 million), Eastern Europe (27 million), and the rest of the world (35 million). The iron and steel industry was at the heart of postwar economic cooperation in Continental Europe, which led to the *European Coal and Steel Community* (ECSC), proposed in 1950 by French Secretary of Foreign Affairs Robert Schuman, signed in 1951, ratified in 1952, and effective in 1953. The Schuman Plan had Jean Monnet as its chief architect.[17] The success of the ECSC led to even closer economic cooperation among the six participating countries, Belgium, Luxembourg, France, West Germany, Italy, and the Netherlands, which in 1958 formed the European Economic Community. The United Kingdom stood aloof during long negotiations but, facing a *fait accompli,* responded by forming with the Scandinavian countries (Denmark, Norway, Sweden) and Austria, Switzerland, and Portugal the European Free Trade Association (EFTA). This trade organization was thought of as an instrument that would enable its members to join the Common Market. But in February, 1963, President de Gaulle of France vetoed a British application for membership in the EEC, temporarily halting the large-scale integration of West European economies.

THE COMMON MARKET. The European Economic Community (EEC) is second only to the United States in its steel production capacity. Four of the participating countries, Germany, France, Belgium, and Luxembourg, are iron and steel producers of long standing. The Heavy Triangle of continental Western Europe, with apexes at the Ruhr, at Dunkerque, and at Lorraine, includes the coal basins of Nord-Pas de Calais, Sambre-Meuse, Campine-Limburg-Aachen, Ruhr, and Saar, and

[16] The United States has, until recently, been dependent on Europe for new iron and steel techniques, with rolling mills the great exception. Since the war American steel firms have moved into research, maintaining large metallurgical research centers.

[17] Monnet also designed the *Plan français de Modernisation de l'Équipement,* which went into operation in 1947 to facilitate the rational use of American Marshall Plan aid in the reconstruction of French economy. The success of the reconstruction plan turned it into a permanent institution, *le Plan,* which sets out guideposts for the French economy, including its geographic aspects.

in addition, the Luxembourg-Lorraine minette ore deposits. The natural unity of enormous industrial capacity in this relatively small area was a major argument in favor of the ECSC. The institutions of the ECSC, placed under the High Authority, with headquarters in Luxembourg, were designed to facilitate economic functioning of the Heavy Triangle.

The rapidly expanding steel industries of Italy and the Netherlands represent a new type of location (which is also coming into use in the old steel nations) [18]: large integrated works on tidewater using imported ore and coal, carried in huge bulk carriers which, since 1955, have revolutionized the concept of economic distance for water-transported bulk cargo. The iron ore imports of the ECSC increased from 13 million tons in 1954 to 33 million in 1962. West Africa, Latin America, India, and Canada accounted for rapidly increasing quantities, but Sweden remained the largest single supplier (40 per cent in 1962).

In a sense, international organization of the European steel industry antedates World War I, when large corporations and cartels operated across national borders. But the cooperation realized within the ECSC is much more ambitious; with a common heavy industry, wars between France and Germany will hardly be repeated. The Community aims at removing all internal obstacles concerning both raw material and marketing in the steel industry: quotas, embargoes, tariffs, export taxes, subsidies, and discriminatory pricing and freight rates will all be abolished.

BELGIUM.   Well-known for its iron and steel industry, Belgium is a major steel exporter. It has in Antwerp, ideally located to serve the Heavy Triangle of Western Europe, the world's leading steel port. Many of the shipments through the preferred steel port of the EEC originate in neighboring countries.[19] The steel shipments have helped make Antwerp the leading general cargo port of Europe.

The heyday of the Belgian iron industry came in the 1830's and 1840's.[20] But unfavorable geological conditions and complex mining rights eventually led to a relative decline in the efficiency of Belgian coal mines. By the end of the century almost all iron ore was imported. A railroad was built across the Ardennes to carry minette ore and pig iron from Lorraine to the Liège and Charleroi areas, the major Belgian steel centers. Blast furnaces were built in the extreme south of Belgium within sight of the minette deposits of Lorraine, and Luxembourg and Belgian interests were engaged in iron works established elsewhere on the minette field.

---

[18] D. K. Fleming, *Coastal Steel Production in the European Coal and Steel Community 1953 to 1963* (Dissertation, Geography), University of Washington, 1965.

[19] The importance of the export market varies widely among EEC countries, ranging from nearly 80 per cent of total deliveries in Belgium and Luxembourg to 20 per cent in Germany and only 12 per cent in Italy. Exports to outside countries represented nearly 20 per cent of total EEC deliveries in 1960.

[20] The Englishman Cockerill had come to Belgium at the end of the eighteenth century and established a successful factory for textile machines at Seraing, near Liège. His son integrated backwards, and started to make iron for his machine factory. The Cockerill firm became the largest industrial empire in Europe, and the iron-smelting industry of Belgium was the envy of most of continental Europe at the middle of the nineteenth century. The Cockerill firm was one of many testimonies on the European continent to Britain's position as the innovation center during the early phase of the Industrial Revolution.

Basic changes in the Belgian heavy industry pattern after formation of the ECSC include cutting out ten million tons of annual coal production at uneconomic mines in southern Belgium, and the establishment of an integrated steel mill at Zelzate on the Gent-Terneuzen Canal, incorporating the latest trends in steel making: large sintering capacity, giant blast furnaces, and oxygen converters. This works is being built by SIDMAR (Sidérurgie Maritime), a joint venture of several steel groups represented in the traditional steel districts of the Heavy Triangle, including Cockerill-Ougrée (formed in 1955 through the merger of Belgium's two leading steel companies), ARBED, the dominating steel group in Luxembourg, and Schneider, one of the three leading French companies.

WEST GERMANY. Germany surpassed Britain as a steel producer at the turn of the century, and remained second to the United States until surpassed by the Soviet Union in the 1930's. Only a small portion of the interwar output was produced outside present West Germany. After a rapid postwar recovery, West Germany produces almost half of the EEC steel output, but an even faster expansion of the Japanese steel industry has placed West Germany in fourth place on the world list of steel producers.

The German iron and steel industry is concentrated in the Ruhr, the second largest iron and steel producing area in the world. The Ruhr forms a conurbation approaching Paris in size, heavily dependent on manufacturing and mining, and forming the leading coal-steel-heavy engineering complex in Europe.[21]

The rise of the Ruhr to European eminence in iron and steel manufacturing occurred after 1850; the first coke-fired blast furnace went into operation in 1849. Data on coal production mirror the change: from 1800 to 1849 output increased from 0.2 to 1.4 million tons; between 1850 and 1899 it grew from 1.7 to 55.1 million tons. Germany, like the United States, virtually stepped directly from charcoal iron to mass-produced steel. It was not so hard pressed as Britain to switch to coke-fired blast furnaces, which produced a cheaper but less versatile iron.[22]

The forested highlands to the south of the Ruhr was one of the oldest and largest iron working regions in Europe. Entrepreneurs and technicians were thus available for the new development, and so was capital; Cologne was a major banking and financial center. The market location of the Ruhr was excellent, in the midst of the most densely populated part of Europe. The Rhine River connected the area with the North Sea, making cheap water transport available for imported iron ore and for exported coal; riparian upstream areas also benefited from water connection with the new industrial district, and chemical and other heavy manufacturing industries were established. The Rhine Valley, including the Ruhr, became the manufacturing heartland of Europe, and the small Rhine River one of the busiest waterways in the world.

21 Ruhr (excl. Düsseldorf) has 1.3 per cent of West Germany's land area, 9 per cent of its population, and produces 80 per cent of its coal and 60 per cent of its steel.

22 It should also be noted that the German view in the decades before 1850 was that Germany could not compete with Belgium and England, which had "richer coal fields and more abundant iron ore." This conclusion is drawn in a contemporary survey of German rail production, published in 1845. Pounds and Parker, *op. cit.*, p. 239.

The coal seams, exposed at the Ruhr River in the southern part of the area, dip relatively steeply northwards. The exposed coal is lean or anthracitic; the more valuable coal can be reached only by shaft mines, which become progressively deeper northwards in the Hellweg, Emscher, and Lippe zones. Local iron ore was available in the early years of Ruhr industrial expansion: high-grade, low-phosphorous ore from the Siegerland hills in the south, the raw material base of Germany's largest concentration of blast furnaces in the 1840's,[23] and "blackband" ironstone found in the coal field. In the 1870's, Spain for a time became a major supplier of low-phosphorous ore from deposits at Bilbao; after the introduction of the Thomas process, Swedish ore became the major ore base of the Ruhr industry.

As a complementary route to the natural waterway of the Rhine, a canal was constructed in the 1890's between Dortmund, in the eastern part of the Ruhr, and Emden, which was made a "German Rhine estuary port." Canals were also built within the Ruhr area, along the Emscher (the Rhine-Herne Canal, completed in 1914), and along the Lippe, opened for barge traffic in 1928. Both connected the Rhine and the Dortmund-Ems Canal. Blast furnaces established from the 1870's lay in the Hellweg zone [24] north of the Ruhr Valley, and later in the Emscher zone, at the sources of the best coking coal. About 1.7 tons of coke were needed to melt one ton of iron ore. By-product coke ovens were built at the pits; in the 1870's the German coal-tar chemical industry, producing dyes and drugs, began its climb to world eminence. By World War II the chemical industry, based on coal, had become extremely complex, with one of its major concentrations in the Ruhr. In the postwar years this industry has switched, to a large extent, from coal to petroleum.

Points near the two access-routes for iron ore, the Rhine and the Dortmund-Ems Canal, were favored for steel works; Duisburg in the west and Dortmund in the east attracted several works. But Oberhausen, Essen, Gelsenkirchen, and Bochum, more centrally located in the Ruhr, also benefited from barge-transported ore after the completion of the Herne Canal. Many works in this part of the Ruhr were established while the industry had a local or regional ore base. Sites on waterways gradually became more attractive as blast furnace performances improved. Today

[23] Much Siegerland pig iron was manufactured elsewhere, e.g., in the Sauerland, where each small district had its local specialty. Solingen, of medieval fame for its swords, was known for cutlery. Separation of iron smelting and manufacturing was common in other parts of Europe; scarcity of charcoal and water-power sites was the rationale behind such separation. The coal-based iron and steel industry was quite different; it favored geographic concentration not only of blast furnaces, steel mills, and rolling mills but also, at least initially, of heavy engineering works. But industrial inertia helped many old manufacturing towns survive and become major centers of metal manufacturing.

[24] The Hellweg zone, the core of the Ruhr, is marked by a string of large cities, dominated by steel works and engineering industries and less by coal mining (Duisburg, Essen, Bochum, and Dortmund). The present areal differentiation in the Ruhr reflects the march of coal mining and manufacturing industry from south to north. Almost all manufacturing industries in the area are there more or less directly because of coal deposits. Oil refineries had their predecessors in prewar and wartime works producing synthetic gasoline from coal. The strong apparel industry and the electrical machinery and electronics industries, which all employ many women, were attracted to the Ruhr by the uneven sex balance in the labor force of traditional Ruhr industries.

some 0.8 to 0.7 tons of coke, but two to three tons of ore, are needed for one ton of pig iron.[25]

The August Thyssen Works at Hamborn, in the northern part of present Duisburg, established in 1890 and the core of the large Thyssen concern, is the largest steel works in Germany, with more than four million tons of ingot production. The Gutehoffnungshütte was first in the Ruhr with an integrated works in which iron passed from blast furnace to rolling mill "in one heat" (Oberhausen, 1888). The large integrated works of the Krupp organization in Essen, best known of the Ruhr cities and home town of the Krupp dynasty, has not been rebuilt after it was dismantled in the postwar years. The concern still produces steel at Rheinhausen, but its main interests are now in heavy engineering and other steel consuming industries.

Other large steel corporations with major operations in the Ruhr area are Mannesmann, Rheinische Stahlwerke, Phoenix-Rheinrohr, Hoesch, Dortmund-Hörder Hüttenunion, and Hüttenwerk Oberhausen.

Small blast furnaces and steel works were established at the turn of the century in coastal cities, and on the large deposits of low grade ore on the north German plain. A much larger blast furnace expansion occurred in German Lorraine as a result of the decreasing pull of coal in the steel economy. The economy of the continuous process, however, soon discouraged the spread of blast furnace capacity. Germany saw no migration of large integrated works to the coast before World War I. In the 1930's, the Nazi government built a large steel works at Salzgitter, similar to the British works at Corby, and based on low-grade ore. It was planned to serve the market in the nearby Volkswagen plant at Wolfsburg. Both plants were owned after the war by the West German government, until the Volkswagen works was sold in 1961 to the public. The first integrated tidewater plant was established after the war at Bremen (Klöckner).

Before World War I, the Saar was closely associated with German Lorraine, and after the two wars it was, for a long time, under French control. It was closely associated with the adjacent French industry even before the creation of the postwar iron and steel community. The steel output from this area exceeds three million tons.

FRANCE. The French steel industry is concentrated in two small areas. Two-thirds of the steel and four-fifths of the pig iron is produced by some fifteen steel works within a small triangle in Lorraine, marked by Nancy and Thionville in the Moselle and Longwy in the Meuse river systems. The area is adjacent to the steel district of Luxembourg. In 1871-1914 it was cut through by the Franco-German border, which greatly influenced the location of steel plants; some were built in Germany, others in France. The steel works—all but one established before World War I—were attracted by large deposits of low-grade iron ore (minette) made available by the introduction of the Thomas process in

[25] Günter Mertins, "Die Entwicklung von Bergbau und Eisenindustrie im westlichen Ruhrgebiet," *Geographische Rundschau*, Vol. 17 (May 1965), 171-79; Hans Knübel, "Die Eisenhüttenindustrie des Ruhrgebiets," *Geographische Rundschau*, Vol. 13 (May 1961), 193-203.

1879. Steel production increased from 100,000 tons in 1880 to 4.6 million in 1913, the tonnage equally divided between the two countries. Lorraine accounted for 13 per cent of Germany's steel output in 1913, and for 22 per cent of her pig iron. German Lorraine received most of its coal and all its coke from the Ruhr; iron ore and pig iron moved in the opposite direction. This exchange between the Ruhr and the Lorraine was never re-established on any important scale after World War I. The newest and largest steel works in Lorraine, Seremange, was completed in 1953, and had an ingot production in 1961 of 1.8 million tons. The new Moselle canal has given Lorraine cheaper access to the Rhine and to the sea.

The other major steel region is near the Belgian border, with the largest works at Denain and Valenciennes on the Scheldt, and Dunkerque on the North Sea. The first two represent older location decisions than the works of Lorraine, established before 1850 and French examples of coal field-oriented iron works. All three works are now operated by USINOR, the leading French steel company. Denain, the largest steelworks in France, with a 1960 production of 1.9 million ingot tons, will be surpassed by the new works at Dunkerque, which is expected to grow from an initial capacity of 1.5 million tons (1962) to five to six million tons in the early 1970's. The Dunkerque works should be a dynamic example of a long overdue trend in the economic geography of French steel production. A large coastal mill is also planned for the Marseille area.

LUXEMBOURG. With a raw material base of minette ore for its iron and steel industry, closely associated with the Lorraine deposits, Luxembourg has been economically tied to Belgium since World War I through a customs union. Since World War II it has been associated with both Belgium and the Netherlands (Benelux). The small country is dominated by its large iron and steel industry, located in the southern border area. Luxembourg is the seat of the High Authority, governing body of ECSC.

ITALY. Characteristic of the prewar steel industry in Italy were many small mills near important markets in Milan, Turin, and other industrial cities in the north.[26] An unusually high percentage of electric and open-hearth furnace capacity created a heavy demand for scrap; Italy and Japan ranked among the leading customers in the international scrap market.

Since the war the industry has expanded rapidly, primarily at large integrated coastal plants. The state-controlled sector of the industry represents 60 per cent of the steel capacity, much more than in any of the other ECSC

[26] Norman J. G. Pounds, *The Geography of Iron and Steel*, 2nd ed. (London: Hutchinson, 1963), pp. 98-100.

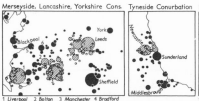

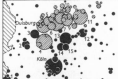

Merseyside, Lancashire, Yorkshire Cons.   Tyneside Conurbation   Ruhr Conurbation

1 Liverpool   2 Bolton   3 Manchester   4 Bradford
5 Preston   6 Blackburn

1 Aachen   2 Mönchengladbach   3 Krefeld   4 Düsseldorf
5 Oberhausen   6 Mülheim   7 Essen   8 Gelsenkirchen
9 Bochum   10 Recklinghausen   11 Dortmund   12 Hagen
13 Wuppertal   14 Solingen   15 Remscheid

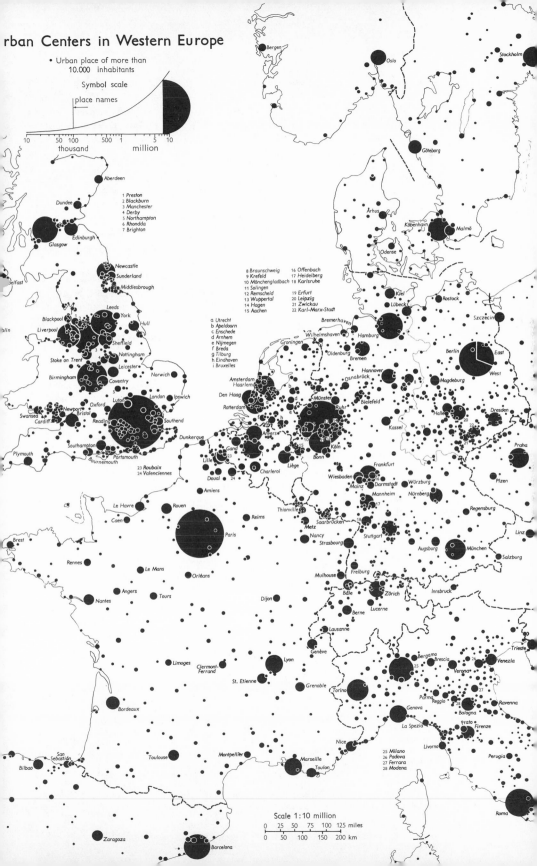

rban Centers in Western Europe

• Urban place of more than 10.000 inhabitants

Symbol scale

place names

| 10 | 50 | 100 | 500 | 1 | 5 | 10 |

thousand   million

1 Preston
2 Blackburn
3 Manchester
4 Derby
5 Northampton
6 Rhondda
7 Brighton

8 Braunschweig   16 Offenbach
9 Krefeld   17 Heidelberg
10 Mönchengladbach 18 Karlsruhe
11 Solingen
12 Remscheid   19 Erfurt
13 Wuppertal   20 Leipzig
14 Hagen   21 Zwickau
15 Aachen   22 Karl-Marx-Stadt

a Utrecht
b Apeldoorn
c Enschede
d Arnhem
e Nijmegen
f Breda
g Tilburg
h Eindhoven
i Bruxelles

23 Roubaix
24 Valenciennes

25 Milano
26 Padova
27 Ferrara
28 Modena

Scale 1:10 million

| 0 | 25 | 50 | 75 | 100 | 125 miles |

| 0 | 50 | 100 | 150 | 200 km |

countries. Italsider owns four of eight large integrated coastal plants in the ECSC: the new works at Taranto, Bagnoli at Naples, Piombino, and Cornigliano at Genoa.[27] Such enormous projects as the Taranto works would probably have been beyond the financing and planning capabilities of a smaller, privately-owned concern, which would hardly have ventured such a radical geographic departure from the established steel areas.[28]

The Italian coastal works have sold a remarkably high percentage of their output in the domestic market, helped by the rapid growth of Italian per capita steel consumption. Italsider's Cornigliano plant at Genoa sells four-fifths of its rolled products domestically, chiefly in the Genoa-Turin-Milan industrial triangle. FIAT of Turin absorbs 30 to 40 per cent of the works' output. Only a trickle of exports is shipped by sea; most of it moves by rail to continental Europe.[29]

The new Taranto works, the first stage of which was opened in 1964, may become an exception, as the steel-using industries of the South, in spite of all efforts, are still rather small. Like many modern works, it is built exclusively for oxygen converters. It has its own tube mill and should take advantage of its strategic location for supplying pipe to Black Sea ports, the Middle East, and the Saharan oilfields. Cargo liners on several major shipping routes may call without making long detours. Taranto seems to have a better geographic location than two state-owned steel mills in the opposite periphery of Europe, built for similar social and political reasons, the Luleå works of Sweden and the Mo-i-Rana works of Norway.

THE NETHERLANDS. The least metal-oriented of the ECSC countries, the Netherlands has a somewhat lower per capita consumption of steel than Italy. The only Dutch steel works, the large integrated mill at IJmuiden, at the seaward end of the North Sea Canal to Amsterdam, pioneered the new trend of tidewater location. But plans of the early 1920's for an integrated steel works were not realized until after World War II.

[27] Over 60 per cent of Italsider's capital is held by Finsider (Società Financiaria Siderurgica), a holding company established in 1937 to manage iron and steel concerns which the Italian government had acquired in 1933 under IRI (Istituto per la Ricostruzione Industriale). IRI owns some 50 per cent of Finsider's capital. The Italian state, through IRI, *owns* some 30 per cent of the Italian steel capacity and *controls* some 60 per cent. Fleming, *op. cit.*

[28] The Taranto works represents a major effort by the Italian government to promote industrial development in the South and thus help to reduce the large difference in standards of living between the southern and northern parts of the country. This enormous national task is tackled in two ways: 1) *Cassa per il Mezzogiorno* (the Fund for the South), set up by law in 1950 and with a status somewhat similar to the American TVA, carries out land reclamation projects, provides public utilities, including roads and railroad facilities, and promotes private investments in manufacturing. 2) Through its two holding companies, IRI and ENI, the government directs a certain percentage of new investments in basic industries to the South. IRI, in addition to its interests in steel, has, through Finsider, sub-companies that are cement, ore, fertilizer, electrochemical and electricity producers as well as construction, shipping, sales, and research organizations. ENI is chiefly engaged in the petroleum and natural gas industries. Giuseppe di Nardi, "The Policy of Regional Development: A Case Study—Southern Italy," *Banca Nazionale del Lavoro, Quarterly Review*, Vol. 70 (September 1960), 215-44; Friedrich Vöchting, "Considerations on the Industrialization of the Mezzogiorno," *B.N.L., Quarterly Review*, Vol. 68 (September 1958), 325-76.

[29] Allan Rodgers, *The Industrial Geography of the Port of Genova* (Chicago: Univ. of Chicago, Dept. of Geography, 1960).

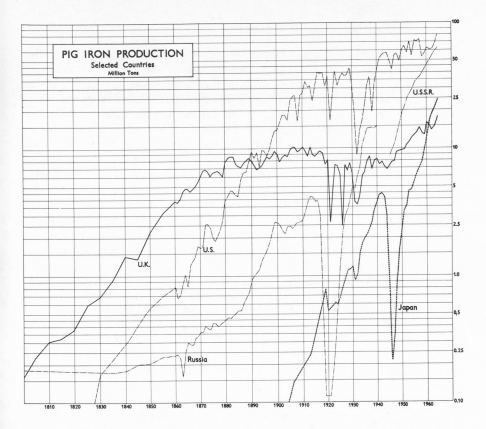

PIG IRON PRODUCTION
Selected Countries
Million Tons

In the nineteenth century, Britain was the workshop of the world, building iron ships, railroad equipment, and textile machinery for other nations. With a time lag of some thirty years, the United States surged ahead and in the late 1880's passed Britain as the leading iron and steel producer. The industrial revolution was roughly contemporary in Continental Europe and the United States. Russia, a world leader in iron production in the late eighteenth century, established a modern iron and steel industry after 1870. In the United States and Russia, the opening of continental land masses required tremendous railroad construction, and the railroads were big customers of the steel industry. In Japan, now the third largest iron and steel producer in the world, the history of modern industry is almost entirely confined to this century.

The Europoort project at Rotterdam includes sites for a large steel industry adjacent to Europe's deepest ore quays, capable of handling the largest ore carriers afloat.

THE UNITED KINGDOM. The birthplace of the iron technology based on coal, and later of the methods for mass producing steel, has a scattered industry distribution, legacy of a long industrial past. Seven steel districts each account for at least two million metric tons of crude steel. There are remarkable functional differentiations among steel districts, the mills of which are medium-sized or small. Some 70 per cent of British pig iron is made from imported ore. The major foreign ore-using steel works are located on the coast, but they are not able to handle ore directly from large carriers into the blast furnaces. The only ore quay (Newcastle) capable of handling a bulk carrier of 25,000 tons dwt, the size of the largest boats on the Great Lakes, serves the inland mill of Consett in Durham. The large integrated mill of the Steel Company of Wales at Margam, near Port Talbot, can only handle 10,000-tonners. Some competing steel mills on the Continent, in Japan, and in tidewater United States can receive much larger ore carriers at mill site, in exceptional cases up to 100,000 tons. In 1963, a Royal Commission found the lack of quays with depth to handle modern ore carriers to be a major handicap of the British steel industry. The physical geography of British coasts makes it an expensive handicap to overcome. A recent study by the British Iron and Steel Federation indicates that, when all factors are taken into consideration (depths at ore shipping ports, distances of ore hauls, costs of port construction in Britain, and so on), the optimum size of ore carriers serving the British industry in the next decades will be between 35,000 and 65,000 tons.

Since the Depression of the 1930's, the British steel industry has often been under government pressure in the location of new steel capacity. When, for example, Richard Thomas planned to build Britain's first integrated wide strip mill at Scunthorpe, the government persuaded the company to construct the new mill at Ebbw Vale in South Wales, one of the most depressed areas in Britain.[30] Nationalization of the industry by the Labor government immediately after the war proved abortive, but the government retains a considerable degree of control through the Iron and Steel Board. One of the largest steel corporations, Richard Thomas & Baldwins, remains publicly owned; imports of iron ore for all British mills are handled by one government organization. Since the war, public funds have been used in several instances for investment in mills located in unemployment areas.

South Wales, Britain's leading steel district, accounting for about a quarter of its output, has seen a shift away from small iron and steel works in the coal valleys, based on local coking coal and ironstone ore. The change has been to large integrated mills at the coast, where major locational assets are (potential) deep water quays for ore receipt, and reasonably short rail and trucking hauls to the two largest, most expansive markets, the London and Midland areas. These are the major domestic markets for the traditional specialty of South Wales, thin flat steel used in automobiles and consumer durables. Industrial expansion in South Wales, depressed by decline in production and export of coal, has met with government blessing. Some expansion has been the result of government pressure, but favorable market trends have had even greater influence. The Ebbw Vale mill, given a controversial location in the 1930's in a narrow valley with little room for expansion and efficient plant layout, has already proved unsuited for major expansion; in 1962 a new mill on a greenfield site at Newport was completed. Other major integrated mills are at Cardiff and Port Talbot. Tinplate continues to be a specialty of South Wales, with a large export. The industry changed its geographic pattern with the introduction of large continuous electrolytic

---

[30] D. C. D. Pocock, "Iron and Steel at Scunthorpe," *The East Midland Geographer,* Vol. 3 (1963), 124-38.

plants; many small units in the Swansea-Llanelly area were closed in the postwar period. Tin smelters based on British ores were started early in this coal field, but for a long time the copper, zinc, and tin smelters and refineries have treated imported raw material. Steel is now by far the most important part of the Welsh primary metal industry.

The Northeast Coast, or Tees-side (Middlesbrough) district, second largest in Britain, intimately associated with shipbuilding and heavy engineering, developed on the basis of Durham coking coal and ore from nearby Cleveland Hills. The local ore production reached a peak before World War I, but is now insignificant. Like South Wales, this district is almost entirely dependent on imported ore. It is dominated by the Dorman Long Company, whose major mills are at Cleveland (Middlesbrough) and West Hartlepool.

The East Midlands have two major steel towns, Scunthorpe and Corby, which, in contrast to other British steel centers, are entirely dependent on local ore from the vast but lean deposits of Jurassic ironstone. They are one-sided steel towns. Scunthorpe is a town of 70,000 people, of which over 20,000 are employed in three integrated steel works turning out 2.5 million tons of steel per year (and somewhat less pig iron). When exploitation started in the middle 1860's, the iron content was around 30 per cent; today the figure averages 20 per cent, probably the leanest ore mined in the world. For a quarter century the output was confined to pig iron. Recent decades have seen a complete switch to sintered ore and greatly improved blast furnace performances; most of the steel is made in oxygen converters. These advances should help this ore field-located steel industry face competition from new coastal steel works using rich imported ores. The three integrated works at Scunthorpe are operated by three major British steel concerns—Richard Thomas & Baldwins; Guest, Keen, and Nettlefolds; and the United Steel Company—which are all represented in several steel districts. The large integrated works at Corby was established by Stewarts & Lloyds in 1934. Corby's status as a company town was changed in 1950, when it was designated a new town. Corby has some 35,000 inhabitants.

Birmingham in the Black Country, well-known in Britain's early iron and steel history, has only one integrated steel works, of less than one million tons capacity. In addition, there are two nonintegrated works and three rolling mills near Birmingham. The Black Country of today is less deserving of this name than other manufacturing regions in Britain.

Sheffield, famous for its cutlery, is Britain's chief producer of alloy steels and other high value products. It has a small blast furnace capacity, and receives pig iron from the East Midlands and bar iron from Sweden. Sheffield's prominence in special steel manufacture is a legacy of a long history of steel making.

The iron and steel industry of the Lanarkshire coal field in Scotland was originally based on the "blackband" ironstone found with the coal, but this soon had to be supplemented with imported ore, first from Spain and later from a variety of sources. As in the Northeast, the steel industry from the beginning was closely associated with shipbuilding and heavy engineering; as late as 1920 Scotland accounted for one-fourth of the nation's steel, but this share has fallen below 10 per cent. Until World War II, the Scottish industry consisted of small plants located inland on the coal field in the Glasgow area, and specialized in heavy products. The decline of the staple industry of the Clyde Valley, ship-building, contributed to the region's depressed economy. After the war, an integrated steel complex was created at Motherwell, where the Ravens-craig works of Colville & Co. serves a continuous strip mill, designed to supply new automobile plants. Both the strip mill and the auto plants were attracted to Scotland through government intervention.

Scattered iron and steel plants form the Northwest district, stretching from the small North Wales coal field to Cumberland. Included are the Cumberland-Furness area, originally based on local hematite ore but now dependent on imports. Workington, in Cumberland, and Shotton, on the Dee south of Liverpool, are among the major works.

SWEDEN.   In Sweden, with the world's highest per capita consumption of steel, the metal manufacturing industries, including steel, now surpass the forest industries in value of exports. The metal sector approaches 50 per cent, the forest sector some 30 per cent, and iron ore only 6 per cent.

Most of the steel works and many engineering works are located in the Bergslagen district, stretching from Gävle to Lake Vänern. The steel mills are small measured by output tonnage, but are usually part of business concerns which are rather large in the European context. ASEA, SKF, the Johnson group, Bofors, Uddeholm, and Sandviken are a few examples. Sweden ranks among the leading world producers for some high-grade steels. Some steel mills would have a higher ranking if measured by value of output, since special steels for watch springs, razor blades, tools, and ball bearings command much higher prices than ordinary steel for construction, automobiles, and so on. The Bergslagen district has several hundred years of iron making tradition, based on exceptionally pure ores and, earlier, plentiful charcoal. Stora Koppar-bergs Bergslag, of early copper fame, "incorporated" in 1347, is the oldest existing manufacturing company in the world, and one of the largest in Sweden. Its Domnarvet steel works, the home works of the Kaldo-process [31] and other innovations in iron and steel making, has the largest ingot capacity in the country. Like the other steel works of Bergslagen, it has an inland location.

The two steel works at Luleå and Oxelösund have a different background and type of location. Both places have been shipping ports for iron ore since the end of last century. Luleå ships high-grade but phosphoric iron from Gällivare; Oxelösund handles the same type of ore from the Grängesberg mine. The Luleå works, built by the government during World War II when Sweden was cut off from traditional sources of tonnage steel, is icebound for several months and is far away from

[31] Named for Professor Bo Kalling and Domnarvet. Among other innovations are the Dored-process for making pig iron in a rotating "blast furnace" into which oxygen instead of air is blown, substantially shortening the time of each heat. The first experimental Dored-installation was opened in 1965. See *Iron Age,* Vol. 192 (October 31, 1963), 104-5 and *Journal of Metals,* Vol. 16 (April 1964), 337-39.

domestic markets and large liner ports. The controversial steel plant is a cornerstone in the government's plans for the economic development of Norrland.

The Oxelösund works, built by the Grängesberg Company after 1957, when the government used its option to buy most of the company's 50 per cent share in the Lapland iron mines, has a favorable location at ice-free quays that can handle 60,000 tonners, the largest vessels that have entered the Baltic. Its market location is far superior to that of the Luleå works. But the optimum location for a large steel works in Norden would be the Göteborg-Uddevalla area, strategically located to serve shipyards of Sweden, Norway, and Denmark, and, in addition, engineering and construction markets from Copenhagen to Oslo.[32] By comparison, Stockholm, which is near Oxelösund, is a small market. The choice of Oxelösund for the new works was influenced by its being the terminal of the ore railway from the company mine at Grängesberg, and the existence of small blast furnaces, coke ovens, and a glass works there since pre-World War I.

EASTERN EUROPE. The Communist countries of Eastern Europe are poorly endowed with iron ore, most of which is imported from Krivoi Rog. The large Upper Silesian coal field, one of the oldest centers for coke-fired blast furnaces in Europe and a major European focus of coal mining and heavy manufacturing, has exceptionally thick coal seams, which makes mining profitable, but the coal usually makes a soft coke, unsatisfactory in modern blast furnaces. The coal field, straddling the borders between Russia (Poland), Germany, and Austria-Hungary before World War I, and the borders between Germany, Poland, and Czechoslovakia in the interwar period, is now mainly within Poland. The Polish conurbation, centered on Gliwice, Bytom, and Katowice, is in the northern part of the coal basin. But the largest Polish steel works was built in the 1950's at the new town of Nowa Huta, east of the coal field near Kraków. Poland has developed a sizeable shipbuilding industry; much of the production is exported to the Soviet Union.

Czechoslovakia's steel industry is shared by a region centered on Moravska Ostrava, in the southern outlayer of the Silesian coal field, and the coal basins of Bohemia. In contrast to Poland, Czechoslovakia was one of the most advanced industrial nations of Europe before the war. It is a major supplier of machinery within the Communist Bloc.

In Hungary, the new integrated steel mill at Dunaujvaros on the Danube south of Budapest is largest. This mill was originally planned for Mohacs in southern Hungary on the Danube, near good Hungarian coking coal at Pecs and Komlo, and near Yugoslavian iron ore. The ideological dispute between Hungary and Yugoslavia in 1948 severed economic relations between the two countries, and Hungary decided to turn to the Soviet Union for its iron ore and, at the same time, build the steel works closer to the dominating Budapest market.

---

[32] Göteborg also has excellent liner services to the four corners of the world; deep water quays for modern super carriers can be provided. The absence of steel works at Göteborg indicates how slowly heavy industry may adapt itself to changed locational premises. The late growth of steel capacity at Detroit is another example.

COMECON (Council for Mutual Economic Aid) appears to have achieved little in bringing about a division of labor in Eastern Europe; every participating country wants to develop its own iron and steel industry irrespective of the economic rationale. The most rapid recent growth in steel production is reported for Romania, originally designated by COMECON planners to specialize in agricultural products and petroleum.

SOVIET UNION. The Russian iron and steel industry has experienced three periods of remarkable expansion. Russia was well endowed to meet rapidly increasing demand for charcoal iron in the eighteenth century, and production increased from 25,000 tons in 1718 to 183,000 tons in 1800. For some time Russia was the largest producer of iron in the world; three-fourths of the iron was produced in the Urals.

Modern development in Russia started in the 1870's, when Belgian and French capital was invested in a coal-based iron industry in the Ukraine. The coal field of the Donets Basin and Krivoi Rog iron ore were connected by rail in 1886.[33]

The third expansion period started with the five-year plans, which emphasized the iron and steel industry. The large Magnitogorsk works, built during the first five-year plan (1928-1932), had an ingot capacity of six million metric tons [34] in the late 1950's. For several years it produced more iron and steel than any other plant in the world, although it had a smaller capacity than two American works (Sparrows Point and Gary).

The Soviets have tried to overcome handicaps of long distances and expensive rail hauls for at least one raw material and for the finished product by economies of scale in production and transportation. Four of the new works, Magnitogorsk, Kuznetsk, Nizhni Tagil, and Zaporozhye, produced some 40 per cent of 1956 pig iron.

Magnitogorsk and Kuznetsk were built simultaneously, one at the rich ore of the Magnet Mountain and the other at the Kuznetsk coal basin, Kuzbas. Heavy trains in shuttle traffic were to carry coal in one direction and ore in the other within the Ural-Kuznetsk combine. In the late 1950's, almost two-thirds of the coking coal for Magnitogorsk came from Kuzbas, and one-third from Karaganda. The rich ores are almost depleted, and Magnitogorsk blast furnaces are being fed concentrates from large ore bodies around Kustanay, in Kazakhstan. Markets are far away; the closest metal-fabricating center of importance is Chelyabinsk.[35]

The Soviet iron and steel industry is usually grouped in three large regions: the South (Ukraine and the Rostov area), the East (chiefly the

[33] In 1885 the South produced 9 per cent of the pig iron, the Urals 78 per cent, and the Center (Tula, Lipetsk) 13 per cent. In 1913 the South had forged ahead to 74 per cent, the Urals had 21 per cent, and the Center 5 per cent. A. Zimm, *Industriegeographie der Sowietunion* (East Berlin: Deutscher Verlag der Wissenschaften, 1963), p. 118. For definition of regions, see last paragraph, this page.

[34] M. Gardner Clark, "Magnitogorsk: A Soviet Iron and Steel Plant in the Southern Urals," in *Focus on Geographic Activity*, Thoman and Patton, eds. (New York: McGraw-Hill, 1964), pp. 128-34.

[35] Even if the location of the Soviet iron and steel industry is open to question from an economic point of view, especially in view of recent developments in oceanborne transport of bulk commodities, there can be no doubt that the depth provided by the Ural-Kuznetsk combine was a great asset to Soviet strategists during the German invasion of the early 1940's.

Table 2.4. Changes in Location of the Soviet Iron and Steel Industry

	1913	1940	1958
	Pig iron, per cent		
South	74	64	51
East	21	29	42
Center	5	7	7
	Steel ingots, per cent		
South	63	51	42
East	21	32	47
Center	16	16	11

Urals and Kuznetsk), and the Center (Moscow, Tula, Lipetsk, Volgograd). The most remarkable changes in relative location of the iron and steel industry has been expansion in the East, primarily the Urals.

The iron and steel works in the South are located in the Donets coal basin, with Donetsk, formerly Stalino, and Makeyevka the leading centers; at the Krivoi Rog ore deposits; in intermediate positions between the Krivoi Rog iron ore and the Donbas coal along the Dnepr River (Dneprodzerzhinsk, Dnepropetrovsk, Zaporozhye, and Nikopol); at the Kerch ore deposits; and on the coast of the Azov Sea between the Kerch ore and the Donbas coal (Zhdanov and Taganrog). Shortage of water for industrial and urban use is a major problem in the South. Multipurpose power projects on the Dnepr River provide both electric power and industrial water. In 1960 a canal was built from the large Kakhovka Reservoir on the Dnepr to Krivoi Rog, which is rapidly approaching Magnitogorsk as an iron and steel center.

From R. E. Lonsdale and J. H. Thompson, "A Map of the USSR's Manufacturing," Economic Geography, XXXVI (January 1960), 36-52.

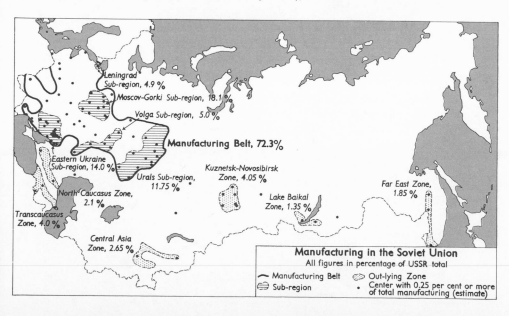

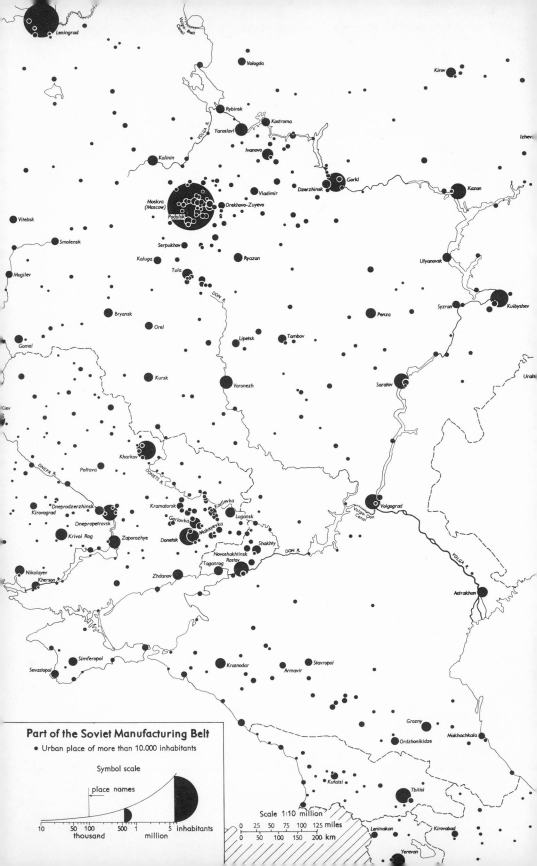

Leningrad

Vologda

Kirov

Izhev

Volga Balt Canal

Rybinsk
VOLGA R.
Yaroslavl
Kostroma
Ivanovo

Kostroma

Kalinin

Kazan

Vladimir
Dzerzhinsk
Gorki

Moskva
(Moscow)
Orekhovo-Zuyevo
Podolsk

Vitebsk

Ulyanovsk

Smolensk

Serpukhov

Kaluga
Ryazan
Syzran
Kuibyshev

Mogilev

Tula

DON R.

Penza

Bryansk

Orel

Lipetsk
Tambov

Gomel

Urals

Kursk

Voronezh
Saratov

Kiev

DNEPR R.

Kharkov

DONETS R.

Poltava

Volgograd
Volga-Don
Canal

Dneprodzerzhinsk
Kirovograd

Kramatorsk
Gorlovka
Kadievka
Lugansk

Dnepropetrovsk
Krivoi Rog
Zaporozhye
Donetsk
Makeyevka

Shakhty

VOLGA R.

Nikolayev
Kherson
Zhdanov
Novoshakhtinsk
Rostov
Taganrog
DON R.

Astrakhan

Simferopol

Krasnodar
Stavropol
Armavir

Sevastopol

Grozny
Ordzhonikidze
Makhachkala

Kutaisi

Tbilisi

Part of the Soviet Manufacturing Belt

• Urban place of more than 10,000 inhabitants

Symbol scale

place names

10   50 100   500 1   5   inhabitants
thousand   million

Scale 1:10 million

0 25 50 75 100 125 miles

0 50 100 150 200 km

Leninakan

Kirovabad

Yerevan

The area around Moscow, the leading manufacturing center in the Soviet Union, is the oldest iron producing district in the country. Production in recent decades has been small by tonnage, and largely specialized in quality steel for precision machinery (Moscow, Elektrostal). The local raw material base has been narrow; there has been no coking coal, and small production of iron ore (Tula). Further south is a tremendous deposit of lean iron ore, the Kursk Magnetic Anomaly, economically accessible only recently with modern techniques of open-pit mining and iron ore beneficiation. Since 1959 the KMA has become a major source of iron ore, favorably located between Moscow and Donbas. Iron and steel capacity has been expanded at Lipetsk and Tula, and new steel works will be built at the KMA.

Most of the steel capacity of the East is concentrated in the Urals, the old Russian iron district opened up in the eighteenth century. In addition to four giant works built in the Soviet period, Magnitogorsk, Nizhni Tagil, Chelyabinsk, and Novo-Troitsk, there are more than two dozen small works, specializing in high quality steel. They are offspring of the old iron industry, and are still based on charcoal and small deposits of iron ore with low sulfur and phosphorus content. The Urals in 1958 produced 13 million tons of pig iron and 19 million tons of steel. Iron ore production from scattered deposits increased from less than two million tons in 1913 to over 27 million tons in 1960.

Steel production at the other end of the Ural-Kuznetsk combine has, for obvious reasons, been less expansive,[36] but West Siberia in 1956 accounted for an impressive 4 million tons of steel. The steel works of Novokuznetsk, formerly Stalinsk, originally received iron ore from Magnitogorsk (1,470 miles) and manganese from Chiatura (3,545 miles).

The Automobile Industry

The basic inventions of the automobile industry were made at the end of the nineteenth century. Steam cars were soon displaced, along with electric vehicles, leaving *chauffeur*, originally applied to the stoker, as the term for professional drivers of automobiles. Despite many basic inventions being German, France was the leading automobile nation in the beginning of this century.

The great breakthrough for the automobile came with the introduction of mass production methods. This development started in the United States, pioneered by Henry Ford, who launched his T-Ford in 1908. The original inventor of mass production technique, Eli Whitney, had started to manufacture standard, interchangeable parts in 1798, when he received an order for guns from the American Army. But it was Henry Ford who exploited the simple concept to the full, and in 1913 introduced the crowning achievement, the moving assembly line, at his new plant at Highland Park, Detroit. The price of the T-Ford was reduced from $950 in 1909 to $295 in 1922. Assembly lines have become

---

[36] The steel works of West Siberia can hardly expand faster than the steel consumption in Siberia; to compete in the European part of the Soviet Union or abroad, they would have to absorb exorbitant freight costs.

more and more complex; the days are gone when, according to Ford, a customer could have a car painted any color he wanted so long as it was black. Orders from car dealers are now fed into computers, which direct the appropriate parts to the assembly line at the appropriate moment; cars of all colors and types in the company's production program are mixed on the assembly line at any given time.

UNITED STATES.   Some major centers of the automobile industry in both Europe and the United States had been established before 1914, although the great decade of the industry came in the 1920's in the United States, and in the 1950's in Europe. Ford, born on a farm near Detroit, was the leading producer of automobiles, followed by General Motors Corporation, which had been organized in 1908 by W. C. Durant, a former carriage manufacturer of Flint. In the late 1920's, GMC emerged as the leading automobile company. The third of the big three, the Chrysler Corporation, founded by a former General Motors executive, produced its first car in 1924.

The American motor vehicle industry is concentrated within or near a midwestern triangle, with apexes at Buffalo, Cincinnati, and Milwaukee, and its heart at Detroit [37] and neighboring cities, including Windsor in Canada.[38] The industry is dominated by the "Big Three," General Motors, Ford, and Chrysler; GMC is the largest manufacturing corporation of all time.[39] The Big Three account for well over 90 per cent of American car production. American Motors, a large automobile manufacturer by European standards, has always produced less than 10 per cent of American cars. All four companies have their headquarters in Detroit, although American Motors is chiefly a Wisconsin firm, with main factories at Kenosha (final assembly) and Milwaukee (body plant). In Canada, Western Europe, and Australia, large shares of the automobile industry are controlled by the Big Three.

The automotive industry has two types of plants, those making components (engines, transmission systems, frames, axles, and wheels), and assembly plants. Both types are highly concentrated within the automotive triangle. In addition, the automobile companies have assembly plants in major market areas throughout the nation, usually on the outskirts of metropolitan cities. Southern California has the largest concentration of final-assembly plants outside Michigan. Eight such plants are located in the Los Angeles area, and two in the San Francisco Bay area.

In spite of a decline in its automotive factory employment, Detroit remains the undisputed automobile capital of the world, followed by its

[37] At the end of last century, Detroit and other cities in southern Michigan were in the transition zone between rich agriculture to the south and the lumber industry of the coniferous forests to the north. This zone got a major concentration of furniture (Grand Rapids) and wagon makers (Detroit, Flint, Lansing, Pontiac). Detroit, in addition, had a boat building industry; many boats were equipped with internal-combustion engines.

[38] For detailed maps of this and some other manufacturing industries, see John W. Alexander, *Economic Geography* (Englewood Cliffs, N.J.: Prentice-Hall, 1963). See also Gunnar Alexandersson, *The Industrial Structure of American Cities* (Lincoln: Univ. of Nebraska, 1956).

[39] The sales of General Motors in 1963 equalled the gross national product of Brazil (80 million inhabitants).

Table 2.5.   Motor Vehicles: Production and Foreign Trade, Selected Countries

Thousands of Vehicles, 1963

| | Trucks and Buses | Cars | | |
	Production	Production	Exports	Imports
World	4.461	16.025	—	—
United States	1.464	7.644	144	409
Canada	99	534	16	60
West Germany	482	2.186	1.217	131
United Kingdom	404	1.608	616	49
France	254	1.453	499	147
Italy	75	1.105	292	187
Sweden	22	146	68	154
East Germany	20	84	29	11
Czechoslovakia	14	56	37	13
USSR	417	170	36	2
Japan	876	408	38	9
Australia	66	308	15	13
Brazil	87	87	—	0

— Stands for information not available.
Source: Automobile Manufacturers Association, *Automobile Facts and Figures, 1965.*
National foreign trade statistics: East Germany, USSR, Brazil (1962).

neighbor city, Flint. Southern Michigan assembles one-third of American automobiles. General Motors has nine factories making components and two assembly plants in Detroit. In Flint it has four components factories and four assembly plants. New automobile factories are always located on the outskirts of cities, oriented to high-speed, limited access highways which enmesh all metropolitan cities in the United States. A steady flow of steel and parts by truck to the components factories, of components to the assembly plants, and of finished cars to the automobile dealers, is an integrated part of the traffic pattern in the automotive triangle.

The large, integrated Ford plant at River Rouge is an exception. Iron ore, coal, and limestone arrive at company quays for blast furnaces and coke ovens in one part of the factory complex, while trucks and cars leave the assembly line in another part. This is the largest factory complex in the United States; peak employment has exceeded 90,000. Normal automobile plants range from 5,000 to 10,000 employed.

The reason for difference in plant size lies in the convictions of the two great founders of the industry, Henry Ford and William Durant. Ford believed in centralized, Durant in decentralized, management; both believed in a high degree of corporate self-sufficiency.[40] General Motors is less integrated vertically than Ford, and is not engaged in the production of steel, plastic products, or glass, but GMC produces more of its own components than Ford, and both produce more than European companies, with the possible exception of FIAT.

WESTERN EUROPE.   Western Europe is approaching the United States

[40] "Cars and Their Components: A Survey by the Economist," *The Economist* (23-29 October 1965), p. x.

in the number of automobiles produced per year.[41] Production is primarily of small cars. The large interwar imports of automobiles from the United States have dwindled to a trickle as the American car manufacturers sized themselves out of the European market.[42] But the American Big Three are active in Europe producing small European cars. General Motors (Opel) ranks as the third largest producer in Germany, and Ford is second largest in Britain. While the large American-built cars are rare on the narrow streets of Europe, the European industry has developed a substantial export of small cars to Anglo-America. Automobiles have become a major item in international trade, and the list of exporters is topped by West Germany and Britain, with France, Italy, and Sweden trailing (Table 2.5). Most of this is intra-European trade, but the westward transatlantic flow has recently amounted to almost 500,000 cars a year.

Cars are usually sent to the export market in assembled form. On the transatlantic route they often move in specially designed vessels which may also carry automobiles as return cargo.[43] In the interwar years, the Big Three American automobile manufacturers had assembly plants in many cities in Europe, but most of these have been discontinued. Belgium is the only European country with a large assembly of foreign-made cars. It ranks after Australia, but ahead of South Africa, among the world's leading assembly countries, accounting for some 300,000 cars a year. The American car manufacturers, which change models every year, have a high threshold value for establishing regional assembly plants, whereas the European manufacturers can use their machine tools longer and thus need a smaller yearly volume. Even so, the regional markets in Anglo-America for European cars are not large enough to warrant the construction of assembly plants. But it is an advantage if the export cars can be assembled in a tidewater plant (Ford at Dagenham, Volkswagen at Emden, Volvo at Göteborg).

In West Germany, a close second after the United States as an exporter of manufactured goods, motor vehicles account for 13 per cent of the export value and in Britain for 12 per cent (1963).

West Germany is second only to the United States in production of automobiles and second to none in export. Production is dominated by four concerns, Volkswagen, Daimler-Benz, General Motors (Opel), and Ford. Volkswagen accounts for over half the national output of cars.

The Volkswagen plant at Wolfsburg, on the *Mittellandkanal* northeast of Braunschweig, is Germany's largest industrial establishment. It was built by the Nazi government (1938-1939) after careful planning. The idea of a *Volkswagen* (people's car), taken directly from Henry Ford, was some years older than the factory. The car, constructed by Ferdinand Porsche, was originally planned to be manufactured at existing German

---

[41] In car registration the United States is still predominant; the Americans make up 6 per cent of the world's population, but they own 58 per cent of the cars.

[42] The leading European market for American cars, Belgium-Luxembourg, ranked fourth in 1962 after Canada, Mexico, and Argentina. Switzerland and Sweden were surpassed also by Australia, Venezuela, South Africa, and Peru.

[43] One large auto carrier can take 1,850 Volkswagens at a time. Volkswagen ships cars to 16 ports in the United States alone.

plants. When it was finally decided to build a new plant, strategic considerations reigned supreme. Maximum distance from the borders, location on the inland waterway system, on a main railroad, and on an *Autobahn* focused attention on the Braunschweig area. This also happened to be equidistant from the Ruhr, Berlin, and Hamburg, the three largest German conurbations. Key personnel were recruited in the United States among German employees of large American automobile corporations. The Volkswagen plant was planned in conjunction with the Salzgitter steel mill, built by the government against the advice of the steel industry after studies of the British Corby mill, which is also located on extremely lean ores.[44]

The first tests with the Volkswagen were made in 1936; basically the same model was still produced thirty years later. (The prototype of all popular cars, the Model T-Ford, was on the production line nineteen years.) Major component plants are in Hannover, Braunschweig, and Kassel, and subcontractors are scattered all over West Germany. Since 1965, Volkswagen cars are also produced at Ingolstadt in southern Germany. An assembly plant for the transatlantic market is at Emden. After pressure from respective governments, Volkswagen has built producing plants at São Paulo and Melbourne, and the company operates assembly plants in South Africa and Mexico. Other assembly plants, operated by local agents, are in Belgium and Ireland.

Daimler-Benz, the second largest automotive company in Germany since a merger in 1926, combines the two earliest names in the automobile industry. Daimler made his first car (1885) at Cannstatt, a suburb of Stuttgart, and Benz (1886) had his shop at Mannheim. Headquarters and main plants of Daimler-Benz are in the Stuttgart area, heavy trucks are made at Gaggenau, south of Karlsruhe, light trucks at Düsseldorf, and buses at Mannheim. The company has assembly plants at São Paulo, Buenos Aires, Bombay, and Melbourne.

The main plant of Opel, a General Motors subsidiary since 1929, is located at Rüsselsheim, between Mainz and Frankfurt. Adam Opel first made sewing machines (1862), then bicycles (1886) and automobiles (1899). The Opel firm was first in Germany with mass produced cars (1924). Most employees in the 1930's lived elsewhere than in the small town of Rüsselsheim, mostly in villages south of the Main.[45] Part of production has been moved to a new plant at Bochum in the Ruhr.

The other American-owned automobile company, Ford, is located in the northern suburbs of Cologne.

France. Paris dominates automobile production in France, with the main factories located in the western suburbs. The experimental period saw many firms, but in the late 1930's two companies, Renault and Citroën, accounted for two-thirds of production. From 1935, aircraft

[44] Prewar Germans who signed up for a Volkswagen and paid advance installments never got any cars; the war broke out when the factory was ready for production and all cars were requisitioned by the *Wehrmacht*. The plant was soon completely turned over to armament production. It was hit by Allied bombs at the end of the war.

[45] W. Hartke, "Das Arbeits- und Wohnungsgebiet im Rhein-Mainischen Lebensraum," *Rhein-Mainische Forschungen*, Heft 18, Frankfurt am Main, 1938. See also Robert E. Dickinson, *City Region and Regionalism* (London: Routledge, 1947).

and armament plants, associated with the automobile industry, were decentralized from the Paris region for strategic reasons. In the postwar period a general decentralization program was initiated by the French government,[46] using the tools of building permits and subsidies.

The government-owned Renault company, France's largest automobile producer, has built new plants since the war at Flins, an outer suburb of Paris, and at Cléon and Le Mans. The most recent addition, an assembly plant built at Le Havre after 1963, has an excellent location for waterborne shipments and for receipt of parts from the Billancourt and Flins plants in the western part of Paris. It is possible to visit all the company's plants in one day, driving from Paris to Le Havre by way of Cléon and Le Mans.[47]

Citroën, in which the Michelin rubber company has controlling interests, has built a new plant at Rennes. The Simca concern, smallest of the four major car manufacturers, produced FIAT cars before the war, and after the war acquired Ford's interests in France. In 1962 Chrysler bought a majority interest in this company. Of France's four automobile companies, only Peugeot has its main plant outside Paris.[48] It is located at Sochaux, near Belfort. Lyon is a major center for the production of heavy commercial vehicles.

The two other American automobile giants have shown interest in the French market. General Motors was refused by the French government, and selected Antwerp; Ford, after negotiations, settled for a German plant site near the French border.

Britain.   British auto production is concentrated in a belt from London to Coventry-Birmingham, with important intermediate centers at Luton and Oxford. London, the most important center of carriagemaking, early became a major producer of automobiles and components. The early British auto industry was also closely associated with the cycle industry, which had established itself in and about Coventry. This town, once known for silk textiles and watches, had attracted small engineering companies which made sewing machines and bicycles. The diversified industrial environment of the Birmingham-Coventry region, with emphasis on metal manufactures, was favorable for the auto industry. Until recently, the British industry was characterized by many "small" manufacturers producing a large number of car models.[49] After many mergers

[46] In spite of successful decentralization efforts, Paris manufacturing employment continues to grow, but the Paris region accounts for a declining share of authorized construction for manufacturing purposes, 37 per cent in 1955 and 13 per cent in 1961. Philippe Pinchemel, *Geographie de la France*, Tome 2 (Paris: Armand Colin, 1964), pp. 542 ff.

[47] A regional concentration of the works of large companies is rather common: Bethlehem Steel in the United States, Michelin in France (old plants in Clermont-Ferrand and Paris, new ones in between at Bourges and Orléans) are two more examples.

[48] Peugeot is a remarkable industrial dynasty of the Belfort area that goes unbroken back to the eighteenth century. Originally they made saws and farm implements; from 1885 they took up bicycle production with great success and, in 1897, automobiles. Out of the ruins of World War II grew three main Peugeot firms: Peugeot automobiles, Peugeot cycles, and Peugeot special steels.

[49] D. W. Fryer, "The British Vehicle and Aircraft Industry," *Geography*, Vol. 33 (April 1948), 136-49; William Goodwin, "The Structure and Position of the British Motor Vehicle Industry," *Tijdschrift voor econ. en soc. geografie*, Vol. 56 (July-August 1965), 145-56.

and consolidations, five large companies now account for 90 per cent of the output of cars and light commercial vehicles: British Motor Corporation (BMC), Rootes Motors, Leyland Motor, and two American subsidiaries, Ford and Vauxhall (General Motors). It may be more appropriate to talk about the Big Two than the Big Five, as BMC and Ford often produce 70 per cent of the output. In comparison with the American industry, British car manufacturers rely much more heavily on independent components manufacturers.[50] Some of these, which grew large by serving many and diverse manufacturers, rank among the large British manufacturing firms: Joseph Lucas (electrical equipment), S. Smith (instruments), and Girling and Lockheed (brakes). Pressed Steel (auto bodies) was taken over by BMC in 1965. These firms strengthen the automotive industry concentration in the London-Birmingham axis. The Birmingham area is no longer the Black Country of last century, but a diversified metalware, engineering, and vehicle manufacturing region.

BMC resulted from the merger in 1952 of the Austin and Nuffield (Morris) concerns. The Longbridge (Birmingham) plant of this company is one of the largest in Britain. The company has several other plants in the Birmingham-Coventry area, and also the former Morris plant at Oxford, home town of the founder of the company. Ford's operations are largely in the Dagenham plant on the Thames in east London. Ford moved from Trafford Park, Manchester, to Dagenham in 1929, and built a fully integrated plant on the model of its River Rouge plant in Detroit. Iron ore and coal are received at the blast furnace, the only one in the London region, and finished cars are exported from the company quays. Rootes Motors have their largest plants at Coventry and Dunstable, near Luton, and Vauxhall is located at Luton and Dunstable.

As in the United States, new automotive plants have been established outside the old manufacturing zone, but there is a fundamental difference between the two countries. In the United States, regional assembly plants are built to save on distribution costs; in England, new automobile plants have recently been built (under government pressure) to create new jobs in the development areas of South Wales, Lancashire, and Scotland. It remains to be seen if this policy will increase the competitiveness of the British automobile industry in the world market.

Italy.   FIAT, with headquarters and two main plants at Turin, is by far the largest manufacturing company in Italy. It accounts for 85 per cent of the automobiles produced, and for 70 per cent of the commercial vehicles. In addition, it produces airplanes. This manufacturing empire acquired its monopolistic position through protection given by the Mussolini regime. Its tradition of self-sufficiency was reinforced during a rapid postwar expansion. Among other things, FIAT has a more elaborate set-up for metal making and shaping than any other car manufacturer in the world.

The small Italian producers, Lancia of Turin and the state-owned Alfa Romeo of Milan, buy many of their components in Germany, France, and Britain.

---

[50] Over half in value of the average British car is bought from outside companies. Elsewhere this percentage ranges from 25 to 40.

Sweden.   Of the two car manufacturers in Sweden, the oldest and largest is Volvo, with assembly plant at Göteborg. It also produces buses, trucks, and tractors, and is Sweden's second largest manufacturing company. SAAB produces cars at Trollhättan and airplanes at Linköping. Both companies are too small to have more than a limited components production of their own; their purchases from outside firms are not limited to the Nordic countries. They also have suppliers on the Continent and in Britain. The EFTA agreements and the structure of the British industry seem to favor British firms as suppliers.

Soviet Union.   Fewer automobiles are registered in the Soviet Union than in the state of Kansas, in Japan, or in Belgium. For every Soviet automobile, there are 75 American cars. Whereas Western Europe, Australia, South Africa, and parts of Latin America are rapidly becoming "Americanized" in their transportation patterns, the government of the Soviet Union has shown few signs of wanting to provide their citizens with the flexibility and efficiency derived from a family car. The current five-year plan sees car manufacturing as one of the most expansive industries, but the 1970 target of 800,000 cars a year is only one-tenth of present U.S. production. In 1966 FIAT was invited to construct an automobile factory in the Soviet Union.

The small Moskvich and the large ZIL are produced in Moscow, and the small Zaporozhets at Zaporozhye. The large plant at Gorki, which produces mainly trucks, also turns out medium-sized cars (Volga and Pobeda). A new all-Soviet auto plant is planned for Izhevsk in the Urals.

The Aerospace Industry

Aircraft manufacture, beginning modestly in 1903, was a minor industry prior to World War II, but in a few years became the world's largest manufacturing industry; at the peak of the war, the United States alone turned out 96,000 planes in a single year. After a temporary cutback, it is again the largest manufacturing industry in the United States. Some 60 years after Kitty Hawk the industry is emphasizing production of missiles and spacecraft. Military contracts account for four-fifths of business in the American aerospace industry. Approximately one-fifth of all scientists and engineers doing research and development work in American industry are employed by aerospace companies. Some 60 per cent of the American Defense Department's weapons requirements are purchased from the aerospace group.[51] In a modern airplane, with its flying control and navigation systems, automatic pilots, computers, and scanners, instruments account for one-half to three-quarters of the total cost of the plane.

The Soviet Union is the only country besides the United States with a full-fledged aerospace industry, but Britain and France are important producers of airplanes. The United States and the Soviet Union are constructing subsonic, jumbo airliners to carry 500 passengers, scheduled for the early 1970's. The Soviets displayed their prototype at the Paris

[51] Robert B. Williamson, "Prospects for the Aerospace Industry in Texas," *Texas Business Review,* Vol. 38, No. 3 (March 1964), 60-64.

air show in 1965. These two countries plan to build supersonic airliners later in the 1970's; Britain and France have a joint program to build the 1,500-mile-an-hour, 150-passenger Concorde.

The large aerospace industry has had considerable influence on American population distribution. More than any other single factor, it contributed to the major increase in manufacturing jobs in peripheral states during the quarter century after 1939. During World War I, when the industry produced at a rate of 20,000 planes a year, cities in the established Manufacturing Belt dominated production: New York, Dayton (home town of the Wright brothers), Detroit (center of the automotive industry), and Buffalo.[52] It was easy to become a builder of airplanes in the early days. Among entrants were Glenn Martin of Santa Ana, a suburb of Los Angeles, who built his first plane in 1906, and William Boeing of Seattle, who was in the lumber business and began airplane manufacture in 1916. The two industries were not incompatible at the time.

By 1940, at the close of the two interwar decades, the industry had moved close to its present distribution pattern. Half the 1940 capacity comprised concerns occupying their original locations (except for local moves), one-fourth had made intraregional shifts, and one-fourth interregional shifts. Three of the industry's larger units had made long moves: Martin from Los Angeles to Cleveland and eventually to Baltimore, Consolidated from Buffalo to San Diego, and North American from Maryland to Los Angeles. In all cases the original plants were abandoned for new ones in distant regions.[53]

The 1940 production of engines and propellers was concentrated at Hartford (in the Connecticut Valley) and in greater New York.[54] Half the airframe assembly sector of the industry, which dominated in employment, was in southern California (Los Angeles and San Diego), with other centers at Baltimore, Long Island, Bridgeport, Buffalo, Wichita, and Seattle.

Climate has played an unusually important role in selection of locations for airplane assembly plants. In pioneer days, flight was attempted only in the best weather. Even today, all-year flying weather is desired when choosing locations for test and delivery flights. In areas of mild climate, without extremes in winter or summer temperatures, the large buildings necessary can be constructed and maintained at lower cost, and outdoor final assembly is possible. The Mediterranean climate of

[52] When the Curtiss Company outgrew the small town of Hammondsport, it moved to the nearest large city, Buffalo. Hammondsport was the home town of Glenn Curtiss, pioneer builder of engines and an early American aviator. He flew between Albany and New York in 1910, the year after Blériot had flown across the English Channel.

[53] William Glenn Cunningham, *The Aircraft Industry: A Study in Industrial Location* (Los Angeles: Morrison, 1951), and "Automobile and Aircraft Industries," in *California and the Southwest,* C. M. Zierer, ed. (New York: Wiley, 1956).

[54] The Curtiss and Wright firms merged in 1929, uniting two of the oldest names in American aviation and two of the largest units of the industry at the time, the Wright engine plant of Paterson, a suburb of New York, and the Curtiss airplane plant of Buffalo. Curtiss-Wright had about half the engine market, and Pratt & Whitney of Hartford, a former machine tool firm that made aircraft engines from 1925, had one-third. Pratt & Whitney was the chief unit of United Aircraft.

southern California was a major location factor for both large indigenous producers (Douglas, Lockheed, Northrop) and companies which moved from other areas (Consolidated, North American).

Southern California was also accommodating to the site requirements of airframe assembly plants. Very few industries demand so much room. At a time when large-scale migration of manufacturing plants from the central parts of cities had hardly started, the airplane assembly plants of southern California acquired large tracts of flat land, usually adjacent to a municipal airport. This, and the similar site requirements of the movie industry, helped make greater Los Angeies a "different" city. With large places of work scattered over a wide territory, and without the dominating focus of a large downtown area, Los Angeles has become a conurbation like the Ruhr, rather than a metropolitan city like London or Paris.

After 1940, strategic considerations were important in the location of new plants. The industry decentralized away from the coasts to the so-called Defense Zone of the interior, and to the Manufacturing Belt. The new plants were branches controlled by established companies of southern California and other production centers; Los Angeles remained the "aircraft capital." Since the war, all of the United States has come within range of potential enemy action; concentration of the aerospace industry to one manufacturing district, however attractive economically, was out of the question. Los Angeles aerospace employment, on a par with automobile employment of Detroit and clothing employment in greater New York, is today much larger than in 1940, but makes up a smaller percentage of the national total. Lockheed, North American, Douglas, and Northrop still have their headquarters and main plants in the Los Angeles area, but their branch plants and subcontractors are scattered over the United States. Hundreds of companies in greater Los Angeles produce parts and components for the aerospace industry; some are branches of well-known Eastern concerns, others have grown up with the local industry. The economy of southern California is extremely sensitive to the vicissitudes of the international situation.

Boeing of Seattle is the largest single employer in the Pacific Northwest, with one-fourth the manufacturing payroll of the state of Washington. It is four times as large as the pulp-and-paper industry, and five times the size of the aluminum industry.

Texas aerospace manufacturing is concentrated in the Dallas-Fort Worth area. The Fort Worth plant of General Dynamics (with headquarters in New York), Ling-Temco-Vought of Dallas, and Bell Helicopter of Fort Worth are the major aircraft plants. Since 1962 the National Space and Aeronautics Administration (NASA) has had its headquarters for manned spaceflight programs in a suburb of Houston. The center is in charge of the Gemini and Apollo (man-on-the-moon) programs, and is NASA's largest contracting division.

Wichita, Kansas, an early center for production of small airplanes (Cessna and others), also has a branch plant of Boeing, deployed there for strategic reasons, when the U.S. government deemed it unwise to produce all its heavy bombers at one location.

The Manufacturing Belt remains a minor influence in the assembly of aircraft compared with the trans-Mississippi United States. The Martin plant at Baltimore, which originated in Los Angeles and moved east before the great western expansion, and which was the training school for Donald Douglas and other Los Angeles airplane manufacturers, is the largest. Others are on Long Island in greater New York. United Aircraft (Hartford, Connecticut), General Dynamics (New York), Grumman (New York), and Curtiss-Wright (New York) are large eastern corporations with main interests in the aerospace industry; others, like General Motors and Bendix, are interested in some facets of the industry. The Manufacturing Belt remains important as a supplier of motors, instruments, and components.

In Western Europe, Britain and France have been the only large postwar producers of airplanes. SAAB, in neutral Sweden, produces military aircraft, chiefly for the Swedish Air Force, and the Italian FIAT works produces light military aircraft. No West European country is large enough to participate in "the race to the moon," and the integration of their economies has not proceeded far enough to participate on a cooperative basis.

Greater London is the undisputed center of Britain's aircraft industry, which before World War II was closely associated with automobile production. There is a broad coincidence between the distribution patterns of the two industries, with London dominating in the manufacture of aircraft. The Rolls Royce Company of Derby and Crewe is as well-known for its airplane engines as for its automobiles. British producers were too small to take advantage of their early lead in the production of jet planes, but the industry has since been concentrated into two combinations, Hawker Siddeley (De Havilland, Blackburn, Avro) and British Aircraft (Bristol, English Electric, Vickers).

The French government-owned Sud Aviation produces both supersonic fighters and medium-sized jet liners (Caravelle). Main production centers are Toulouse and Paris.

Germany was a great pioneer in the production of airplanes and airships. The tragic fate of the transatlantic zeppelin Hindenburg in New York in 1937 put a stop to the construction of dirigible airships; World War II temporarily brought to an end German construction of commercial airplanes.

The aerospace industry should be the largest manufacturing branch of the Soviet Union, but few reliable data are available on its location. A decentralized distribution pattern, desired by strategists, should be easier to achieve in the Soviet Union than in the West. The Soviets, in addition to military airplanes, missiles, and spacecraft, produce commercial planes for a vast network of airlines in the Communist Bloc. These plane types are named for their constructors (Tupolev, Iljushin, and, prototype of the world's largest passenger plane, Antonov). Lenin showed interest in aviation and founded the Central Aerodynamic Institute in 1918, later followed by other academic institutions for training and research. With German assistance, a Junker airplane factory was built near Moscow in the 1920's. In the early 1930's, Soviet-trained constructors made planes that flew across the North Pole to North America. After several other feats came the first missile in orbit (1957) and the first man in space (1961). The Russian *sputnik* became a household word in most languages. The major Soviet space center is at Baikanur in Central Asia.

Shipbuilding and Ship Repair

The complete dominance of the two postwar superpowers, the United States and the Soviet Union, in the aerospace industry, and their relative insignificance in the shipbuilding industry, which for centuries has been dominated by Northwestern Europe and now also by Japan, is explained chiefly by the different nature of the customers. Most ships are ordered by private shipowners, operating in a competitive international market, who place their orders where they obtain the best conditions, at home or abroad. Shipbuilding for an export market is common. Space research and construction of space craft is a government matter with military applications, although handled in the United States largely by private, domestic firms on government contract. International contacts, including some U.S. invitations to the Soviet Union for cooperation in space exploration so as not to duplicate extremely heavy costs, are made at government level. International trade is unimportant in the aerospace industry, except in the small sector producing commercial aircraft.

The large postwar changes in the geography of Europe's shipbuilding industry, a major decline in Britain, and expansion in Scandinavia and the Continent, have been eclipsed by the spectacular emergence of Japan as the leading shipbuilding nation. The United Kingdom, having launched more tonnage than any other country for about a century, has seen its share of world production dwindle.

British shipyards are concentrated in two areas, the Northeast Coast and the Clyde Valley. The northeastern district comprises Blyth, the lower Tyne, with Wallsend, Walker, Hebburn, and South Shields as leading centers, Sunderland on the lower Wear (with no less than six medium-sized yards), and the lower Tees and adjacent coast, with yards at Haverton Hill, Middlesbrough, and West Hartlepool. At the turn of the century about half of British tonnage (and almost one-third of world tonnage) was launched in this concentrated district.[55] In 1959 the northeastern area launched 45 per cent of British tonnage, about the same share as in the late 1920's, but during the Depression of the 1930's it was surpassed by the Clyde district. The Northeast Coast was the world's leading shipbuilding district in 1959, followed by Hamburg, the Clyde Valley, and Göteborg.

The other large shipyard district in Great Britain, the Clyde Valley downstream from central Glasgow, developed with iron-and-steel vessels, whereas the Northeast Coast was a leading center when ships were built of wood. The Clyde has long been known as the leading shipyard river in the world, but at the end of the 1950's the same tonnages were launched on the Elbe and the Göta älv. Many famous British passenger liners, such

[55] L. Dudley Stamp and Stanley H. Beaver, *The British Isles* (London: Longmans, 1941) p. 382 ff.

Shipyards of the World
Tonnage Launched
Each sector represents one yard launching more than 100 tons in 1959

1

M Middlesbrough

Glasgow
Aberdeen
Dumbarton
Greenock
Dundee
Port Glasgow
Blyth
Walker
Wallsend
Belfast
Clydebank
Hebburn
South Shields
West Hartlepool
Sunderland
Barrow
Haverton
M
Rotterdam
Birkenhead
Schiedam
Amsterdam
Vlissingen
Heusden
Alblasserdam
Dunkerque
Tamise
Hoboken

0   100   200 KM

2

Bergen
Oslo
Stockholm
Fredrikstad
Stavanger
Uddevalla
Göteborg
Oskarshamn
Landskrona
Kiel
Helsingör
Malmö
K
Flensburg
Lübeck
Gdańsk
Rendsburg
W
Bremerhaven
Wismar
Szczecin
Emden
Hamburg
Bremen

K Köbenhavn
L Lervik
W Warnemünde
O Udense

0   100   200 KM

A

Collingwood
Quebec
Quincy
Camden
River Rouge
Port Weller
Chester
Sparrows Point
Newport News
San Francisco
Pascagoula

0   500   1000 KM

B

1
2

Rauma
Turku
Helsinki

Le Trait
Monfalcone
St. Nazaire
Nantes
Muggiano
Rijeka
Bordeaux
Genova
Split
El Ferrol
Port-de-Bouc
Bilbao
Pula
La Ciotat
Livorno
La Seyne
Napoli
Cadiz
Palermo

Thousand Gross
Register Tons

— 300
— 200
— 100
— 50
— 10
— 1
— 0.1

0   200   400   600 KM

C

Hakodat
Kawasaki (Tsurumi)
Maizuru
Kobe
Tokyo
Innoshima
Nagoya
Yokohama
Hiroshima
Osaka
Yokosuka
Nagasaki
Kure
Uno (Tamano)
Aioi
Sakurajima

0   100   200 KM

Keelung
Hong Kong
Whyalla

0   2500   5000 KM

Data from the Glasgow Herald Trade Review, January 1960

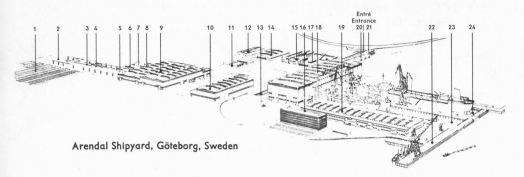

Arendal Shipyard, Göteborg, Sweden

The radically new shipyard of the Götaverken Shipbuilding Company is designed on the assembly-line principle. Vessels are built indoors and pushed outdoors, section by section, as completed. They are built from stern to bow, instead of from keel to stack. Construction indoors avoids losing time during bad weather. A crew constructs a ship in little more than half the time required in traditional shipbuilding methods. 1. Plate yard (long-term stock yard). 2. Plate yard (for immediate use). 3. Conveyor belt. 4. Straightening roller. 5. Shot blasting (plates). 6. Mold shop. 7. Optical marking. 8. Shot blasting (profiles). 9. Plate shop. 10. Welding shop. 11. Central kitchen and canteens. 12. Cold store. 13. Buffer store. 14. Heated store. 15. Production shops. 16. Office. 17. Acetylene generating plant. 18. Hull assembly hall. 19. Equipment shops. 20. Changing rooms and swimming pool. 21. Staff amenities building. 22. Fitting-out pier. 23. Building dock II. 24. Building dock I. (Götaverken.)

as the *Queen Mary* and the *Queen Elizabeth*, were built on the Clyde.

In addition to the two dominant British districts there are large yards at Belfast, Birkenhead near Liverpool, and Barrow-in-Furness. The Thames Valley has no construction yards of any importance, but before the days of iron-and-steel ships the lower Thames was a leading shipbuilding district. The Thames estuary declined as a shipbuilding center in the latter half of the nineteenth century. The Northeast district and the Clyde Valley, centers of heavy manufacturing based on local coal fields, had advantages at a time when heavy ship plates, machinery, and other components could not be transported as easily as now.

Since 1929, British launchings have never exceeded 1.5 million tons a year. World production in 1964 was 10.3 million tons. In the peak years 1913 and 1920, British yards accounted for about 2 million tons. In the 1890's they produced about 1 million tons per year but world production then was only 1.2 million tons.

British stagnation stands in sharp contrast to rapid development in other European countries. Sweden launched less than 10,000 tons at the turn of the century, but 857,000 tons in 1959. Most of this expansion occurred in the postwar period. The Swedish curve for launched tonnage shows an even growth rate from about 1910, with dips for the two interwar depressions and a standstill during World War II. Swedish yards have specialized in tankers and bulk carriers, with the large Norwegian merchant fleet as the leading foreign customer. The Danish shipbuilding industry, about the same size as the Swedish in the interwar period, grew slowly in the 1950's, whereas the Norwegian industry expanded rapidly and is now larger than the Danish. Both the Danish and Norwegian yards, especially the latter, have the advantage of a large domestic merchant fleet and the disadvantage of smaller and less diversified base industries than the Swedish yards.

German yards compete with the British and Swedish for second largest output in the world after Japan. The German expansion to a peak of 1.4 million tons in 1958 occurred after German yards were again allowed to build ships in 1949. Compared with the 0.5 million tons produced in the peak years of the interwar period, German expansion is smaller than the Swedish and much smaller than the Japanese. In 1964 German yards launched 890,000 tons. Other European countries with a rapidly expanding shipbuilding industry at the end of the 1950's were the Netherlands, France, Italy, and Yugoslavia. All of these, especially the Netherlands, have experienced setbacks in the 1960's.

The tremendous shipbuilding increase in European countries other than the United Kingdom—evident in the interwar period but accentuated after World War II—is basically a result of Great Britain losing the monopoly created by an early start in new techniques of steel making

The two building docks of the Arendal Shipyard, with a 56,000 dwt ton tanker to the right and a 70,000 ton tanker to the left. To cut down on production costs, modern shipyards offer ships of standard design. A series of twelve 70,000 ton vessels is being built at Arendal. Götaverken has also prepared standard designs for tankers of 95,000, 125,000, and 150,000 dwt tons. (Götaverken.)

and steel ship construction. Behind this development are factors which are difficult to separate and assess. Conservatism may have prevented the British yards from accepting innovations which led to lower production costs for her competitors. Swedish yards, for instance, were quicker than the British to accept techniques developed in the United States during the war: to weld instead of rivet the hulls, and to subassemble sections. These techniques considerably shorten the time a ship occupies a slipway. Swedish and some continental yards started early to offer standard vessels made in series, with resultant lower costs. The British labor market, with trade unions organized according to occupation or craft rather than industry, has not functioned as smoothly as its Swedish counterpart.[56] The British industry is divided among a large number of medium-sized yards, which has adverse effects on costs. The new distribution pattern of the world's steel industry, which shows considerably reduced dependence on coal and increased attraction to coastal locations, has altered the premise of the shipbuilding industry. It has reduced the advantage that the two British shipyard districts had at the beginning of this century. Steel works making ship plates have been built in coastal locations at other points in Europe, and low shipping rates sometimes make it advantageous to import plates from the United States or Japan.

Japan in the feudal period had a lively coastwise traffic by small vessels, but ocean-going ships were outlawed in the interest of the Japanese seclusion policy. After the Restoration in 1868, the government made efforts to build up an engineering industry and a mercantile marine. Some government yards taken over from the Shogunate were transferred to private ownership in the early 1880's, and new private yards were established.[57] The first steel ship was built in the 1890's; in 1896 the Government started to subsidize builders of steel vessels of over 700 gross tons. However, the shipbuilding industry expanded slowly, since almost all construction material had to be imported and the Japanese engineers lacked experience. In 1901 the first modern steel mill went into operation at Yawata and, by the outbreak of World War I, considerable experience in shipbuilding had been gained. Launched steamship tonnage increased from less than 10,000 gross tons a year at the end of the 1890's to over 50,000 tons in the period 1909-13. The war was a great boom period for Japanese industry, including the shipyards. Launched tonnage increased from 85,000 tons in 1914 to 650,000 tons in 1919. The following depression and competition from abroad turned these achievements into a thing of the past—the Japanese cost level was still high. In the boom year 1929 only 165,000 tons were launched; it was not until the end of the 1930's that production surpassed 400,000 tons. The tremendous Japanese expansion in shipbuilding, which in 1956 placed Japan ahead of all other nations, is thus a postwar phenomenon. Several factors contributed to this development. First, a surprising number of Japanese mili-

---

[56] As Sweden has the highest wage level of the major shipbuilding nations competing on the world market, Swedish shipyards have to be on the alert for new techniques and organizational innovations which may lower costs and thus compensate for the higher wages.

[57] G. C. Allen, *A Short Economic History of Modern Japan* (London: Allen & Unwin, 1946).

tary and civilian yards were still intact after the war, and these soon concentrated on civilian production.

Most world regions, especially Anglo-America and Europe, had a rapidly rising curve in the 1950's for imports of bulk cargo, particularly oil. American (and Greek) shipowners increased their tonnage rapidly, especially of tankers, and registered their vessels under flags of convenience, primarily in Liberia. The Japanese shipyards were in a favorable position to compete for these orders, although their costs were not especially low. They could deliver ships within a short time when European yards were booked for several years. Rapid expansion of Japanese shipyard capacity was possible because of a good supply of ship building engineers from civilian and military yards, a large pool of labor, and rapidly expanding base industries, especially steel works geared to the needs of shipyards. The Cold War made it in the strategic interest of the United States to support and cooperate closely with economic development in Japan.

Japanese shipyards also have a large domestic market. In 1941 Japan had a merchant fleet of 6.1 million tons, third largest in the world. At the end of the war this fleet was on the bottom of the Pacific; only 750,000 tons were left. The Japanese mercantile marine was rapidly rebuilt after the war; in 1964 it was fifth largest in the world, with 10.8 million tons. Demand for maritime transport will increase substantially in Japan in the next few decades. The demand for petroleum alone was expected to increase from 25 million tons in 1959 to 70 million in 1970, and 130 million tons in 1980, according to the Japanese long term plan.[58] Present trends indicate even larger quantities. Long distances from the Middle East, where most of the oil will probably emanate, means that much tonnage will be employed in this transport. Japanese yards are building tankers of 276,000 dwt tons, and ore carriers of 100,000 tons. Even larger tankers have been ordered.

A large percentage of Japanese (and Swedish and German) launched tonnage is accounted for by super tankers and bulk carriers, cheaper per ton than the dry cargo liners and passenger liners which are the mainstay of British yards. Measured by value, British decline and Japanese expansion in shipbuilding would be less drastic.

The United States, from the beginning of the nineteenth century to the Civil War (1861-65) the leading shipbuilding nation in the world,[59] has a small construction of merchant ships, kept alive in peacetime by large government subsidies. In the heyday of American shipbuilding, when Yankee Clippers were among the finest ships on the seven seas, shipping was an important American industry, especially in New England. As long as wooden hulls were in use, the Atlantic seaboard had abundant raw materials for shipbuilding. During the Colonial Period and again from 1800-1861, ships were built for export.

[58] *Prospects of Japan's Economy in 1980* (Tokyo: Economic Planning Agency, 1960). Here quoted from Saburo Okita, "Japan's Economic Prospects," *Foreign Affairs*, Vol. 39, No. 4 (October 1960), 129.
[59] E. B. Alderfer and H. E. Michl, *Economics of American Industry*, 3rd ed. (New York: McGraw-Hill, 1957).

Two basic changes are responsible for the weak position of American shipbuilding after the Civil War. In Great Britain in the 1850's and 1860's, ships were increasingly built of iron and, later, steel. Britain was several decades ahead of the United States in the iron and steel industry; wood accounted for only 4 per cent of the tonnage launched in Great Britain in 1880.[60] The change to steel ships did not occur on a large scale in the United States until the turn of the century. Throughout this period, maritime activity was on the decline in America. Investment of domestic and European capital was concentrated on railroad construction and the development of mining and manufacturing. Shipbuilding was neglected. At the outbreak of the First World War, 90 per cent of America's foreign trade was carried in foreign ships.

American manufacturing has been highly competitive in the world market in mass production of machinery, durable consumer goods, and so on. The United States has often produced 70 per cent of the world's automobiles, but normally less than 5 per cent of tonnage launched. Cars are mass-produced, while ships have traditionally been custom-built. During World War I, and even more during World War II, conditions were favorable for mass production of ships. Increased demand for tonnage had to be met as quickly as possible, and ships lost in war had to be replaced. The American mass production technique was mobilized and remarkable results were achieved. Shipbuilding temporarily became the second largest American industry after airplane manufacturing. In the peak year 1943 no less than 11.6 million gross tons were launched, compared with 75,000 tons 12 years later, the lowest figure for the postwar period.

In peacetime, American shipbuilding and shipping are not competitive in the world market. The high American wage level does not reflect a correspondingly high efficiency in these two industries. The Merchant Marine Act of 1936 instituted Federal government subsidies, amounting to from one-third to one-half the construction cost of new ships built according to standard patterns at American shipyards. American ship operators receive other types of subsidies as well.[61]

The five largest American shipyards are located on the Atlantic seaboard, one in Boston (Quincy), two in Philadelphia on the Delaware River (Chester and Camden), one in Baltimore (Sparrows Point), and one at Hampton Roads (Newport News).

The American shipbuilding industry is larger than indicated by the yearly launchings of merchant vessels. Civilian yards participate in construction of naval vessels of all kinds, and their repairing activity is substantial. Measured in "value added," repairs exceed construction in the United States. The ranking of countries according to the value of ship repairs differs drastically from ranking by new buildings, as exemplified by the following selection: United States—435 million dollars, United Kingdom—210 million, the Netherlands—112 million, West Germany—

[60] Stamp and Beaver, *op. cit.*, p. 383.
[61] For more details on government support to American shipbuilding and shipping see H. Gerrish Smith, "The Shipbuilding, Ship Repairing and Shipping Industries," in *The Development of American Industries*, 3rd ed., J. G. Glover and W. B. Cornell, eds. (Englewood Cliffs, N.J.: Prentice-Hall, 1951).

100 million, Japan—93 million, Belgium—40 million, and Sweden—29 million.[62]

Repair docks have a distribution pattern different from that of construction docks. They are scattered along the main shipping routes of the world, but there is a strong concentration of dry docks and floating docks in northwestern Europe, northeastern United States and Japan, the main terminals of shipping lines as well as bulk transportation. Rotterdam, Hamburg, Antwerp, Newcastle, London, Liverpool, and New York have many repair docks. Wherever possible, shipyards combine construction and repair work, and repairs often account for a considerable share of the shipyard's total income. As operating costs are high, ships usually go to ports on their routes for repairs. Shipyards in big ports are therefore in a better position than those of smaller ports to attract ships for repair.

Machinery, Appliances, and Tools

The manufacturing of machinery, appliances, and tools is a major sector of the manufacturing industries in most industrialized nations, covered by three main headings: *a*) general machinery, *b*) electrical machinery, and *c*) electronics. Some geographic generalizations are valid for all three groups.

It has always been easier to use a machine than to make one, which means that machine manufacturing is concentrated in the old manufacturing regions of the world. Within these regions, makers of a machine are likely to be found close to the users of that machine. Juxtaposition of discriminating buyers and a skilled metal manufacturing industry creates a fertile milieu for inventions and good engineering. For instance, textile machines are made in Lancashire, West Germany, New England, eastern Pennsylvania, Switzerland, Moscow, and Japan.

Even when the machine-using industry shifts geographically, machine makers tend to remain in the old region. Almost two-thirds of the textile workers in the United States are in the South, but four-fifths of the textile machines are made in the North, primarily in Massachusetts and Pennsylvania. Britain has lost most of its textile markets but is still a large exporter of textile machines, surpassed only by West Germany.

Most machines that enter the international market move between industrial nations. The flow to the underdeveloped world is small by comparison, but machine imports, vital to the economic development of poorer countries, are usually given high priority. The United States, West Germany, Britain, France, U.S.S.R., Italy, Japan, and Sweden account for the largest exports of machinery. A large factory anywhere in the world is likely to have machinery from several of these countries. A major domestic market is no prerequisite for success in this field (e.g., Switzerland); high development costs may be recovered, not only by a large export volume, but also through branch plants and licensing agreements.

[62] The figures refer to one year around 1957. They were taken from different sources and are not strictly comparable, but should give a rough idea of the magnitudes.

FARM MACHINERY. The mechanization of farms, pioneered by the United States, illustrates many principles of geographic interaction between machine using and machine producing industries. With the relative decline of agriculture in the economy of industrialized nations, many firms, originally making farm machinery, may now primarily produce other types of machines; but the story of the farm machine industry, one of the oldest and most widely spread machine making industries, is intimately associated with the growth of important metal regions and centers in the industrial countries of the world.

United States. The American farm machine industry is concentrated in the Midwest, especially northern Illinois and adjacent areas. Here, the westernmost part of the Manufacturing Belt overlaps the eastern half of the Corn Belt, the world's richest area of commercial agriculture. The industrial revolution in this region was propelled to a large extent by an agricultural revolution. Land suitable for large-scale farming and mechanization was plentiful, but labor was scarce. Repeal of the English Corn Laws of 1846 and rapid construction of railroads after 1850 opened large markets. The American Midwest took the lead in development of labor-saving devices, just as northwestern Europe led the development of land-saving devices (scientific animal and plant breeding, fertilizers, weed control). The Civil War made the shortage of labor acute, and speeded up mechanization.

The farm machine factories of Peoria, Chicago, the "Tri-Cities" (Davenport–Rock Island–Moline), Rockford, Milwaukee, Racine, and other centers usually originated with inventions made by blacksmiths, mechanics, and foundrymen of the last century. Problems were often tackled by several inventors simultaneously, but only a few had the business acumen and financial backing to develop an empire on the basis of such inventions.

A classical example is John Deere, who in 1837 developed a strong, light, steel plow that would scour in the prairie soils.[63] The earlier plows of wood or cast iron, developed in regions with a native vegetation of trees, could not turn over the tough sod of the grassland, the native vegetation of most of the present Corn Belt. Deere, a blacksmith of Grand Detour, moved his business to a central location at Moline, and by the 1850's Deere plows were the yardstick of quality in Illinois and Iowa. The only drawback was the price—almost double that of a cast-iron plow. James Oliver of South Bend, Indiana, made a cast-iron plow in 1867 with a mould-board that had a hard surface and scouring properties similar to those of steel. Oliver, too, built his business into an industrial empire. Both the Deere and the Oliver firms developed sulky gangplows in the 1870's.

The grain drill, which originated in Britain, did not work very well in prairie soils, and was not widely accepted until the late 1870's. Hand seeders were used on small and medium-sized farms, and horse-powered broadcast sowers on large farms.

[63] Allan G. Bogue, *From Prairie to Corn Belt* (Chicago: University of Chicago, 1963).

The reaper was a real labor-saving device. The first practical reapers were patented by Obed Hussey (1833) and Cyrus McCormick (1834). McCormick was the better businessman of the two. After manufacturing and improving the reaper in his farm workshop in the Shenandoah Valley of Virginia, he moved to Brockport on the Erie Canal in 1845, and to Chicago in 1848. Five fieldhands were required to bind after the reaper. In 1858 the Marsh brothers of DeKalb, Illinois, patented a harvester on which two men could ride and bind the cut grain. The self-binder, invented by John Appleby of Beloit, Wisconsin, eliminated even these men. The inventions of Marsh and Appleby were acquired by William Deering, who combined them in the first successful binder. The Deering Company, then the world's largest farm-implement factory, merged with the McCormick firm of Chicago in 1902 to form the giant International Harvester Corporation. The first combines, which replaced both binder and thresher, were used in California at the end of last century, but the great breakthrough came with the labor shortage of World War I. Today much wheat in the Great Plains is harvested by teams that follow the wheat harvest from northern Texas to the Canadian border, operating several self-propelled combines and trucks to bring the wheat from field to elevator.

In the first stage of farm mechanization, which started long before the Civil War but developed most rapidly between 1860 and 1910, men were displaced by horses as suppliers of farm energy. The horse population of the Midwest increased tremendously. But experiments with steam tractors were made early on large prairie farms, and by 1905 it became obvious that the internal combustion engine was superior to both steam and horsepower. Draft animals have now all but disappeared from the farms of the Midwest, making available for other purposes land formerly used for feed production. The largest tractor company, Caterpillar Tractor, was originally a California concern. It moved from Oakland to Peoria, Illinois, at the end of the 1920's to be in the center of its market.

The agricultural implement industry tallies some 1,500 companies in the United States. In addition to the few giants there are hundreds of highly specialized producers working for a regional market. For example, California's specialized agriculture is served by producers turning out asparagus and cotton pickers, and grape, lettuce, and tomato harvesters, to mention just a few examples.[64]

The Commonwealth. The British accounted for many early innovations in farm machinery, but the industry depended on export markets. When Britain was the workshop of the world, domestic agriculture dwindled and England became the leading market for international trade in farm products. Canada, particularly the Ontario Peninsula, was a good overseas testing ground for British inventions. The large Massey-Ferguson concern, with headquarters in Toronto and subsidiary plants in the United States, Europe, and other parts of the world, resulted from

[64] In the South, the postwar switch to mechanical cotton pickers, produced near the market, has removed hundreds of thousands of jobs for Negroes, which has created social problems not only in the cotton-growing counties but also in those urban areas to which many poorly educated Negroes migrated.

the merger of the oldest and largest Canadian farm machinery companies. It is similar to the full-line American giants. Australia also saw an indigenous farm implement industry assist the spread of grain farming in the continent.

Western Europe.   Heavy mechanization of farm operations, with subsequent disappearance of draft animals, is chiefly a postwar phenomenon in Western Europe. Many agricultural implements were developed simultaneously in Europe and the United States; others were introduced soon after production started in America. Acceptance of the new technique was much slower in Europe, where farm labor was still relatively plentiful until World War II. Western Europe's contribution has been chiefly to dairy technology. The separator, for instance, was invented by

The first "gasoline traction engine" made in 1906 by International Harvester weighed 13,500 pounds, developed 20 horsepower, and was capable of speeds of 1.75 or 2.12 mph. Its 1964 successor, the four millionth tractor produced by the company, weighs 9,125 pounds, develops 95 horsepower, and can travel at speeds of from 1.75 to 19.25 mph. Miniaturization of transport devices and other machines has stepped up power and flexibility and reduced size and mass. (International Harvester.)

the Swede Gustaf de Laval [65] in 1878. The widespread farm implement industry of Western Europe includes both domestic producers and subsidiaries of large North American corporations.

Soviet Union. Mechanization of farm operations in the Soviet Union has received much publicity, but it is in fact extremely uneven. Over 40 per cent of the gainfully employed population is still engaged in agriculture, whereas the figure is less than 10 per cent in some advanced free-market countries.

Tractors and combines were much emphasized in the first five-year plans. The first modern tractor factories were opened in Volgograd (1930) and Kharkov (1931), and the first combine factory at Zaporozhye (1930). Production of bulky farm machinery is market-oriented in the Soviet Union, as elsewhere. Since extensive farming is typical of the Soviet Union, the centers producing farm machines, including tractors, are widely scattered.

Japan. Postwar developments in the Japanese farm implement industry may, in the long run, be of greatest interest to the majority of the world's farmers. The Japanese have tackled the problems of mechanizing wet-rice cultivation in areas where a high yield per acre is a necessity. The advanced technical equipment used on the American Great Plains may be of academic interest to the rice farmer of Monsoon Asia, but the small tractors and threshing machines developed by the Japanese are different. They are a necessity in Japan if large-scale transfer of people from farming to urban industries shall proceed according to plan, and this technology is also directly applicable in most of Monsoon Asia.

ELECTRICAL MACHINERY. Electrical engineering, from the outset, has been a metropolitan industry dominated by a few large firms. In the United States General Electric, Western Electric, and Westinghouse rank among the largest manufacturing firms in the nation. The same holds for Germany (Siemens, AEG, Bosch), the Netherlands (Philips), Japan (Hitachi, Tokyo Shibaura, Matsushita), Britain (AEI, English Electric, General Electric), France (Cie Générale d'Electricité, Thomson-Houston, CSF), Switzerland (Brown Boveri), Sweden (ASEA, LM Ericsson), and Canada (Northern Electric). Most of these firms are global in their operations. Many of them were organized by leading inventors, e.g., General Electric by Edison, Western Electric by Bell, and so on. Most decisions about location of main factories, research laboratories, and headquarters were made before World War I, in many cases in the nineteenth century. Some inventors had ties with universities in metropolitan areas, which offered a more practical orientation than small town universities. The large city provided rentable premises for the first, experimental shops of the inventor, and the metropolitan labor market had the special skills needed by the infant industry. Not least important, the product was developed before the demand; the big city market is concentrated and innovation-prone.

---

[65] Laval also invented the first practical steam turbine. The Alfa-Laval Company of Stockholm, formed in 1883 for the production of separators, has established subsidiary companies in many parts of the world.

Philips Plants in the Netherlands

Groningen

Drachten

Stadskanaal

Hoogeveen

Zwolle

Amsterdam

Weesp   Huizen

Hilversum   Baarn

Amersfoort

The Hague   Utrecht

Borne

Hengelo

Doetinchem

Gorinchem   Nijmegen

Dordrecht   Oss

Oosterhout   Uden

Roosendal   Tilburg

Middelburg   EINDHOVEN

Geldrop

Valkenswaard   Venlo

Weert

Roermond

Sittard

Heerlen

• 50—200 employed
● 200—1,000 "
● 1,000—3,000 "
◎ Headquarters and main plant

0   50 Km

After P. George

The large Philips group in electronics and electrical equipment more than doubled its total employment in the 1950's. In 1960, its domestic and foreign plants employed 211,000 workers, 75,000 of them in the Netherlands. Much of the domestic expansion took place in decentralized plants, many of them in areas of structural unemployment. The 3-million conurbation stretching from Rotterdam to Amsterdam and beyond, including The Hague, was almost completely avoided. (From P. George, "Les Establissements Philips aux Pays-Bas: une politique de la répartition géographique des usines," Bulletin de l'association de geographes francais, 1961, pp. 198-205.)

However, electrical engineering is not exclusively a metropolitan industry. A few of the big companies have locations in small cities (Philips in Eindhoven, Brown Boveri in Baden, ASEA in Västerås). When the industry has reached a certain maturity, standardized products made in large volume and manufactured by unskilled labor can advantageously be made in small or medium-sized towns. The large companies have branch plants scattered over the country and abroad; these are often in small cities. The branch plant is sometimes classified under a heading other than electrical machinery. Both General Electric and Westinghouse, for instance, make washing machines, which in the language of the Bureau of the Census are "machinery, except electrical."

The second half of the nineteenth century saw a series of revolutionary inventions and innovations in the use of electricity, all made in northeastern United States or western Europe. The first practical telegraph was built in 1844 by Samuel Morse. The first transatlantic cable (1858) failed, but from 1866 there was a cable connection between Europe and America. The telephone was patented in 1876 by Alexander Graham Bell. In 1877 Edison invented the phonograph, and in 1879 the incandescent lamp.[66] Guglielmo Marconi of Italy was able to send signals by radio-telegraphy across the English Channel in 1898, and across the Atlantic in 1901.

[66] Thomas Alva Edison, the greatest name in electricity in the final decades of the nineteenth century, first established himself in Boston, but in 1870 moved to greater New York, where most of his inventions were made. To get space for expansion, the Edison Machine Works were moved to Schenectady in 1886. In 1892 Edison's companies and Thomson-Houston of Boston (Lynn), a leading firm in the arc lighting industry, merged and became the Edison General Electric Company, ancestor of the present General Electric. The new company had headquarters in Manhattan and major factories at Schenectady (generators and other heavy and non-standardized equipment), East Newark (lamps), and Lynn (other light standardized equipment).

The electrical industry in the United States got its start in New York, Pittsburgh, Boston, and Chicago. These four industrial areas accounted for 62 per cent of 1899 employment, but none of them has maintained its share. In 1957 they had only 32 per cent of the total. Philadelphia was in fourth place after New York, Chicago, and Boston.[67]

The first branch to develop in Britain was manufacture of cables. Much of the material for this heavy trade was imported, and the ocean bed was often the destination of the final product. Plants were in need of elbow room, and the industry was logically given waterside sites in outer suburbs of London, where land was cheap (Woolwich, Greenwich). But in the present pattern cable making is an exception. The heavier sections of the industry are primarily in the Midlands (Birmingham), and the lighter sections in the London region. Electrical engineering and electronics are among the growth industries that have helped the London region and Birmingham to a faster population growth than the rest of Britain in recent decades.

In Germany, Berlin is the dominant center, with Nürnberg and Stuttgart (Bosch) as secondary centers. The postwar division of Germany has hampered expansion at the headquarters and main factories of the large Siemens company in Siemensstadt, a suburb of Berlin, but electrical engineering is still the leading manufacturing industry in the divided city, accounting for roughly one-third of the manufacturing employment in both zones.

Leningrad, the leading center for electrical engineering in the Soviet Union, accounted for more than half of the production of turbines and generators in the mid-1950's, and was outstanding in the production of motors, transformers, and telephones. In pre-revolutionary times, most of the factories were assembly plants. For instance, the present *Elektrosila*, which employs about 10,000, was an assembly plant of the Siemens-Schuckert company in 1914,[68] with 1,000 employees. Other centers of electrical engineering are Kharkov, Sverdlovsk, and Novosibirsk.

The Soviet Union is a leader in the construction of large electric power plants, and, along with Sweden (ASEA), in the long-distance transmission of electric power.[69]

ELECTRONICS. In 1960 the electronics industry, reaching for top position among American industries, was surpassed only by automobiles, steel, aerospace, and chemicals in annual sales. It is so new that the 1963 Census of Manufacturing was the first to single out electronics as a separate industry. There is more justification for calling this the Electronic Age than the Nuclear Age; together the two industries may justify talk

---

[67] Robert Rider, "Electrical Machinery," in *Region in Transition*, Vol. 1, Economic Study of the Pittsburgh Region (Pittsburgh: The Pittsburgh Regional Planning Association, 1963), 348-81.

[68] A. Zimm, *Industriegeographie der Sowjetunion* (East Berlin: VEB Deutscher Verlag der Wissenschaften, 1963).

[69] A master plan for the 1960's involves connecting the European grid with the Central Siberian grid by 1,400 kv-DC lines. This unified power system, with its apex at Lake Baykal, will make low-cost coal and water-power in Central Siberia economically accessible in the Urals and in areas further west. David J. M. Hooson, *A New Soviet Heartland?* (Princeton: Van Nostrand, 1964), 124. The existing high-voltage lines in 1965, mostly of 400 and 500 kilovolts, include a European grid of 800 kilovolts. Water power accounts for 20 per cent of the Soviet electric energy output.

of a second Industrial Revolution. To the consumer the electronics industry has brought radio, television, and high fidelity; to office and factory it has brought data-processing equipment and automated machinery; to national defense it has brought radar and myriad control devices for operation of aircraft, missiles, space satellites, artillery, and naval vessels.[70] Giant computers and machines that make factories increasingly automatic would not have been possible were it not for the transistor, nor would it have been possible to send man into space. The invention of the transistor was announced by Bell Laboratories in 1948, when the vacuum tube had become a bottleneck in the road to miniaturization of electronic devices.

In an electronic device, a controlled and variable flow of electrons results in a signal containing information. To be classified as electronic the product must therefore contain vacuum tubes of some kind, or transistors. Until World War II electronics was almost synonymous with radio. Patents that foreshadowed the vacuum tube were registered by Fleming (1904) and de Forest (1906), men closely associated with pioneers of the electrical industry, Edison and Marconi. The North Atlantic was the great testing place for new inventions in the field of wireless communication. Marconi interests, with American factories in greater New York, controlled wireless equipment; the American Telephone and Telegraph Company (A.T.&T.) controlled developments in telephony. But no company could, on the basis of its own patents, produce the equipment for modern radio. The Radio Corporation of America (RCA), organized in New York in 1919, absorbed the assets of American Marconi and, within a few years, served as a patent pool for General Electric, A.T.&T., and Westinghouse.

Greater New York was the birthplace of much of radio technology; it was also the principal center for broadcasting. The first national networks (NBC and CBS) were formed in 1926 and 1927; before that broadcasting was conducted on a local scale. Demand for radios grew in New York earlier than in other places. At the beginning of 1923 the United States had 1.5 million radio sets, 75 per cent of which had been assembled by the owners. Some 750 manufacturers of radio sets entered the market in the four years beginning with 1923, but very few survived for any length of time. The shift to large-scale production of radio sets was evident in the late 1920's. National networks widened the market to include areas outside large cities. A national market for radio sets was better served from Chicago than from New York, as was the case in many other consumer goods industries.

In the television boom after World War II, starting with 1947, large and established radio manufacturers were best equipped to take up this new industry. In the late 1950's ten manufacturers, all located in the Manufacturing Belt, had 85 per cent of the market: six were in the Midwest, four in the Chicago area. Other large production centers were

70 James M. Hund, "Electronics," Made in New York, Max Hall, ed. (Cambridge: Harvard Univ., 1959), pp. 243-325; R. C. Estall, "The Electronic Products Industry of New England," Economic Geography, Vol. 39 (July 1963), 189-216; W. B. Harris, "Electronics Business," Fortune (April 1957). The first of four articles on the U.S. electronics industries.

New York, Syracuse, and Philadelphia. Few radio and television manufacturers make most of their own components; parts are made by component manufacturers in the United States and abroad, many in Japan.

Consumer electronics, however, has been minor in a postwar boom industry dominated by military and industrial electronics, which is closely associated with the aerospace industry. Electronics is a major growth industry in many parts of the United States (New York, Chicago, Philadelphia, Boston), particularly in the fast growing peripheral states— California, Texas, and Florida. Texas and Florida are still small compared with the old manufacturing states, but California is one of the leaders. Radio and TV manufacturers employ many women, and get along with a small proportion of skilled employees, but firms making military and industrial electronics often need to be in close contact with the most advanced research institutions in the field. The large concentration of such firms at Boston (Highway 128), on Long Island, in Los Angeles, or around San Francisco Bay is no coincidence. The academic, climatic, and recreational assets are stressed when Los Angeles or San Francisco companies want scientists to join their staff.

The electronics industry in Europe has a similar pattern. Standardized output of components and products is often located in an area with a surplus of female labor, e.g., the Ruhr, but research, development, and the most advanced production is concentrated in metropolitan areas (London, Paris, and so on). In France, Grenoble and the Riviera, with good universities and scenic and climatic amenities, have attracted a sizeable electronics industry, helped by the government decentralization program.

The Cotton Textile Industry

Clothmaking was a widely spread usufacture until modern times, but it was also the leading industry working for local and distant markets. In medieval Europe it was an important factor in the growth of towns, especially in Italy and the Low Countries. This industry spearheaded the Industrial Revolution in England, and in almost every country has been among the pioneers of modern manufacturing. Between 1760 and 1790, a series of inventions put the spinning of yarn and weaving of cloth on a mechanical basis. John Kay's flying shuttle, invented in 1733 but commonly used after 1760, increased the output of the handloom weaver. James Hargreaves' spinning jenny (1764), Richard Arkwright's "water frame" (1768) and carding machine (1775), and Samuel Crompton's "spinning mule" (1779) moved spinning from cottage or workshop into the factory. Arkwright stands out as a pioneer of major status. His mill at Cromford near Nottingham, built in 1771, can be seen as the first factory of mechanized production. But the mechanization of weaving was slower. Edmund Cartwright's power loom (1784) was no immediate commercial success. It took several decades in the new century of agonizing social adjustment before the power looms had superseded the hand looms. A cheap fiber needed for the new power machines was provided by Eli Whitney's invention of the cotton gin (1793), which mechanized removal of seeds from lint. Britain forged ahead in cotton manufacturing on the basis of her new machines and cheap cotton from the United States. Cotton, an unimportant export in colonial America, became the leading export item for the United States. Cotton cloth was soon mass produced in British factories for markets all over the world; the spinning wheel and the hand loom were gradually put out of commission by the cheap factory products. The market for cotton cloth was ubiquitous, and factories were soon established in the four corners of the world, using Lancashire machinery and, as a rule, protected by a tariff. The manufacture of cotton textiles is now one of the few manufacturing industries in which poor nations, such as Egypt, India, and Hong Kong, produce a surplus for export.

THE RISE AND FALL OF AN INDUSTRY. The British cotton industry, concentrated in the Lancashire region centered on Manchester, was the first of the great modern industries. The Lancashire region, where the industry was mature by 1840, has normally accounted for over 80 per cent of British cotton production. In our day of new growth industries in old industrial nations, the Lancashire cotton district is a prime example of a major industry on the decline, about 50 years after its zenith.[71] It now employs fewer people than in 1840, and less than one-fourth of the 650,000 peak employment just before World War I, when the British cotton industry accounted for 25 per cent of United Kingdom's exports. Shrinkage of export volume to 5 per cent of the 1912 peak is the chief cause of the industry's decline.

In its first growth period, the 60 years before 1840, power seems to have been the most important location factor of the Lancashire cotton industry. Lancashire was rich in water power, but the availability of power sites was restricted. By 1840 water power provided only 13 per cent of the industry's energy, although the waterwheels were more powerful and reliable than the steam engines of the day. Steam-powered mills were virtually tied to the coal field or its margins. An overland trip of eight miles doubled the price of coal, and since the cost of fuel was about one-fifth the cost of labor—the largest cost item—such a distance was equivalent to a wage difference of 20 per cent.

The pre-industrial economic geography of Britain strongly influenced the coal field-industry association. Farmers of the sterile Pennine hillsides had been dependent on the textile trade for generations before the

[71] All the problems brought to an over-specialized region by the decline of its dominating industry are found in the Lancashire district.

Lancashire was not only the plant school of the industrialized world. Life in the new factory towns of the 1840's and '50's provided the empirical background for the writings of Karl Marx and Friedrich Engels, which a hundred years later laid the theoretic foundation for the Communist Revolution on the Eurasiatic Continent. In the contemporary writings of the Manchester school, advocating free trade and *laissez faire*, the same reality was seen from a different angle. The two opposing economic systems of the present world, the centrally planned economies of the Communist countries and the free-market economies of the West, may thus both look to Manchester as a place of pilgrimage.

An American or Canadian worker from an industrial park with "campus atmosphere," driving his car through a grim and depressing cotton town in Lancashire, does not have to stretch his imagination to understand the pessimistic views of Karl Marx a hundred years ago. That time has not borne out Marx's predictions is another matter. Marx was neither the first nor the last social scientist to err in prediction.

Industrial Revolution. In part of Lancashire they changed from woolen cloth to fustian at an early stage, and in another they switched to cotton at the turn of the century, but in Yorkshire they continued with woolen cloth. The concentration on cotton west of the Pennines, and on woolen and worsted east of the hills, became stronger as the Industrial Revolution proceeded. Central Scotland had a similar historic background as Lancashire, and its physical milieu was also similar (coal field and high humidity).[72] Merchants of Glasgow built cotton mills on the Lanarkshire coal field, but this district declined after 1860. It specialized in finer goods for the domestic and continental markets, but coarse goods for the colonial market was the most expansive trade at the time. The Clyde district became increasingly specialized in steel and engineering industries, especially shipbuilding.

By 1840 the Lancashire cotton district [73] had a distribution which differs only in detail from that of the present day. After 1840 new growth was simply added in areas already associated with cotton manufacture. The geographic differentiation of spinning and weaving into separate districts began to crystallize. Once developed, it has persisted mainly for external economies. The specialization went even further. Some towns (e.g., Oldham, Rochdale, and Bury) were coarse-spinning towns, others (Bolton, Leigh, Stockton, and Manchester) had fine-spinning mills; some were weaving coarse goods (Blackburn and Darwen), and others fine goods (Nelson and Colne). Bleaching, printing, and dyeing were concentrated in special districts. The finished cloth market was in Manchester, the natural commercial focus of the region. Liverpool became the chief European market for raw cotton, most of which was imported from the United States.

The geography of contraction between 1931 and 1951 draws attention to the traditional specialization in Lancashire. Losses in employment were greater in weaving than in spinning, and were lowest in the finishing trades. The towns of the weaving belt in the north suffered greater distress than the spinning towns in the south. Since Asian competition was keenest in the coarser goods, weaving towns in the Blackburn area, producing coarse gray-cloth for tropical markets, suffered most, losing an average two-thirds of their employment in textiles. Eastern towns of the weaving belt produced fine cloth for the domestic market and selected export markets, and were shielded from the full impact of Asian competition. In the spinning belt the same observations could be made. Coarse-spinning towns around Oldham were more seriously hit than fine-spinning towns centered on Bolton.

Postwar recovery reached a peak in 1951, followed by the most acute crisis in the industry's history. Employment, output, and exports showed

[72] Before artificial humidifiers were introduced, natural humidity was of great importance in textile districts.

[73] Wilfred Smith, *An Economic Geography of Great Britain* (London: Methuen, 1949); W. Smith, "Trends in the Geographical Distribution of the Lancashire Cotton Industry," *Geography*, Vol. 26 (January 1941), 7-17; H. B. Rodgers, "The Lancashire Cotton Industry in 1840," *Institute of Brit. Geogrs., Trans. and Papers*, Vol. 28 (1960), 135-53; H. B. Rodgers, "The Changing Geography of the Lancashire Cotton Industry," *Economic Geography*, Vol. 38 (October 1962), 299-314.

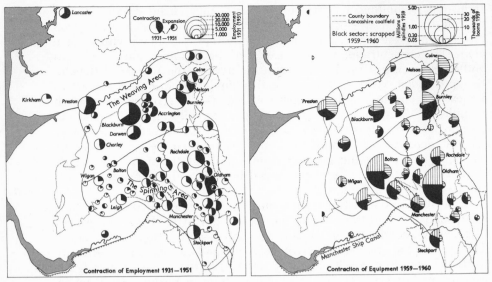

The Decline of the Lancashire Cotton Industry

From H. B. Rodgers, "The Changing Geography of the Lancashire Cotton Industry," Economic Geography, Vol. 38 (October 1962), 299-314.

a steeply downward trend, but imports of cloth, chiefly from Hong Kong, increased rapidly. By 1958 Britain had a net import of cotton cloth. Most imports were grey-cloth, which was dyed and printed in Lancashire and then in part re-exported. A plan for voluntary rationalization through scrapping excess machinery and closing of redundant mills was presented by the government at the end of the decade. It was two-thirds financed by the Treasury and one-third by the industry. As a result, 40 per cent of the looms and 49 per cent of the spindles were scrapped—but much of this machinery had been idle for years. The old separation of weaving from spinning is no longer an advantage to the industry; geographically and commercially, the two branches are becoming more integrated.

Industrial diversification has made steady progress in the Lancashire region since the early 1950's. Much of the region has been listed as development area in need of government assistance in the attraction of new industry. Old mills have been converted to other uses. Some 550 mills were closed between 1951 and 1960; 380 have been reoccupied by other trades. Some 120,000 people were employed in the converted mills, equal to two-thirds of the loss in textile employment since 1951. The single-story weaving sheds have been more easily converted than the multistory spinning mills, which influences the location of new industry. The latest contraction of the cotton industry in Lancashire means that it has lost its capacity to inflict serious damage on the regional economy, especially since two-thirds of the mill workers are women. Further decay would, in general, not hurt the primary income of the family, but only the supplementary income.

A MIGRATING INDUSTRY. The first American cotton mill was built in 1790 at Pawtucket, Rhode Island, by Englishman Samuel Slater, who was trained at an Arkwright factory near Nottingham. After a slow start because of British competition, the industry expanded rapidly following the War of 1812 and the new tariff.[74] Mills were built at many small waterfalls of southern New England and the Middle Atlantic States. Later, larger falls were dammed and provided with lateral canals, which served as millraces along which a great number of mills received their power. The Merrimack River saw the growth of three great textile towns: Lowell and Manchester in cotton, and Lawrence in woolen and worsted. Much capital made in shipping and whaling was invested in textile mills; New England turned its interest from "wharf to waterfall." After 1860 the cotton industry of New England switched to steam for power, but there were no coal fields in this region. Coal was received by schooners, and later by steamers, from Hampton Roads and Baltimore, which led to the rapid expansion of Fall River and New Bedford on the coast of southern Massachusetts.[75] At the peak of New England's cotton manufacturing in the early 1920's, these two towns had almost two-thirds of the region's capacity.

The map of the New England cotton industry in 1924 reflects three stages in the history of the industry: (1) numerous mills on small waterfalls; (2) concentration of mills at the large falls in Lawrence and Lowell, Massachusetts, and Manchester, New Hampshire, on the Merrimack River; and (3) concentration of mills at the coal-receiving ports of Fall River and New Bedford, Massachusetts. (From J. R. Smith, M. O. Phillips, and T. R. Smith, Industrial and Commercial Geography, 4th ed. New York: Holt, 1955, p. 536.)

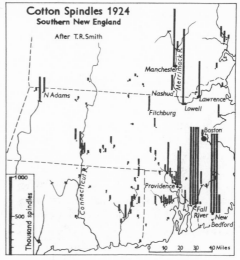

After 1880, production of cotton cloth in the South increased steadily. This was first concentrated on coarser grades produced for a poor Southern market. It is often presumed that liberated slaves formed the pool of low-wage labor that attracted the cotton industry to the South. But this is not correct; the main Southern industry excluded Negroes, except for limited menial purposes. The Piedmont area, where the cotton mills were built, had a large supply of white workers. Others were recruited from the overpopulated valleys of Appalachia. The first cotton mills were not built by individual enterprise alone. Citizens' committees often raised

[74] Imports of British textiles were still heavy; roughly one-third of the nation's imports between 1820 and 1850 consisted of English textiles. Benjamin Chinitz, *Freight and the Metropolis* (Cambridge: Harvard Univ., 1960), p. 10.
[75] T. R. Smith, *The Cotton Textile Industry of Fall River, Massachusetts* (New York: King's Crown, 1944).

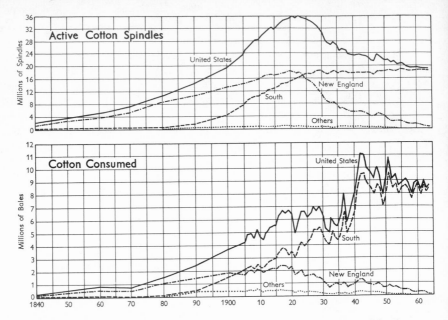

The South surpassed New England as a cotton textile area in 1924, if measured by active spindles, or in 1902 if measured by raw cotton consumed. The time lag can be explained by the southern mills' initial production of coarse fabrics for the poor southern market. For many decades following the Civil War, differences between northern and southern standards of living and wages far exceeded the present differences.

funds through special cotton mill campaigns to promote industrial growth in the war-ravaged South. Entrepreneurs were dependent on the backing of white citizens, and the white workers soon acquired a vested interest in keeping the cotton mills white.[76]

Southern industry was initially attracted by water power; later it could procure cheap coal by rail. Rather early in the history of the Southern cotton industry there was a change to electric power, which made possible single-storied plants, often located in small towns or the countryside. In addition to low-cost labor and power, the Southern industry thus had the advantage of more efficient plants and new machinery. By 1925 the Southern mills had passed New England in number of spindles, and by 1940, 90 per cent of the American cotton industry was in the South. After a temporary recovery during the war, the New England cotton industry has continued its southward migration. Only an insignificant capacity remains in New England. The Southern industry in the 1950's ran into a period of stagnation in employment after seven decades of expansion, partly because of technical advances, partly because of foreign competition (Japan, Hong Kong, Italy). In addition to lower wages, the competitors had the advantage of an export subsidy paid by the U.S. Department of Agriculture to American raw cotton exporters, and thus not enjoyed by the domestic industry.

A STABLE PATTERN. Cotton manufacture, the dominating industry of Czarist Russia, was concentrated in the Moscow region (Moskva,

[76] Gunnar Myrdal, *An American Dilemma* (New York: Harper, 1944).

Orekhovo-Zuyevo, Serpukhov, Ivanovo, Kalinin), with a secondary center in St. Petersburg. About half of the raw cotton was imported, and half came some 3,000-4,000 km by rail from domestic sources in Central Asia and Transcaucasia. Most of the textile machinery was imported.

The distribution pattern has not changed much during the Soviet period; some capacity has been built in Sibiria to save on long rail hauls (Barnaul, Novosibirsk), and the cotton growing districts have also expanded their capacity (Tashkent, Fergana, Ashkhabad, Kirovabad, Leninakan). But the Moscow region in 1960 still produced more than three-fourths of the cotton cloth (90 per cent in 1913). Almost all of the raw cotton now comes from domestic sources. The Soviet Union produces her own textile machinery.

The Apparel Industry

Fashion is the key to the apparel industry, its organization, and geographic distribution, especially to women's clothing in countries with a high standard of living. Manufacturers of high-priced women's dresses must be prepared to make significant changes in their products within a few days; their production cycle is often shorter than a week. The mode followed by women of the Western world is dictated by a few *maisons des hautes coutures* in Paris, which produce apparel for a selected group of customers, and make two full lines every year for spring-summer and fall-winter shows attended by designers from all parts of the world. Although the primacy of Paris as world fashion capital is uncontested,

New York's Garment Center in Midtown Manhattan

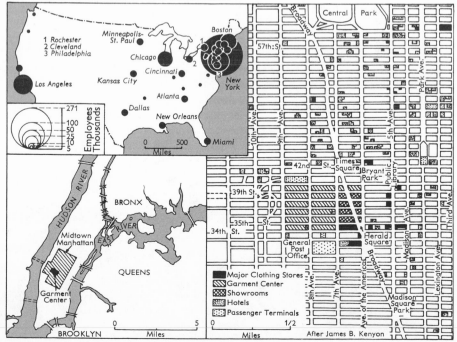

After James B. Kenyon

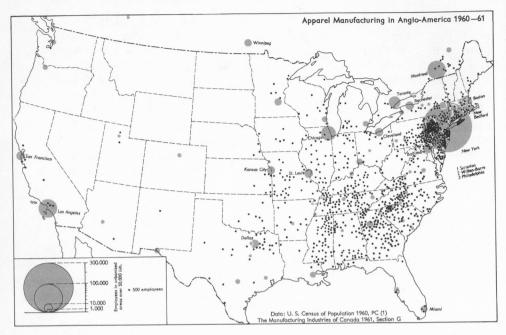

Two influences in the geographical distribution of the American clothing industry are conspicuous: New York's dominance as a directing center, and the trend toward low-wage areas. Had the industry been directed from Chicago or Los Angeles, for example, the pattern would have been different.

Employment in apparel manufacturing during three consecutive census years. Inset scale shows figures for nation.

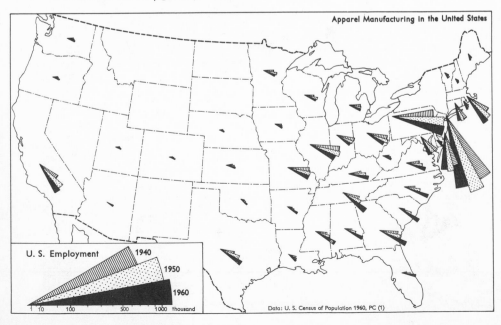

every country has its own fashion center, usually in the economic capital (which is often also the art center). Here Paris fashions are adapted to meet national preferences. Women who pioneer new styles are to be found among the very wealthy, concentrated in the economic capital. The Paris shows are widely publicized, and national style pioneers are always in the public eye; new styles become almost instantly known and desired. To meet this demand, the clothing industry must be organized in a way that allows great flexibility.

The industry is characterized by small and highly specialized firms, but its geographic concentration is stronger than industries dominated by a few, large companies. There are more garment industry employees within urbanized New York than employees of any single manufacturing industry in any urban center on earth. About 100,000 apparel workers are employed in the famous Garment Center, comprising 18 blocks between 34th and 40th Streets, and Ninth and Sixth Avenues in Manhattan. In 1960 total apparel industry employment in Greater New York was 306,000, or 26 per cent of the U.S. total. As labor costs are important in the clothing industry, and wages are normally highest in metropolitan cities, these data indicate the strong pull of the fashion center. However, just as in the printing and publishing industry, it has been possible to take advantage of both lower wages and rents outside the metropolitan cities and the external economies offered by the big city. Much of the actual sewing has been moved, first to smaller towns, often depressed mining and textile towns, within overnight trucking range of New York,[77] and later to places in the deep South. Showrooms, model shops, wholesaling, and other key functions remain near the central business district, where many ancillary goods and services required by the clothing industry are readily available. The need to keep in touch with the world of fashion urges many American firms producing popular-priced women's garments to locate their headquarters in the Garment Center, though their plants are distant from Manhattan. They buy designs from model houses or "pirate" them from style-innovators in the neighborhood. New York's leadership in fashion remains unimpaired; its share of American clothing sales has decreased only moderately in recent decades, and still exceeds 60 per cent. But as a center of production New York has been slipping since the First World War.[78]

HISTORY. The transfer of garment making from home to shop and factory has been a slow process. Nowhere has it been completely accomplished, and in some areas it has hardly begun. Tailor shops existed in antiquity, and quantities of uniforms have been made at least since the seventeenth century, but large shops in which machinery was used date back only to the early nineteenth century. The modern apparel industry got under way in the United States, where sailors provided a market for ready-to-wear clothing at New York, Boston, and New Bedford from about 1825. The garments were designed and cut in shops,

---

[77] Generally regarded as 300 miles.
[78] Roy B. Helfgott, "Women's and Children's Apparel," in *Made in New York*, Max Hall, ed. (Cambridge: Harvard Univ., 1959); James B. Kenyon, "The Industrial Structure of the New York Garment Center," in *Focus on Geographic Activity*, R. S. Thoman and D. J. Patton, eds. (New York: McGraw-Hill, 1964).

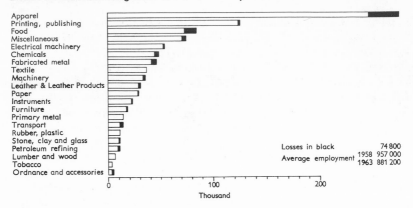

Losses of Manufacturing Jobs in New York City 1958–1963

Apparel
Printing, publishing
Food
Miscellaneous
Electrical machinery
Chemicals
Fabricated metal
Textile
Machinery
Leather & Leather Products
Paper
Instruments
Furniture
Primary metal
Transport
Rubber, plastic
Stone, clay and glass
Petroleum refining
Lumber and wood
Tobacco
Ordnance and accessories

Losses in black   74 800
Average employment 1958 957 000
                    1963 881 200

0   100   200
Thousand

Data refer to New York City, not to the SMA. Long-distance migration of production capacity has been conspicuous, especially in the apparel industry's moves to the South.

but sewing was done by housewives in their homes (putting-out system). European production and sale of ready-to-wear clothing conflicted with the legal monopoly of the tailors' guild, but ready-made clothing for men became common in England after 1850. The sewing machine, invented by Elias Howe (1846) and later improved by Isaac Singer and others, and the band saw for cutting many layers of cloth simultaneously, invented in 1858 by John Barran, a wholesale clothier of Leeds, had put the clothing industry on a sound mechanical basis when demand for uniforms during the Civil War started a major boom. Physical measures of millions of soldiers provided statistical knowledge of the male body that made possible improved fitting qualities. The putting-out system gave way in the following decades to the workshop, using machines and employing mostly women.

Manufacture of clothing is overwhelmingly a female industry, with women accounting for 82 per cent of 1954 employment in Britain (440,-000). But in 1851 there were 115,000 males and 17,000 females in England and Wales with tailoring as their occupation. Most of them were village tailors, itinerant tailors, or dressmakers who made clothes that were beyond the skill of household members. One craftsman made a product from beginning to end. It was division of labor, pioneered by the Jewish wholesalers of Manhattan and London's East End, that made possible the switch to predominantly female labor with a few weeks training on the job. New York had become an American leader in the manufacture of men's ready-to-wear clothing by 1850. Between 1860 and 1910, the city's apparel industry employment grew from 30,000 to 236,000, and the number of plants from 600 to 10,000. New York by 1910 had over 60 per cent of the American garment industry (measured by employment). Two events marked the beginning of a new stage for the industry after 1880: *a*) American women turned to ready-to-wear clothing, and *b*) there was a great inflow of immigrants from eastern and southern Europe. About 1.5 million Jews came to the United States before World War I, especially in the early 1880's, following pogroms in Russia and eastern Europe. Tailoring had been a Jewish occupation in Europe. Many immigrants were skilled, but the majority were poor, illiterate, and unskilled, so it was considered a moral obligation for Jewish tailors to take poor, co-religionist immigrants into their shops and teach them the trade. A large ghetto developed on the lower East Side of Manhattan, near the point of debarkation for immigrants. The contracting system spread rapidly at this time. The contractor, or "sweater," was actually an organizer of immigrants. For a set price he had garments sewn that had been designed and cut by the clothing jobber; this work was often done in the contractor's tenement. Working conditions in the "sweatshops" of the 1880's were appalling. Beginning in 1892 work in the tenements was outlawed. The factories, often occupying unattractive loft space, were not much better, but at least home and working place were separated.

By the middle 1920's the apparel industry had completed its migration within Manhattan from the lower East Side, near the heaviest colony of Jewish immigrants, to its present location, better served by rapid transit from the Bronx and Brooklyn. Jewish labor and management dominated the apparel industry at the outset, but clothing workers were soon recruited among the Italians and, more recently, Puerto Ricans and Negroes.

The system of merchants or *jobbers*, who buy and cut the fabrics and subsequently sell the finished product, and *contractors*, who for a set price convert cut cloth into clothing, is still common in New York, especially in the high-priced lines. More standardized garments are often made by manufacturers in their own shops. In either case, the average clothing firm on Manhattan is small, employing about 20 people.

GREAT BRITAIN. The English pattern is similar to the American, but London used to be a less pronounced leader than New York. In 1861 Greater London had barely one-quarter, and in 1951 barely one-third, of the clothing workers in England and Wales.

Clothing manufacture in London is largely concentrated in certain narrowly-defined areas in central parts of the city.[79] Persistent tailoring and dressmaking centers have been found during the last hundred years in both West End (Westminster) and East End (Whitechapel in Stepney, with an outlier in Hackney).

The Westminster concentration was based on streets famous for highest-class men's tailoring, e.g., Savile Row, which long dominated the tailoring quarter of West End. Tailors and other producers (dressmakers, shoemakers, saddlers), catering to wealthy Westminster customers, had to work close to their market. Since the end of the nineteenth century, ready-made clothing has been produced in Westminster, chiefly by manufacturers working directly for retail outlets located on Oxford, Regent, and Bond Streets, confirmed as London's leading shopping streets by construction of the tube in the beginning of the century. The clothing shops, and the host of subcontracting firms for buttonholing, pleating,

[79] P. G. Hall, "The Location of the Clothing Trades in London, 1861-1951," *Institute of British Geographers*, Transactions and Papers, Vol. 26 (1960), pp. 155-78. P. G. Hall, *The Industries of London Since 1861* (London: Hutchinson, 1962).

The Industrial Structure of London

The industrial structure of Greater London is compared with that of Britain. (From M. J. Wise, "The Role of London in the Industrial Geography of Great Britain," Geography, XX, 1956, pp. 219-32.)

embroidering, buttoncovering, and ancillary firms supplying textiles, buttons, zippers, hooks, belts, decorations, thread, lining materials, and sewing machines, are found in the side streets. This apparel industry complex provides the small firm with external economies, in Marshall's sense,[80] which are large enough to offset wage and rent differences between central London and smaller towns.

East End has been dominated by wholesale ready-made clothing of low quality. The history of the East End clothing industry is similar to that of Manhattan: the key role played by the Jews in organizing the industry, the influx of Jews from eastern Europe following the pogroms of the early 1880's, and availability of cheap labor (wives of dock workers, construction workers, and others with irregular employment). East End was the traditional home of the Jews since Cromwell lifted the medieval ban on their residence in England, and it had for centuries been the home of the poor. The Jewish clothing industry of Whitechapel in the late 1880's was confined to an area of about one square mile, completely isolated from the English population that surrounded it on all sides. Ready-made clothing had been made there since about 1850 by old clothes dealers who became wholesale clothiers. They subcontracted the sewing of garments, which had been cut in their warehouses, to "sweaters" who organized housewives, and later immigrants, for the work. Even after the great Jewish immigration, homeworking women often undersold male labor in "sweatshops." This industry, aimed for a working class and colonial market, was oriented to cheap labor. With restriction on immigration after 1911, workshop legislation, increased standard of living, and assimilation of the Jewish population group, working conditions have improved and quality of output has been upgraded, but the industry tends to remain where it was, enjoying the same external economies as the West End industry.

[80] Alfred Marshall, *Principles of Economics*, 8th ed. (London: Macmillan, 1961). First edition, 1890.

Leeds and Manchester are important secondary clothing centers in Britain. Leeds, the center of England's wool textile district, specializes in products made from woolen and worsted, while Manchester, economic capital of the Lancashire cotton district, primarily makes products of cotton and rayon. London, a world style capital for men's clothing, is surpassed by Leeds as a producer of men's outerwear. As in the United States, the clothing industry has expanded in towns where labor and factory space were made available by contraction of the textile industry, and in towns with predominantly male jobs (coal mining, steel works). Many factories were induced by government agencies to move into depressed areas or to open branch plants. As a result, some clothing industry is found in almost all towns in Britain.[81]

INTERNATIONAL TRADE. Clothing enters international trade on a small scale. Only in a few countries (Israel, Japan, France, and Switzerland) does clothing account for as much as 2 to 5 per cent of exports. Hong Kong is a remarkable exception. As an average for 1959-1961, clothing, the leading export commodity, accounted for 24 per cent of Hong Kong's exports.

The Pulp and Paper Industry

Per capita consumption of paper ranges from almost 500 pounds a year in the United States to a few pounds a year in some underdeveloped countries. The average consumer buys very little paper; almost all of it comes to him as an adjunct of other products and services. Manufacturing of pulp and paper is not in the public eye to the same extent as other major manufacturing activities, e.g., steel, automobiles, or machinery, but per capita paper consumption is sometimes used as one of the few meaningful yardsticks for measuring standards of living.

FROM RAGS TO WOOD PULP. The modern technique of making paper antedates the pulp industry. A machine for matting fibers into sheets was invented by Nicolas Robert of France in 1798, and five years later two Englishmen, Henry and Sealy Fourdrinier, constructed the first commercially successful paper machine. Until then paper had been made by hand from rags, one small sheet at a time. The Western world had learned the art of paper-making, originally invented in China (Tsai Lun, A.D. 105), from the Moors in the Middle Ages. Inadequacy of the rag supply was a pressing problem for thousands of small paper mills in Europe and North America, and it was made even more acute by the gradual introduction of paper machines. Research in new raw materials led to practical results in 1840, when F. G. Keller invented the wood grinder in Sachsen, Germany.

Mechanical wood pulp, or groundwood, did not replace rags; for some decades it was used largely as a filler mixed with rag pulp. As the lignin or wood substance is not removed, and fibers are cut in the grinding process, groundwood is confined to papers in which permanency and color are not important, primarily newsprint. Groundwood paper has

[81] For good maps of this and other manufacturing industries in Britain, see *Atlas of Britain* (London: Oxford Univ., 1963).

the great advantage of taking ink even at high printing speeds. Raw materials for this industry are nonresinous woods such as spruce, balsam, fir, and western hemlock; it is a major consumer of electrical power and clean water.

In continued attempts to get a better substitute for rags, a chemical method was sought which could dissolve the lignin and separate out the cellulose fibers.[82] In 1867 B. Ch. Tilghman's works in the United States laid the foundation for development of the *sulfite process*, which was developed commercially by C. D. Ekman, Sweden, in 1872. Chips of non-resinous wood are boiled under pressure in an acid liquid, chiefly bi-sulfite of lime. Sulfite pulp in unbleached form is used in newsprint, wrapping paper, and food-container board, and in bleached form in a host of high-grade papers and boards. Further refined sulfite pulp, which has lost its fiber structure, is the raw material for rayon, plastics, lacquers, and other products (dissolving pulp).

The *sulfate process*, using a basic cooking liquid of sodium sulfide and caustic soda, will pulp any kind of wood. The method was first commercially developed by the Swede A. Müntzing and the German C. F. Dahl. When boiled long under low pressure, a strong but dark colored fiber is produced which makes a very strong paper (Swedish *kraftpapper*). The sulfate process, now the largest by tonnage, accounts for 60 per cent of United States pulp production, and is used chiefly in regions with ample supply of resinous pine wood. In unbleached form it is used for kraft papers of all types, including wrapping paper, bags, cardboard cartons, and boxes, and in bleached form is applied to food-container boards, white wrapping paper, book paper, and so on.

The bleaching technique for sulfate pulp, developed in the 1930's, makes possible the production of pulp that is as white and cheap as sulfite pulp, but stronger. At the same time the new *magnefite process*, patented by large Canadian and U.S. companies and first described in 1958, has widened the wood base for converted sulfite mills to include pine and hardwoods and has increased the strength of the pulp so it approaches that of sulfate pulp.

The *soda process*, actually tried in 1851 but commercially practicable much later, is a basic method using a solution of caustic soda for pulping short-fibered hardwoods, such as aspen, poplar, and cottonwood. The weak but easily bleached pulp produced by this method is employed in books and magazines; the tonnages produced remain small. In many paper mills it has been replaced by waste paper pulp.

The *semi-chemical processes*, in which the wood is softened by chemicals and then subjected to mechanical defibrating, return higher yields than the chemical processes (60 to 90 per cent of the wood) and provide a market for hardwood. They were originally developed in the Forest Products Laboratory at Madison, Wisconsin, and account for rapidly increasing production in the United States and Europe. These pulps are well suited to corrugated boxes and cartons.

---

[82] About half the weight of coniferous wood consists of cellulose fibers, over one-fourth of lignin, and the rest of resins, sugar, and hemicellulose. Only the cellulose fibers are desired for paper making.

Pulpwood accounts for about 90 per cent of the primary fibrous material used in paper manufacture.[83] Waste paper is not included in this estimate, as it is actually wood pulp in a waste form.

The superiority of wood as a raw material in paper making rests on economic grounds. An acre of wheat land in the Pacific Northwest yields one or two tons of straw, but annual growth on an acre of forest land is three or four tons.[84] The forest, when completely logged off, represents the accumulation of many years' increment, and this compact yield can be cheaply handled, stored, and transported. There has been a tendency in many regions for pulp mills to follow in the wake of lumber mills, usually a few decades after the introduction of modern sawmills.

The costs of collecting waste paper limit its use to areas with high population density; almost one-third of American paper output is made of waste paper. For paperboard mills in the American Manufacturing Belt, waste paper is an important raw material. High quality waste paper, mixed with sulfite pulp, is also used in book paper.

Straw, corn stalks, bagasse, and similar agricultural waste products are unable to compete with wood as a cheap source of cellulose in industrialized countries, which are favorably located with regard to coniferous forest regions. Historically, straw preceded wood as a paper making material in the United States and several other countries. Straw paper was used for printing and wrapping during and after the Civil War. After a steady decline, straw accounts for about 1 per cent of American fiber consumption. It is limited to certain grades of cheap board in which the entire stalk is used. Bagasse, for obvious reasons, has become a major source of cellulose fiber in many tropical countries.

Fine paper mills, producing short runs, draw upon a wide assortment of fibers, whereas newsprint or kraft paper mills use only one or a few. This difference has great implications for the locational pattern of the industry.

In India, bamboo pulping became commercially practicable about 1922, and since the war bamboos have supplied most raw material for the paper industry, with grasses second and waste paper third. Wood pulp has been almost negligible in that country.

The process of converting pulp into paper and board is essentially the same for all grades. The Fourdrinier machine is used in paper making, and the cylinder and inverform machines are used in board making. Within limits, it is possible to make many different kinds of paper or board on the same machine; grade shifting is a recognized practice. Productivity increases sharply with increase in size of machine. Fine papers are made on small machines, and newsprint and kraft paper on large ones. Large Fourdrinier machines are among the most expensive machines in industry.

[83] Louis T. Stevenson, "The Pulp and Paper Industry," in *The Development of American Industries,* J. G. Glover and W. B. Cornell, eds. (Englewood Cliffs, N.J.: Prentice-Hall, 1951), p. 526.

[84] John A. Guthrie, *The Economics of Pulp and Paper* (Pullman: State College of Washington, 1950), p. 32.

From headquarters in the Manufacturing Belt, many large paper concerns (e.g., International Paper and St. Regis in New York, Scott in Philadelphia, Mead in Dayton, Kimberley-Clark in Neenah, Wisconsin) operate mills in the South, the Northwest, Canada, and other parts of the world. Two leading paper corporations operate from the West Coast: Crown Zellerbach in San Francisco and Weyerhaeuser in Tacoma. Others are paper divisions of large manufacturing concerns: Continental Can, New York, and Container Corporation, Chicago. The Bowater Company mills were built by European interests. Its plants are located at Liverpool and Corner Brook in Canada, and Catawba and Calhoun in the South. Location of corporate headquarters is subject to extreme inertia. The home mill (above) and headquarters of the large Kimberley-Clark group at Neenah, on the Fox River, originated as an all-rag newsprint mill (two tons a day) in 1872. (Kimberley-Clark.)

PAPER AND PULP IN ANGLO-AMERICA. Wood prices can be expected to be highest in the area of highest market potential, stretching from New York to Chicago. They should decrease as one proceeds north or south, toward points of lower market potential. The producers of low-value paper—by far the most important by tonnage—should be sensitive to even small differences in wood prices. Such paper mills should, theoretically, seek a location either near the market, receiving pulp from peripheral pulp mills, or at pulp mills in the forest areas. A factor of great importance, often forgotten in theoretical discussions centered on weight losses of raw materials in the manufacturing process, is the economy of continuous process. If this is introduced, the scale tips in favor of forest areas, for although pulp can be as easily transported as paper, the equivalent amount of pulpwood cannot. Integrated pulp-paper mills near the market, receiving pulpwood from forest areas, form a third alternative only in areas of low-cost water transport.

Pulp and Paper Mills in Anglo-America 1963

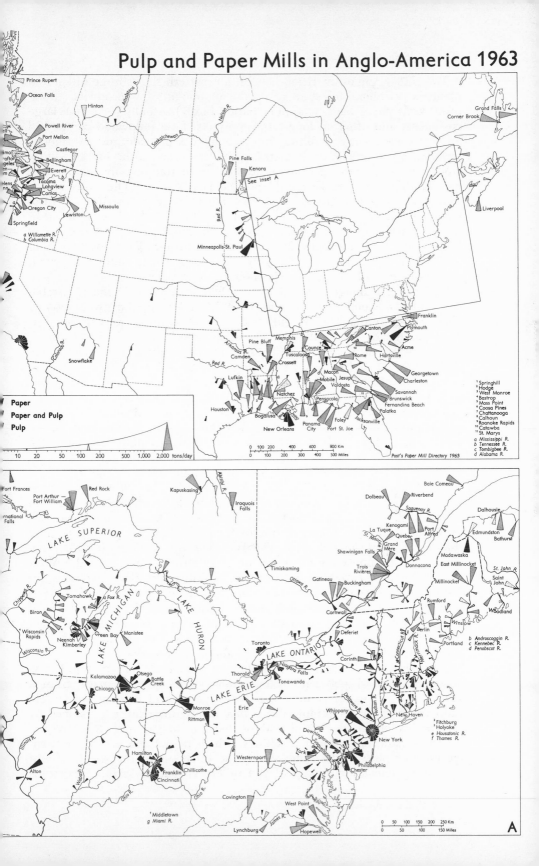

Prince Rupert
Ocean Falls
Hinton
Powell River
Port Mellon
Castlegor
Bellingham
Everett
Tacoma
Longview
Camas
Oregon City
Springfield
Missoula
Lewiston

a Willamette R.
b Columbia R.

Minneapolis-St. Paul

Grand Falls
Corner Brook
Liverpool

See inset A
Pine Falls
Kenora

Red R.
Saskatchewan R.
Athabasca R.
Nelson R.

Snowflake
Colorado R.

Paper
Paper and Pulp
Pulp

10   20   50   100   200   500   1,000   2,000 tons/day

Franklin
Canton
Plymouth
Pine Bluff
Memphis
Counce
Acme
Tuscaloosa
Rome
Hartsville
Camden
Crossett
Macon
Georgetown
Lufkin
Jesup
Charleston
Natchez
Mobile
Valdosta
Savannah
Pensacola
Brunswick
Houston
Bogalusa
Foley
Fernandina Beach
New Orleans
Panama City
Jacksonville
Port St. Joe
Palatka

Arkansas R.
Red R.

1 Springhill
2 Hodge
3 West Monroe
4 Bastrop
5 Moss Point
6 Coosa Pines
7 Chattanooga
8 Calhoun
9 Roanoke Rapids
10 Catawba
11 St. Marys

a Mississippi R.
b Tennessee R.
c Tombigbee R.
d Alabama R.

0   100   200   400   600   800 Km
0   100   200   300   400   500 Miles

Post's Paper Mill Directory 1963

Fort Frances
Port Arthur Fort William
Red Rock
International Falls

Kapuskasing
Abitibi R.
Iroquois Falls

Baie Comeau
Dolbeau
Riverbend
Dalhousie
Saguenay R.
Kenogami
Port Alfred
Edmundston
Bathurst
La Tuque
Quebec
St. Maurice R.
Shawinigan Falls
Grand Mère
Madawaska
East Millinocket
St. John R.
Trois Rivières
Donnacona
Millinocket
Saint John
Timiskaming
Ottawa R.
Gatineau
Buckingham
Rumford
Woodland

LAKE SUPERIOR

Chippewa R.
Tomahawk
Fox R.
Biron
Wisconsin Rapids
Neenah Kimberley
Green Bay
Manistee
Wisconsin R.

LAKE MICHIGAN
LAKE HURON

Cornwall
Deferiet
Winslow
Berlin
Portland
Merrimack R.

b Androscoggin R.
c Kennebec R.
d Penobscot R.

Toronto
LAKE ONTARIO
Corinth
Niagara Falls
Thorold
Tonawanda
Kalamazoo
Otsego
Battle Creek
Chicago
Monroe
Erie
LAKE ERIE
Rittman

Illinois R.

Whippany
New Haven
Downingtown
Hudson R.
Delaware R.

Fitchburg
Holyoke
e Housatonic R.
f Thames R.

Alton
Hamilton
Franklin
Cincinnati
Chillicothe
Westernport
York
New York
Philadelphia
Chester

Wabash R.
Ohio R.

Middletown
g Miami R.

Covington
West Point
James R.
Lynchburg
Hopewell

0   50   100   150   200   250 Km
0   50   100   150 Miles

A

The actual Anglo-American distribution pattern shows huge integrated plants in peripheral forest areas, producing one or a few products (newsprint, kraft paper bags, wrapping paper, boxes), usually for a few large customers, and often on long-term contracts. Low pulpwood prices and low conversion costs, resulting from economies of scale and continuous process, apparently offset high transportation costs to the market. Pulpwood prices in these peripheral regions have traditionally been about half of those in New England and the lake states.[85] The mills of the Manufacturing Belt are either board mills, based primarily on waste paper, or special paper mills (book and writing paper, tissue). In addition to waste paper, soda pulp, and semichemical pulp made from local hardwoods, they use many kinds of pulp from other regions and from abroad. These mills are only slightly affected by cheap sources of wood; close contact with the market is their prime concern.

The cost advantage enjoyed by the South and the Pacific Coast because of low wood prices is considerably greater in the production of chemical pulp than in groundwood. Almost twice as much wood is used per ton of chemical pulp. Canada's specialization in newsprint is partly a result of American tariff policy with no duty on newsprint, pulp, and pulpwood, but high tariff for paper and board.

Separate pulp mills are rare in Anglo-America, but many integrated mills sell pulp on the market. Interregional trade in pulp is relatively small, at least in comparison with Europe. The Pacific Northwest ships much sulfite pulp to the Manufacturing Belt, and before World War II the eastern part of the Belt imported large quantities of pulp from northern Europe, which helps to explain the concentration of paper mills in southern New England and the Middle Atlantic states.

The remarkable expansion in American pulp and paper production in recent decades has been accompanied by large changes in the distribution pattern of the industry. In the early 1930's the South was still on a par with New England, but in the early 1960's it produced more than eight times as much pulp. The West has also had a large expansion. The South accounts for 60 per cent of American pulp, and the West almost equals the rest of the country. Sulfate pulp alone accounts for 60 per cent of American tonnage, with mechanical pulp second (13 per cent) and sulfite third (10 per cent), closely followed by semichemical pulp (9 per cent). In Canada, groundwood makes up 50 per cent. Sulfate pulp used to be unimportant in Canada, but in 1961 it slightly exceeded sulfite, each accounting for about 20 per cent.

PAPERBOARD. Paperboard, the largest branch of the paper industry, accounting for 47 per cent of U.S. tonnage in 1964, is made from a variety of raw materials, of which waste paper and unbleached sulfate pulp are the most important. The choice of raw material is influenced by the quality of board desired and by location of the mill. Most paperboard is made on cylinder machines, which permit the use of different qualities of pulp in the same sheet; the thickness of the sheet is built by adding one layer on top of the other. The outer surface may thus

[85] Guthrie, *op. cit.*, p. 144.

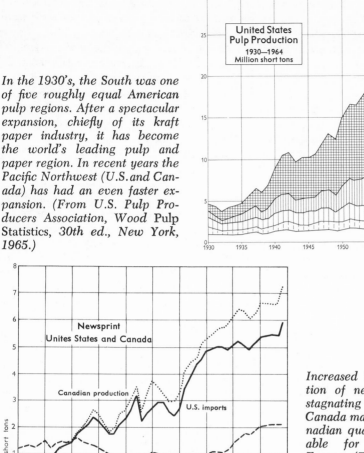

In the 1930's, the South was one of five roughly equal American pulp regions. After a spectacular expansion, chiefly of its kraft paper industry, it has become the world's leading pulp and paper region. In recent years the Pacific Northwest (U.S. and Canada) has had an even faster expansion. (From U.S. Pulp Producers Association, Wood Pulp Statistics, 30th ed., New York, 1965.)

Increased U.S. production of newsprint and stagnating imports from Canada make larger Canadian quantities available for export to Europe. (From the Statistical Abstract of the United States.)

be made of better quality pulp than the rest. The new inverform machine, used for some types of board, has the advantage of high operating speeds.

American consumption of paperboard was seven times as large in 1960 as it was 40 years earlier. This spectacular increase surpassed that of any branch of the paper industry except the relatively minor tissue and sanitary paper. It reflects two important developments in the transport and distribution of goods in modern society: substitution of paperboard containers and cartons for wooden boxes, jute sacks, and so on, and a shift from retail sale of goods in bulk to packaged selling.[86]

NEWSPRINT. The newsprint industry was first established in New England and the state of New York, and later moved into the lake states, Michigan and Wisconsin, and eventually into the Pacific Northwest. The

[86] *Ibid.*, p. 61.

great migration of this industry has been across the national boundary into Canada, a move stimulated by an embargo on exportation of Canadian pulpwood imposed by the Canadian provinces before World War I, and by American removal of duties on newsprint in 1913. After that year Canadian newsprint production, financed largely with American capital, rose steadily. It was one-third of American production in 1913, passed the American in 1925, and was more than three times that of the United States in 1940. On both sides of the Canada-United States border, the composition of species is favorable for the newsprint industry, which uses about 80 per cent groundwood and 20 per cent unbleached sulfite pulp, added to give the paper greater strength. Non-resinous wood, such as spruce, predominates in this region.

Newsprint mills are usually fully integrated, and the pulp is handled in slush form in a continuous process. Traditionally, the paper companies have also engaged in large-scale generation of electric power. Low production costs, achieved by constructing large mills in remote locations where other users do not compete for wood and hydroelectric power, are partly offset by high transportation costs. Most newsprint is shipped to the market by rail, since mills located on tidewater or on the Great Lakes are blocked by ice for as long as five months. In recent years Montreal has had some winter traffic; if the St. Lawrence were kept open, it should benefit the many pulp and paper mills on the north shore.

"Migration" of the newsprint industry did not, of course, involve transfer of the physical plant, but it did often mean a reclassification. Take a modern newsprint mill of 1880 in southern New England. A few decades later it was obsolete and found it necessary to shift to some other groundwood paper, such as wallpaper, and after another decade or two may again have shifted to groundwood specialties. Increasing costs of pulpwood may eventually have forced the same mill to discontinue operation of its pulp mill and buy pulp in the market. This time it may also have shifted to fine sulfite or sulfate paper.[87] This characteristic series of shifts toward higher grade papers lies behind today's neat regional differentiation within the paper and pulp industry of Anglo-America. Shifts are possible since the basic machines are the same for all sectors of the industry.

KRAFT PAPER. The vast belt of yellow pine forests in southeastern United States, stretching in a wide crescent from Virginia to eastern Texas, did not get their first sulfate mill until 1911, when a 20-ton-a-day mill was built at Orange, Texas. Considerable doubt remained for some time among industrialists as to the adequacy of the wood supply for huge, modern mills.[88] But after 1930 great strides were made in the South, based on research by C. H. Herty, who proved that a steady supply of pinewood could be maintained, and that the exceptionally high resin content of southern pine did not preclude its use for pulping. The market stimulus provided by the pulp mills has led to markedly improved silvi-

[87] E. B. Alderfer and H. E. Michl, *Economics of American Industry*, 2nd ed. (New York: McGraw-Hill, 1950), p. 301.

[88] Sven A. Andersson, "Trends in the Pulp and Paper Industry," *Economic Geography*, Vol. 18 (July 1942), 195-202.

Table 2.6. *Wood Pulp Production by Major Countries in Selected Years*

	1923	1929	1937	1948	1956	1964
Mechanical pulp						
World, mill.m. tons	4.71	7.13	9.67	9.70	16.11	20.81
World, per cent	100.0	100.0	100.0	100.0	100.0	100.0
Finland	4.4	4.9	7.4	5.6	6.1	7.6
Sweden	8.0	9.2	7.6	7.0	5.7	5.9
Norway	7.9	7.2	5.6	4.5	4.1	4.3
Canada	29.2	33.0	35.1	42.6	33.4	29.0
United States	30.3	21.0	15.1	20.4	23.7	23.6
Chemical pulp						
World, mill.m. tons	6.10	10.02	14.59	18.86	33.12	53.09
World, per cent	100.0	100.0	100.0	100.0	100.0	100.0
Finland	5.2	6.2	10.1	5.7	5.6	7.0
Sweden	16.3	18.8	19.1	12.3	9.6	9.7
Norway	5.4	4.5	3.8	2.0	1.8	1.7
Canada	15.6	14.1	11.3	15.1	13.2	12.1
United States	33.1	29.1	30.8	51.5	49.0	55.0

Sources: *Statistical Yearbook,* League of Nations and United Nations.

culture and reforestation, which has created pulpwood increments sufficient for many additional mills. Since the end of the 1940's, the South has accounted for more than half of United States pulpwood cut; in 1963 it produced no less than 60 per cent of American pulp. The southern forest region is ideally suited to a high degree of mechanization, but the availability of low-wage Negro labor has kept mechanization at a moderate level. Yearly increments per acre are some three times those of eastern Canada or Sweden. The South is an unexcelled natural tree farm.

The integrated pulp and paper mills of the South are very large. The plant of the Union Bag–Camp Paper Corporation at Savannah, Georgia, has long ranked as the largest pulp and paper production unit in the world. It has a daily capacity of 2,400 tons of kraft paper, primarily wrapping and bag papers and board. Located on the tidewater section of the Savannah River, it receives pulpwood by truck, barge, and train. Within a 120-mile radius south-southwest of this plant, more than 90 per cent of the area is woodland, a percentage greater than 30 years ago. In location and pulpwood-source management, this mill is representative of the older mills in the region.[89] It receives a larger share of its pulpwood from company land than do the newer mills.

PULP AND PAPER IN WESTERN EUROPE. The neat differentiation in Anglo-America between special paper and board mills in the region of highest market potential and large, integrated pulp-paper mills for standardized products such as newsprint, wrapping paper, paper bags, and board in peripheral forest areas is less conspicuous in Europe, where national legislation often prohibits ownership of land by foreign companies. Large newspapers, magazines, paper companies, and other heavy consumers of pulp in the densely populated Paris-Liverpool-Ruhr Tri-

[89] Merle Prunty, Jr., "Recent Expansions in the Southern Pulp-Paper Industries," *Economic Geography,* Vol. 32 (January 1956), 51-57.

angle have not been able to integrate backwards and locate their integrated plants in the peripheral forest areas of northern Europe. On the other hand, customs barriers have prevented Nordic pulp mills from integrating forwards. Instead, large paper mills producing newsprint, wrapping paper, and board have been erected at tidewater locations, such as Rouen near Paris, the Lower Thames and Medway near London, and in the Liverpool-Manchester area.

France and Germany are pulp producers on a par with Norway. Former beach and oak woods have been turned into spruce or pine "fields" in large areas of Europe north of the Alps; remaining deciduous forests may be pulped by new semichemical processes. But all countries on the Continent have sizable imports of pulp and paper, chiefly from the Nordic countries.

Britain is the largest market for international trade in pulp. Traditionally strong economic ties between Britain and Norden, now strengthened by the EFTA agreements, are based on complementarity in economies and natural resources. British coal and industrial products were changed early for Nordic products of forest (Finland, Sweden, Norway) and farm (Denmark). Bowater Paper, a leading British concern in the paper industry, has mills in Canada and the United States, and some interests in the Nordic pulp and paper industry. With rapidly increasing American newsprint production in the South and Northwest, Canadian producers are forced to look to Britain and EEC as outlets for their growing output; Southern kraft paper mills export marginal quantities to Europe.

The pulp and paper industry of Norden, with a combined export tonnage exceeding that of Canada, is primarily located at the Gulf of Finland (Kotka at the Kymi river), the Gulf of Bothnia (Oulu and Kemi in Finland; the Sundsvall and Härnösand districts in Sweden), Lake Vänern, and the Oslofjord (Sarpsborg, Drammen). The lower reaches of the rivers provided ideal sites for forest industries during the pioneer period: lumber was floated down to the mill from a vast hinterland and finished products were shipped by tramps or liners directly to customers with tidal location. The hydrology of Finland makes it favorable to locate forest industry plants at inland lakes and rivers. With recent changes in cost relations between floating and trucking, increasing quantities of lumber are trucked to the mills; only the major tributaries are being used for long-distance floating. In southernmost Sweden, which has a relatively high yearly increment, icefree ports, good roads, but no large rivers, several coastal pulp mills have recently started producing for the export market.[90]

[90] Sweden south of the sixtieth parallel, which runs somewhat north of Uppsala, accounts for half the yearly increment, but southern Sweden has exported pulpwood in the form of pitprops to England and Germany, and later in the form of pulpwood to Norway and Germany. The large cellulose companies of the north, which traditionally draw much of their pulpwood from company land, have not dared establish export mills on the coasts of Småland and adjacent provinces, where farmer-owned forests prevail. The establishment of these mills had to await postwar initiatives by the farmers' cooperatives. In spite of a favorable location with regard to the continental market, they have not yet been integrated.

This is just another example of irrational distribution patterns in manufacturing. Such patterns cannot be understood as a simple function of transport economy only.

Forest industries have traditionally been heavy contributors to exports of the Nordic countries: over 80 per cent in Finland, some 40 per cent in Sweden, and less in Norway. These percentages have been declining since the war. In Sweden, engineering industries now make a larger contribution than forest industries, and in Finland they are rapidly expanding their share. The Swedish pulp industry suffers from being a pioneer in the field; e.g., the average sulfate mill has a capacity of 109,000 tons a year, whereas the average in Finland is 197,000 tons, and in the southern United States 203,000.[91] In Sweden the sulfate industry expanded rapidly from the turn of the century, in Finland from the 1920's, and in the American South from about 1930. A conspicuously large number of Nordic mills are pulp mills, but paper (including newsprint) and board are increasing their share of export tonnages, helped by the economies of continuous process and, recently, by EFTA agreements. Finland and Norway now export more paper and board than pulp, measured by value.

Petroleum Refineries

The first oil well was drilled at Titusville, Pennsylvania, in 1859; a hundred years later (1960), world production of petroleum for the first time exceeded 1,000 million metric tons. This quantity surpasses by a wide margin those of coal, iron ore, lumber, wheat, rice, and the other products of mine, farm, and forest which, transformed by the manufacturing process, are the material basis of our civilization. What is more, world oil production has continued to increase at a steady 6 to 7 per cent per annum decade after decade, whereas production of some other major raw materials (coal, wheat, rice) increase at much lower rates. Petroleum refining as a major manufacturing industry (measured by investments and as a generator of traffic flows) is thus a later phenomenon than the recent centenary of the modern petroleum industry might indicate. The 1960 production of crude petroleum was twice as large as ten years earlier, and the aggregate production of the ten years of the 1950's equalled that of the 90 previous years. The chief petroleum deposits are, as a rule, distant from the chief areas of consumption, making petroleum the leading product in long-distance trade.

TUG-OF-WAR BETWEEN OILFIELDS AND MARKETS. Early refineries, based on simple heating and distillation, produced kerosene, for which a flourishing market was rapidly developed. The Pennsylvania oil contained a high proportion of kerosene, but since as much as 50 per cent of the crude was dumped or burned as waste, refineries were restricted to locations on or near the oilfields. Petroleum became an important source of lubricants in about 1870, but quantities used in this way have always remained a small proportion of total refinery output. The internal combustion engine, invented in 1860 (J. J. E. Lénoir) and applied to motor vehicles on a large scale in the beginning of this century (with the introduction of the Model T-Ford in 1908 as the great landmark),

---

[91] The largest mill in the South, at Savannah, has a pulp capacity of almost 700,000 tons.

provided demand with tremendous growth potentials for a new light fraction. The problem of increasing surplus of heavier fractions was eased by development of the cracking process, but there were limits to this costly method. The best refinery location was still on or near the oilfield.

The situation changed with the opening of markets for the heavier fractions. Diesel and fuel oils for homes and factories, ships, locomotives, and road vehicles made heavy inroads into the traditional markets of coal. This development was well under way in the interwar period in the United States, was repeated in the old coal nations of Western Europe from the 1950's, and appeared somewhat later in the Soviet Union. During World War II, the petrochemical industry had its great breakthrough in the United States; after the war it superseded the traditional coal-tar based chemical industry in the old industrial nations of Europe. A modern refinery gets saleable products from 90 to 95 per cent of the crude oil, and uses about half of the remainder as fuel in the refinery.

These developments had a great influence on the economy of different oil refinery locations. Demand in major market areas has increased tremendously since World War II, the demand structure gradually coming to match the most economic pattern of refining. Only if there is demand for practically all the yields can refineries be built near the market. and market refineries do not have to be large. With a throughput of two million tons a year they are reasonably economic; above three million tons a year, the economies of scale become very small.[92] In transportation the economies of scale are striking; freight rates per ton decrease substantially with increasing tanker size. Since the war there has been a spectacular increase in the size of tankers. Ships of over 200,000 tons, much too large to pass through the Suez or Panama Canals, are hauling crude from the Middle East to Japanese refineries. Many supertankers of the early 1950's are now employed in coastwise hauling of products. Traditionally there has been a difference of freight between dirty and clean tankers, with dirty oil paying some 10 per cent less. This helped to justify the construction of refineries in selected market areas in the interwar period. Difference in transport costs between crude oil and products has grown with increase in tanker size. Few customers, besides refineries, handle enough oil to take advantage of the very low freight rates offered by mammoth tankers.

Introduction of mammoth tankers influences the location of refineries within consuming areas, especially in northwestern Europe, which is surrounded by shallow seas and where few coastal points can economically be made ready to accommodate vessels drawing 45 feet or more. Several established refineries on the European coast already have to be supplied with crude through pipelines from other ports.

Like other heavy industries, an oil refinery is a considerable nuisance, and in densely settled consuming areas may lead to conflicts with residential and recreational interests, while also irritating prospective manu-

[92] P. H. Frankel and W. L. Newton, "The Location of Refineries," *The Institute of Petroleum Review,* Vol. 15 (July 1961), 197-201.

facturing neighbors. The recent selection of refinery sites at Göteborg, Sweden, is a case in point. First a refinery was prevented from choosing a site at a popular beach area near the city, and later an automobile assembly plant contested the right of an oil company to build a refinery within one of the manufacturing zones of Göteborg, claiming that gases emitted from the refinery would hurt the finish of cars.

This inconvenience of refineries tends to prevent their being located close to the core of metropolitan cities. The advantage of trucking products direct from refinery to customers within the metropolitan area makes locations close to the city attractive. Refineries located outside economic trucking distance send oil products by coastal tankers, barge, rail, or pipeline to depots in metropolitan areas. As all oil companies cannot economically operate a refinery in every metropolitan area, both solutions are common, which means much crosshauling of petroleum and petroleum products. In some cases market refineries have been located *between* metropolitan areas to minimize this crosshauling (e.g., Fawley, England). Oil depots are also found at strategically located smaller towns.

International firms are especially noteworthy in the petroleum trade. Vertically integrated, international petroleum corporations own, rent, or otherwise control most means of production, transportation, and distribution from oil wells to neighborhood filling stations.[93] They usually have refining facilities near the oilfields and near the market. Seven such groups own some 70 per cent of refining capacity outside Anglo-America and the Communist World; in the early 1950's the Big Seven had about 90 per cent of the business.[94] Within Anglo-America, their share is smaller. The Soviet oil industry is on a par with the largest of international oil companies in volume of operations. Hardly any organization is more global in scope than the international oil groups.[95] Final decisions about

[93] Five of the Big Seven are American: Standard Oil of New Jersey (Esso), Gulf Oil, Standard Oil of New York (Socony Mobil), Standard Oil of California (Socal or Stancal), and Texas Oil (Texaco). The Royal Dutch/Shell group (Shell) is a private Anglo-Dutch company, whereas British Petroleum is jointly owned by state and private interests.

[94] Complete vertical integration in the oil industry is a comparatively recent development. Standard Oil of Ohio, organized in 1870 under the direction of J. D. Rockefeller, specialized in refining and marketing, leaving the hazardous prospecting and drilling to others. At the end of the decade the company controlled 95 per cent of American refining capacity, with refineries in Cleveland, Pittsburgh, Philadelphia, New York, etc. When Standard Oil of New Jersey was split into 33 separate companies by a decree of the U.S. Supreme Court in 1911, having violated the American anti-trust laws, it controlled 90 per cent of the pipelines, 85 per cent of the refining capacity, and 85 per cent of the market. Alderfer and Michl, *op. cit.*, pp. 276 ff.

[95] In volume of sales Standard Oil (N.J.), with 10 billion dollars, ranks second after General Motors (16 billion) among American industrial corporations. Among 49 such firms with sales exceeding one billion dollars in 1963, 11 were oil companies. But the four largest oil companies in 1958 accounted for only 32 per cent of the American market, a smaller concentration than in many other trades, which reflects both the enormous size of the American oil market and the international engagements of some of the largest companies. Standard Oil (N.J.) produces three-fourths of its crude oil and two-thirds of its refined products outside the United States. Jersey and its affiliates operate in 140 countries, employing over 147,000 people and producing about 13 per cent of the world's crude oil. With 26 wholly owned refineries and interests in another 32, this group has a global refining capacity exceeding 175 million tons. Eight Jersey refineries are rated at more than 5 million tons a year: Aruba, Amuay Bay, Baton Rouge, Baytown, New York (Bayway), Fawley, and Augusta. About two-

construction of new refineries or expansion of old ones will be made in New York, London, or Pittsburgh, where the corporate headquarters are located. In these decisions economic geography may yield to political geography, as consuming countries and producing countries exert conflicting pressures on the international companies.

ANGLO-AMERICA AND THE CARIBBEAN. Prior to World War II the United States accounted for over two-thirds of the world's refinery capacity, and almost two-thirds of the oil production. With rapid postwar expansion of oil production in other areas, the American share of oil production has dropped to less than one-third, but the share of refinery capacity stands higher, approaching 45 per cent. Three-fifths of American capacity is located on tidewater, an increase from less than half in the early 1930's. Ports of the Gulf Coast account for 30 per cent of the total U.S. refinery capacity; this percentage almost doubled between 1931 and 1961. Market-oriented refineries of the Atlantic Coast account for an almost unchanged 15 per cent share, and the Pacific Coast, which has changed from an important surplus region for petroleum to a deficit area, has declined from 19 to 15 per cent.[96]

The Gulf Coast, the tidewater face of the dominating American oilfields, now ships relatively small amounts of crude to East Coast refineries, which are supplied chiefly from Venezuela and the Middle East. The large, low-cost refineries on the Gulf Coast supply the growing Southern market, ship products by tanker to the East Coast[97] by pipeline and barge to the western part of the densely settled Manufacturing Belt, and by tanker to the Pacific Coast. Geographically associated with the oil refineries of the Gulf Coast is the rapidly expanding heavy petrochemical industry, producing raw materials for the predominantly market-oriented light chemical industry. The close geographic association of these two and the natural gas industry is economically beneficial to all three. The deep-water channels, originally constructed to accommodate tankers shipping crude from the shallow Gulf Coast, are now lined with recently constructed manufacturing establishments. This complex of

thirds of Jersey's refining capacity is now located near crude oil sources, no less than 43 per cent around the Gulf of Mexico and the Caribbean, which is the core area of the company's refining activity. Four regional groups control most of Standard Jersey's foreign operations: Esso Europe (headquarters in London), Esso Africa (Geneva), the Far East (New York), and Latin America (Coral Gables, Florida). *The Fortune Directory*, August 1964. Robert B. McNee, "The Economic Geography of an International Petroleum Firm," in *Focus on Geographic Activity*, R. S. Thoman and D. J. Patton, eds. (New York: McGraw-Hill, 1964), 98-107.

[96] Gunnar Alexandersson and Göran Norström, *World Shipping: An Economic Geography of Ports and Seaborne Trade* (New York: Wiley, 1963), p. 298.

[97] In 1962, construction was started on a 36-inch pipeline to carry products from Houston to New York, with feeders to smaller southeastern markets en route. It will traverse 1,400 miles, as against 2,120 miles for competing tankers. This pipeline is expected to be competitive by virtue of its size (the economies of scale are very great in pipeline transportation), and by virtue of being one-third shorter than the shipping lanes. Rates will be adjusted so that New York users will pay less per ton-mile than users along the line, a standard practice for tidewater terminals of overland transportation lines that compete with cheap ocean transportation.

The first oil pipelines to connect Texas and the East Coast, the "Big Inch" and "Little Big Inch," were built during World War II, more for strategic than economic reasons. After the war they were sold to natural gas transport companies, and all petroleum between the Gulf Coast and the East Coast was again carried by tankers.

Population

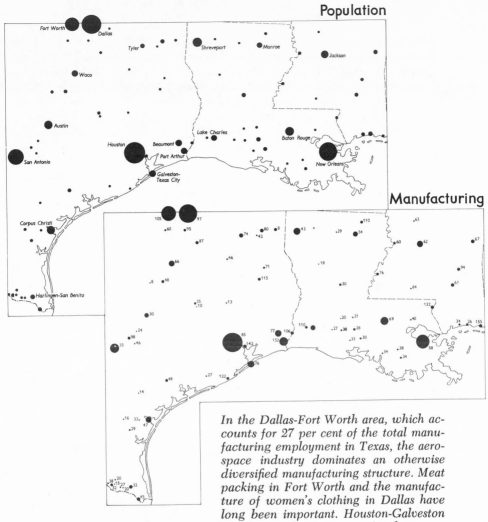

Manufacturing

In the Dallas-Fort Worth area, which accounts for 27 per cent of the total manufacturing employment in Texas, the aerospace industry dominates an otherwise diversified manufacturing structure. Meat packing in Fort Worth and the manufacture of women's clothing in Dallas have long been important. Houston-Galveston employs 22 per cent of those in manufacturing, and it is a center for the manufacture of machinery—much of it oilfield machinery—and for the production of chemicals, mostly petrochemicals, including synthetic rubber. Petroleum refining is also important in this area. The Beaumont-Port Arthur area, with 7 per cent of total manufacturing employment, produces petrochemicals, and it is one of the world's largest, most concentrated regions of petroleum refining. (Compare the low index values for most cities on this map with those of the Manufacturing Belt.)

manufacturing industries has turned the Gulf Coast into a top-ranking area for manufacturing investments.[98]

[98] The three categories of refinery locations, resource-oriented, market-oriented, and intermediate, must be seen as loosely defined generic terms. Many refineries will fit into more than one category. Resource-oriented tidewater refineries have traditionally had a good market location for supplying tankers with bunker oil. On the American Gulf Coast they now also have a big market in the petrochemical industry, although these refineries do not attract other industry on a scale comparable to that of the old coal mines. Many market-oriented refineries have also attracted thermoelectric and petrochemical plants.

The many large oil refineries on the Delaware River, downstream from Philadelphia, receive more crude petroleum, foreign and domestic, than all other ports of the United States combined. The Philadelphia area, with land available for heavy manufacturing industry along the river, has a larger refining capacity than New York, which is right on the ocean at the mouth of the Hudson River. But New York, by far the largest market, is the major destination for petroleum products from domestic and foreign refineries. Many manufacturing and transportation establishments compete for New York's scarce tidewater land. All but one of New York's refineries are in mainland New Jersey, on the Arthur Kill and Kill Van Kull channels fronting Staten Island. In the 1950's, one large refinery moved from New York to the Delaware River (Delaware City) because of lack of expansion space.

Montreal is the only Canadian refining center on the tidewater side of the Manufacturing Belt, and the leading refining center in the country. Its geographic location makes imported crude more attractive than domestic for the refineries. Since World War II, Montreal has received most of its crude by pipeline from Portland, Maine, chiefly imports from Venezuela.

The Great Lakes, despite a key role in the history of bulk transportation in Anglo-America, have never had any significant tanker trade. Chicago and Toledo, leading American refining centers on the Lakes, and Sarnia, leading center in Canada, receive crude by pipeline from domestic fields, and use the Lakes to a limited extent for shipment of products. Other important refining centers in the western part of the Manufacturing Belt are found on the Mississippi-Ohio river systems, e.g., Wood River opposite St. Louis.

Most resource-oriented inland refineries are small and widely dispersed. In some cases petrochemical plants (e.g., Borger, Texas) supplement the regional market, which, in spite of low population density, is quite large, thanks to high per capita consumption.

On the Pacific Coast, Los Angeles is both a large market and a major oilfield district; among its many refineries are all types represented elsewhere in the nation. From being a major surplus region in the 1920's with resource-oriented refineries, Los Angeles, with its rapidly expanding economy, has become a deficit area with primarily market-oriented refineries.

After World War II, large refineries and crude terminals were completed on the west coast of the Paraguaná Peninsula in Venezuela (Punta Cardón in 1947 and Amuay Bay in 1950), connected with oilfields on Lake Maracaibo by pipeline. Nearly all of Venezuela's output had previously been handled in the Netherlands Antilles, where two refineries were constructed in the 1920's on Curaçao and Aruba. Postwar expansion of refinery capacity oriented towards the oilfields of Venezuela was originally caused by increased flows of petroleum products to traditional markets in Europe and Latin America. As Europe turned increasingly to Middle East oil in the 1950's, the Caribbean refining industry became more closely tied with the North American market. American refineries, in this period of rapidly increasing net imports of oil, switched to a higher gasoline yield, opening a large market for imported fuel oil. At the East Coast refineries, residual oil was reduced from almost 22 per cent (1949 output) to less than 11 per cent by 1958. But American import restrictions of the late 1950's put a damper on fuel oil imports, and temporarily postponed some expansion projects at the Caribbean refineries.

Much postwar refining capacity was located in Venezuela as a result of the 1943 Hydrocarbons Act, which required oil companies to refine at least 15 per cent of their crude output within the country. With the completion in 1956 of a deepwater channel through the Straits of Maracaibo, later deepened to 43 feet, the main Venzuelan oil district was accessible to supertankers, greatly changing the premises for refinery location in this region. The earlier alternatives for getting oil out from Lake Maracaibo were by small tankers to the Netherlands Antilles or the Paraguaná Peninsula, or by pipeline to the Paraguaná terminals. Future export refineries may be located at the large crude terminals constructed on Lake Maracaibo after completion of the deepwater channel.

The refineries of British Trinidad have a location similar to those on the Netherlands Antilles. But, in addition to Venezuelan crude, the Trinidad refineries process crude from local oilfields. Pointe à Pierre is one of the largest export refineries in the Caribbean region.

Mexican refineries were resource-oriented export refineries during Mexico's boom period of oil production in the first decades of this century, with a peak in 1921. Tampico for a short time ranked as leading oil port in the world, but the rapidly increasing Mexican population now consumes almost all oil production. Although production is again growing, only marginal quantities are exported. A pipeline was laid in the late 1950's across the Isthmus of Tehuantepec from the new Minatitlan refinery, built to replace an old plant. The pipeline supplies the Pacific Coast with petroleum products which were formerly imported from California.

EUROPE, NORTH AFRICA, AND THE MIDDLE EAST. In 1939 Western Europe had an oil-refining capacity of 17 million tons; in 1962 it was about 250 million. Europe's share of total world capacity in the meantime increased from some 5 per cent to 20 per cent. After continued rapid expansion, capacity was expected to reach 400 million tons in 1966.

The dollar shortage in war-ravaged Europe made it difficult to continue the prewar pattern of importing oil products from refineries in the United States and other countries in the western hemisphere. European governments exerted pressure on oil companies to increase refining capacity: dollars were made available for purchase of American refining equipment, and preferential tariffs were applied favoring imports of crude oil rather than products. Several hundred million dollars of foreign exchange were saved when crude was gradually substituted for products in imports into the Organization for European Economic Cooperation (OEEC) countries.

Another political push towards more refining capacity in Europe was provided by rising nationalism in some oil-producing countries. Nationali-

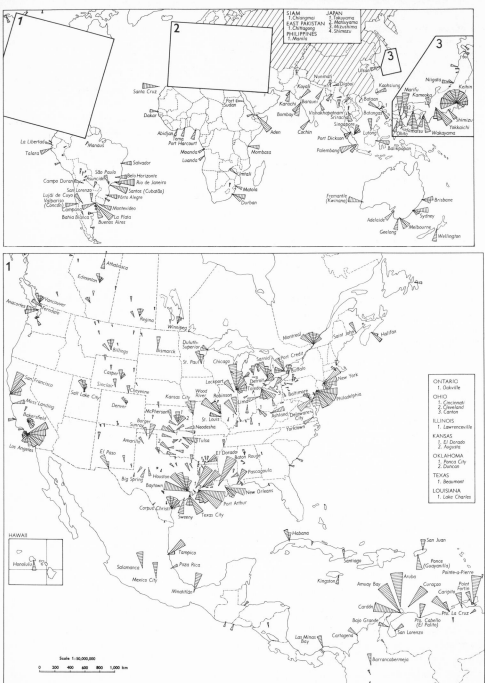

zation in 1951 of Anglo-Iranian's assets, and closure of the world's largest oil refinery at Abadan, demonstrated the dangers of dependence on overseas supplies of refined products. The wisdom of keeping refining operations separate from production was seen during the Suez crisis

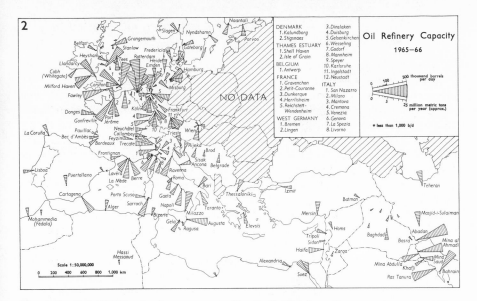

2

Oil Refinery Capacity 1965—66

DENMARK
1. Kalundborg
2. Stigsnaes

THAMES ESTUARY
1. Shell Haven
2. Isle of Grain

BELGIUM
1. Antwerp

FRANCE
1. Gravenchon
2. Petit-Couronne
3. Dunkerque
4. Herrlisheim
5. Reichstett-Wendenheim

WEST GERMANY
1. Bremen
2. Lingen

3. Dinslaken
4. Duisburg
5. Gelsenkirchen
6. Wesseling
7. Godorf
8. Mannheim
9. Speyer
10. Karlsruhe
11. Ingolstadt
12. Neustadt

ITALY
1. San Nazarro
2. Milano
3. Mantova
4. Cremona
5. Venezia
6. Genova
7. La Spezia
8. Livorno

* less than 1,000 b/d

500 thousand barrels per day

25 million metric tons per year (approx.)

NO DATA

Scale 1:50,000,000

0 200 400 600 800 1,000 km

Since the late 1950's, in the economically underdeveloped consuming countries of Latin America, Africa, and Monsoon Asia, expansion of refining capacity has been accomplished by construction of small refineries; only one-fourth of existing or planned units exceed 2 million tons. Great efforts have recently gone into reducing manufacturing costs in small refineries by keeping them as simple as possible, but this makes their output inflexible and prevents the manufacture of special products. Communist Bloc countries (USSR, Romania, Czechoslovakia) have provided loans and technical aid for the construction of state-owned refineries in some underdeveloped countries (Ethiopia, Egypt, Syria), and the Italian state enterprise ENI has built refineries in Ghana, Tunisia, and Morocco. The Big Seven have also faced competition from the American independents, who pool their resources in the international field though competing in the domestic market. (From The Oil and Gas Journal, The Petroleum Times, World Oil, *and* World Petroleum.)

(1956-57). The wave of refinery construction following events of 1951 provided Western Europe with adequate refinery capacity, which greatly simplified the problem of supplying required quantities of oil products at the time of the Suez crisis.[99] Producing regions outside the crisis area could speed up crude production from wells that were, for economic reasons, normally "capped" or inactivated. Large refinery capacity is a strategic necessity in industrially developed areas, as it provides flexibility; in times of crisis it is easier to find new sources for crude than for products.

Postwar political events gave the European refining industry a head start on a course the oil companies would certainly have followed eventually for economic reasons. A major handicap to economic operation of oil refineries in coal-dominated Europe before the war was the concentration of demand for the lighter fractions. Since the war, total demand, especially for fuel oil, has increased rapidly. The demand structure in Europe has thus changed to match more closely the most economic operation of refineries.

[99] Peter R. Odell, *An Economic Geography of Oil* (London: Bell, 1963), pp. 114 ff.

New development was under way before the war, but even then oil companies were exposed to government prodding. A French law of 1928 made it attractive for international oil companies to build refineries on French territory, and in the early 1930's there was a rush in refinery construction along the lower Seine, near Marseilles, and at Bordeaux in anticipation of the opening of French crude terminals on the Levant Coast. The relatively large German and Italian capacity had also been built with priority given to other than economic considerations.

The largest concentration of refining capacity in Western Europe is in the area of highest market potential,[100] centered on the southern North Sea and the English Channel, with Rotterdam, Antwerp, the lower Thames, Southampton (Fawley), and the lower Seine as main production centers. Much German capacity is concentrated inland, in and near the Ruhr area, where oil competes with coal, the *raison d'être* of this outstanding manufacturing region. The refineries are supplied with crude by pipeline from Wilhelmshaven and Rotterdam. Northwestern Europe is now adding a third major element in its fuel balance, in addition to traditional coal and more recent petroleum. Vast deposits of natural gas have been found in the Groningen region of the Netherlands and under the North Sea. Increased competition should, in the long run, lower prices paid for petroleum products by European consumers.

The French refineries and petrochemical plants are located at the tidewater terminals of the main French traffic axis across the "isthmus" from Le Havre-Rouen to Marseilles by way of Paris and Lyon. In the early 1960's a pipeline was constructed from Marseilles (Lavéra) to the Rhine Valley and southern Germany, with refineries at Lyon, Strasbourg, and in southern Germany. Another pipeline has been built from Genoa to refineries in Switzerland and southern Germany. Most of this inland capacity is located on rivers, but river barges can not match coastal tankers in low cost transport of surplus products; the need for tailoring refineries to the local market is therefore greater than in tidewater locations.[101] Inland refineries increased their share of the West European capacity from 15 per cent in 1960 to 30 per cent in 1966.

Italy in the early 1960's emerged as the leading oil refining nation in Western Europe, helped by its strategic location in the Mediterranean and by its active state enterprise ENI. Oil refineries became major vehicles for the economic development of the Italian South, which attracted several "base-load" refineries or large refineries strategically situated to supply a number of deficit areas.

The four Nordic countries, with an oil market as large as that of

---

[100] A map of Western Europe's population potential compiled by W. Warntz and D. Neft can, with due consideration of differences in purchasing power, be used for describing the market potential. See *Europe's Needs and Resources,* J. Frederic Dewhurst, ed. (Baltimore: Twentieth Century Fund, 1961), p. 56. Less generalized maps, like W. William-Olsson's *Economic Map of Europe* (Stockholm: Generalstabens Litografiska Anstalt, 1952), or any of several detailed population maps will permit an even more detailed description of the market potential.

[101] In addition to oil refineries and petrochemical plants on the Rhine, Europe's Chemical River, the Strasbourg-Mulhouse area has attracted other manufacturing capacity, domestic (e.g., a large Peugeot plant at Mulhouse) and foreign, especially American. In anticipation of the full impact of the EEC, Alsace, once an insecure border area, has become one of the fastest growing manufacturing regions in France.

Mediterranean Europe, were untried territory for refineries of the international oil companies until about 1960. Swedish refineries had been built by domestic intrests, but it could be seen in the middle 1950's that large oil companies would soon start a rush of refinery construction in this market area,[102] following a pattern established in the United States and elsewhere. A market area with no producing facilities, supplied from outside by a few competing firms, will rapidly acquire several production units when one of the competitors decides that the growing market can profitably support several plants. A good guess was that refineries would be built as close to the Köbenhavn-Göteborg-Oslo axis as the 45 foot contour would permit. In the actual rush, one refinery was built at Oslo, one built and one acquired at Göteborg, and three built on the Belts.

The first refinery in the Persian Gulf region was completed at Abadan on Shatt al Arab in 1913, to serve as an outlet for newly developed oil-fields in the western foothills of the Zagros Mountains. Total refinery capacity of the Middle East increased from 16 to 42 million tons from 1939 to 1951. Abadan, the world's largest refinery, accounted for 25 million tons. It is the largest city in the world (over 300,000) whose economy is entirely dependent on a refinery.

The 1951 nationalization of the Anglo-Iranian Oil Company, including the refinery at Abadan, was followed by a period of hesitation about refinery construction in the Middle East. This period came to an end in the early 1960's. The refinery at Mina Abdulla expanded from 2 to 7.5 million tons, and the Mina al Ahmadi refinery increased by 3 million tons. Japanese interests, with an offshore oilfield at the Kuwait-Saudi Arabian Neutral Zone, agreed to build a refinery (Khafji) when production reached a fixed level. Other companies seeking exploration rights during the hectic competition for concessions in the late 1950's and early 1960's offered to build refineries to make their offers as attractive as possible. Total refining capacity of the Persian Gulf region is therefore expected to rise considerably in the 1960's. The situation on the American Gulf Coast suggests that this may be an economically sound development, particularly if investments are also made in heavy petrochemical industries, for which there should be a tremendous potential market in Monsoon Asia.

Failure of the Abadan refinery to regain its pre-crisis peak of 25 million tons may be partly ascribed to its obsolete location. Access to Abadan is limited by sand bars in the Shatt al Arab to ships of up to 30-foot draft, which is insufficient for modern super-tankers. The refinery is also grossly overstaffed by modern standards, employing eight times as many men per unit of output as the average in Venezuela.[103]

Chemical Industries

The delimitation of chemical industries must be somewhat arbitrary; chemistry plays some role in practically all manufacturing industries. The U.S. Census of Manufactures divides its major group, *chemicals and allied*

[102] Gunnar Alexandersson, "The Oil Refineries of the World," *Proceedings of IGU Regional Conference in Japan 1957*, p. 264.
[103] Odell, *op. cit.*, p. 195.

products, into three major subgroups: *basic chemicals,* such as acids, alkalis, salts, and tonnage organic chemicals; *chemical products to be used in further manufacturing,* such as synthetic fibers, plastics, solvents, dyes, and pigments; *finished chemical products* ready for consumption, such as drugs, cosmetics, paints, detergents, and fertilizers.

Prior to the 1870's, the chemical industries were extractive in character and relied on simple, empirical techniques. The breakthrough for a scientific approach to new knowledge in applied chemistry came in Germany, although one pioneer in the field of organic chemistry, W. H. Perkin, was British. He discovered the first aniline dye (1856) and established the first factory to produce coal-tar dyes. Some early German chemists worked in England. The British dominated the alkali industry, first of the modern chemical industries.

Germany's educational system, with its scientific tradition and close connection between universities and industry, was better geared to the new growth industry. The organic chemical industry of Germany produced dyes, explosives, and drugs from basic materials furnished by by-product coke ovens developed as early as the 1870's, and perfected (1898) by Heinrich Koppers of Essen, who constructed a new oven for Hugo Stinnes, the German coal tycoon. Before World War I both Britain and the United States depended on organic chemical imports from Germany, but the war made German patents available and provided a great stimulus to United States and British industry.

As a result of the war effort, the United States had the world's largest chemical industry by 1920. American industry gradually took the lead in industrial research, and pioneered the switch in emphasis from coal-tar chemicals to petrochemicals. In the interwar years, but especially after World War II, the tendency in technologically advanced countries to replace natural materials with synthetic ones led to tremendous expansion in production of organic chemicals, including plastics. Synthetic materials can be adapted in the laboratory to meet almost any need. This has weakened the bargaining position of underdeveloped countries in the market place; they usually export only one or a few raw materials, which often have a synthetic competitor or substitute. Synthetic materials, made from such common substances as coal, petroleum, natural gas, salt, sulphur, and wood, are not subject to large fluctuations in price and supply.

Chief economic characteristics of the capital intensive chemical industries are large research budgets, frequent changes in products and processes, giant enterprises, administered prices, and rapid over-all expansion.[104] The average U.S. investment per chemical worker was $2,580 in 1958, compared with an average $980 for manufacturing as a whole. Expenditures on research and development amount to over 3 per cent

[104] American population grew at a yearly rate of 1.1 per cent in the quarter century before 1958, per capita income at 1.9 per cent, gross national product and industrial production at some 3.0 per cent, and industrial chemicals at about 10 per cent. Some old branches such as dyes and industrial explosives had a low growth rate (less than 2 per cent), and new branches, synthetic fibers other than rayon and acetate (36 per cent) and synthetic plastics and resins (17 per cent), had high growth rates. H. J. Barnett and F. T. Moore, "Long Range Growth of Chemical Industries," *Chemical and Engineering News,* Vol. 36 (April 7, 1958), 78 ff.

of sales volume in the United States; the corresponding figure for all manufacturing industry is slightly over 1 per cent. In the early 1950's the chemical industries accounted for one-fourth of basic research outlays made by all American manufacturing industry. By 1970, three-fifths of the sales of American chemical companies will be of products not known to the public in 1960.

The "overhead economies" of the chemical industry stem not only from a large research budget, but also from joint production and economies of scale. Chemical manufacturers are often drawn into new lines of production to provide markets for their by-products; they encourage vertical combinations, integrating forward to secure maximum market for main and subsidiary products, and backward to control the cost of raw materials. Horizontal combinations joining firms producing the same products are also common. Direct economies of scale are great in many chemical industries, especially in basic chemicals, involving the processing of raw materials of large tonnage and low value.

Chemical corporations rank among the largest industrial firms in most industrial countries. Intercorporate relations are extremely complex, and by no means stop at the national border or the traditional demarcation line of the chemical industry. The large oil companies are heavily involved in the petrochemical industry and, to take American examples, such firms as Eastman Kodak, leading manufacturer of photographic apparatus and supplies, and Pittsburgh Plate Glass, primarily a glass manufacturer, are leading producers of chemicals.

In addition to the chemical giants, the industry includes thousands of small or medium-sized firms, most of which blend or process chemicals produced by others.

BASIC CHEMICALS. Basic chemicals are produced in large quantities. World production of sulfuric acid, the leading basic chemical by tonnage, amounts to some 60 million tons. A waterside location is often necessary to handle large quantities of inexpensive raw materials and fuels, because copious quantities of water are used in the manufacturing process and because of the necessity for effluent disposal. The British Alkali Act of 1863 was the first of many regulations to control stream and air pollution, which has become an important problem in the industrialized world and must always be considered when sites are chosen for chemical plants.

Sulfuric acid, one of the barometers of industrial activity, is made by burning sulfur or roasting pyrites to obtain sulfur dioxide, which is processed by either the contact process or the chamber process. The former, discovered in 1831 by Phillips of Bristol, England, was widely used in Germany after 1870 and the United States after 1890, but did not spread in Britain until World War I. It produces a pure and highly concentrated acid, and accounts for over three-fourths of the quantities produced in the United States. The chamber process, introduced in 1746 by Roebuck, is mainly used for making sulfuric acid for industries not requiring very pure or concentrated acid, especially the superphosphate industry.

The major markets for sulfuric acid are the fertilizer industry (about one-third of the U.S. total), the manufacture of other acids, alkalis, and a wide range of organic chemicals, the iron and steel industry, and the rayon industry. Production is strongly market-oriented because of handling and shipping problems. United States and Western Europe each account for about one-third of world production. United States, Britain, and Japan primarily use native sulfur as a raw material, but in Continental Europe and the Soviet Union pyrites are more important; some sulfuric acid is a by-product of coal gasification and petroleum refining, and some originates in lead and zinc smelters.

The Gulf Coast of Texas and Louisiana has held a virtual world monopoly in production of native sulfur since the introduction of the Frasch process in 1898, which made possible low-cost extraction of sulfur from the salt domes. The major producing areas of sulfuric acid in the United States are the Manufacturing Belt, the Southeast (large production and consumption of fertilizers), and the Texas-Lousiana Gulf Coast. Sulfur is shipped in tankers and tank-barges to the large producers of sulfuric acid.

Alkalis are used in the manufacture of glass, textiles, soap, and so on. The two most important are soda ash (or sodium carbonate) and caustic soda (lye) (or sodium hydroxide). Producers are usually located with access to cheap raw materials and fuel.

Modern alkali industries date back to Nicolas Leblanc, a French chemist, who developed a method in the 1780's of making soda ash from salt, sulfuric acid, limestone, and coal. The industry had its greatest success in Britain, where it gravitated to the Cheshire salt field south of the Lancashire cotton district, which became a pioneer region in modern chemical industry. Cheshire was the one great salt field known in Britain at the time, and it had a most fortunate location, near the textile district and the great liner port of Liverpool. The expanding textile industry increased demand for acids, alkalis, soaps, and other chemicals, and increased use of soap in many parts of the world enlarged the market for alkalis.

A more economical method of making soda ash was developed by Ernest Solvay of Belgium, who built the first plant at Charleroi in 1863. Most soda ash, with the glass, soap, fertilizer, and caustic soda industries as customers, is now produced by the Solvay process, after several decades of fierce competition between the two methods. Additional quantities are obtained through electrolysis of salt brine and recovery of natural soda.

Caustic soda can be made from soda ash, but the largest quantities are now made by electrolysis of salt or brine with chlorine collected at the anode as a by-product. Caustic soda is used in the soap and rayon industries, petroleum refining, and several chemical industries. Heavy consumers of chlorine (pulp, paper, and textile mills) began early to manufacture their own chlorine, with caustic soda as a by-product. This seriously affected the Solvay firms, which reacted by building their own electrolytic plants. Fuel economies made possible cheap production of both chlorine and caustic soda.

The making of soap, by boiling fats with caustic soda, is dominated by firms with major interests outside the chemical industries. The British-

Dutch Unilever concern, formed in 1929 through merger of the Lever interests, which had a major soap manufacturing center at the company town of Port Sunlight near Liverpool, and the Margarine Union, is now one of the five largest manufacturing concerns in the world, with some 300,000 employees. The Lever firm was built on the utilization of vegetable oils instead of animal fats for soap-making. The Unilever concern has plantations in Africa, Southeast Asia, and the Pacific islands. Unilever's chief competitor, Procter & Gamble of Cincinnati, has a similar vertical organization, and is also represented by subsidiaries in many countries. Both companies produce soapless detergents which have made heavy inroads on the markets for soap in the last decade, and have greatly affected the prospects for vegetable oils.

Alcohols are widely used as solvents, antifreeze, and fuel, and as raw material for drugs, perfumes, ether, and synthetic rubber. Ethanol and methanol, or ethyl and methyl alcohol, are the most important industrial alcohols.

Ethyl alcohol, the common alcohol in, e.g., whiskey or vodka, is denatured for industrial uses to make it unfit as a beverage. It can be made from molasses, grain, or potatoes—the Soviet synthetic rubber industry was initially based on potato spirits. Increasing quantities of ethanol are produced by synthesis of ethylene, a product of the coal tar or petrochemical industries, and water, with sulfuric acid as catalyst. Sugar contained in the waste liquor of sulfite pulp mills can also be used. During the economic isolation of World War II, neutral Sweden built a diversified organic chemical industry based on sulfite spirits; after postwar expansion it now exceeds the domestic raw material base.[105]

Methyl alcohol is very poisonous, although it has a rather pleasant odor. Traditionally made by distillation of wood (hence the term wood alcohol), it is now made synthetically from carbon monoxide and hydrogen. Methanol is the starting point for the manufacture of formaldehyde, a major raw material in the plastics industry.

Industrial alcohol production is not controlled by the large chemical corporations; nor does the orderly price behavior typical of other sectors of the chemical industries always prevail in the industrial alcohols sector, with its wide raw-material range.

FERTILIZERS. Artificial fertilizers have been used in rapidly increasing quantities in the last century. In the Old World, especially China and Japan, fields have been cropped for thousands of years without being exhausted thanks to composted organic wastes, night soil, green manure, and other natural fertilizers. But modern Japan has succeeded in doubling rice yields per acre since the 1880's, chiefly by applying commercial fertilizers in addition to the traditional manure. Minerals taken out of the soil with the crop must be replaced.

---

[105] Chemical raw materials are also obtained as by-products of sulfate mills (tall oil, turpentine). The bulk of naval stores traditionally produced in southeastern United States are now by-products of sulfate mills. Most products derived from the wood chemical industry can also be produced by the coal or petroleum-based industry, often at lower cost. But the use of the waste liquor, after evaporation, for fuel and as a chemical raw material largely solves the problem of water pollution, which used to be very serious in the sulfite industry.

In 1840 German chemist Justus von Liebig showed that plants need certain minerals to grow. Northwestern Europe pioneered the use of mineral fertilizers, just as the American Middle West led the mechanization of farms. Europe was short of arable land, the United States was short of people. Use of fertilizers in the United States was long limited to the humid southeastern fringe from New England to Mississippi, but since the middle 1930's fertilizers have increasingly been used in the American agricultural heartland, the Middle West. They have contributed substantially to the conspicuous increase of American yields in this period.

Soils need both minerals and water to produce good crops. Usually it is cheaper to supply leached soils in humid areas with minerals (chiefly nitrogen, potassium, and phosphorus) than to supply soils in dry areas with water. Grassland areas of the temperate zones normally yield low increases in crop returns per input of fertilizers. No one would apply fertilizers on steppe or desert soils, where water is the critical factor, but if desert soils are irrigated, they will also be leached and in need of fertilizers.

Large areas of the United States Atlantic coastal plain receive two or three times the national average of fertilizer per acre of arable land. The same holds true of irrigated areas of California and Arizona, but in North Dakota only one-fourth the national average is applied.

Fertilizer factories are highly market-oriented, preferably located in ports with access to cheap water transport for incoming raw materials and outgoing products. The Norwegian saltpeter plant at Heröya near Skien-Porsgrunn is a good example; thousands of cargoes are picked up every year at the factory by small vessels and carried as close as possible to the ultimate consumer in Denmark and southern Sweden. In the United States, major ports between New England and Louisiana have long had fertilizer plants; Baltimore is known as the fertilizer capital (the first fertilizer plant in the United States was built at Baltimore in 1850). Since the 1930's several plants have been established in the Middle West.

For many decades Chile supplied the world market with mineral nitrate from unique deposits in the Atacama Desert. This monopoly was broken when methods were developed before World War I for fixation of atmospheric nitrogen. The first method, the Norwegian Birkeland-Eyde electric-arc process (1903), led to the establishment of factories at two hydroelectric power sites, Notodden and Rjukan, in remote inland areas of southern Norway. The German Haber-Bosch process, perfected in 1913, proved to be a more economic way of producing ammonia. This process now accounts for more than two-thirds of the world's output of manufactured nitrogen compounds. The first British plant went into operation in 1925, and the first American in 1927. Norsk Hydro, a leading manufacturing concern in Norway, rebuilt its Notodden and Rjukan plants for the Haber-Bosch process in 1929, and simultaneously established its large coastal plant at Heröya in the Skien conurbation.

Artificial phosphatic fertilizers are obtained by treating phosphate rock with sulfuric acid; the product is known as superphosphate. Some phosphate is also obtained as a by-product of steel furnaces treating phosphorous iron ore.

Major supplies of potash for the fertilizer industry are a few large salt deposits—at the Harz Mountains near Stassfurt; in Alsace, France, near Mulhouse; northeastern Spain; near Carlsbad, straddling the New Mexico-Texas border; and at Solikamsk in the Soviet Union.

The fertilizer industry holds a key position in the future economic development of poor tropical countries. The tremendous market of India, with its notoriously poor farming practices, located next door to vast deposits of oil and natural gas in the Persian Gulf area, is a challenge to the organizing spirit of the international oil and chemical corporations, as well as to the government of India.

MAN-MADE FIBERS.   Man-made fibers made up 28 per cent of world consumption of apparel fibers in 1964. The cellulose fibers, rayon and acetate, accounted for two-thirds, and the synthetic fibers, which entered the market after World War II, for one-third.

Cellulose Fibers.   The first successful processes imitating the silkworm were patented around the turn of the century. Cellulose converted into a liquid was forced through tiny holes in a metal plate, and then hardened to a solid in a bath or in dry air. The resulting fiber, originally called artificial silk, was regenerated cellulose, not a truly synthetic fiber.

In 1884 French chemist H. B. de Chardonnet announced the first successful method for converting a liquid into a solid thread, the nitrocellulose process.[106] Chardonnet's factory at Besançon, established in 1890, was the first rayon factory in the world. Other methods followed: cuprammonium rayon or bemberg rayon (first made in 1890, commercially successful at the turn of the century), viscose rayon (Cross and Bevan, 1891), and acetate rayon (patented in 1902; factories after World War I).

World production of cellulose fibers, made chiefly from bleached sulfite pulp, was of little significance until the early 1920's. In 1920 they accounted for less than one-third of 1 per cent of the total tonnage for cotton, wool, silk, and rayon. By 1940 this share had risen to 12 per cent, and cellulose fibers competed with wool for second place after cotton among the textile fibers. Though rayon was first made as an ersatz for silk, from about 1930 increasing quantities were produced as staple fiber, or staple. Filaments were cut in appropriate length to be spun on cotton, woolen, or linen spindles, and rayon became a substitute for the other natural fibers. In the 1930's and early '40's the Axis Powers, Germany, Japan, and Italy, which had no domestic sources of raw cotton and wool and needed their foreign exchange for purchases of various strategic materials, pushed the production of rayon staple. They accounted for the bulk of the output of staple.

Viscose rayon makes up almost 90 per cent of cellulose fiber production. Acetate never had any great importance outside the United States

[106] The term *rayon* was substituted for *artificial silk* in 1924. Since 1951 the term rayon has been reserved, in American usage, for fibers made by the viscose and cuprammonium processes; those made by the rival acetate process are referred to as *acetate. Dissolving pulp* commonly designates a special grade of bleached sulfite or sulfate pulp used for the manufacture of rayon, cellophane, plastics, and other non-paper products.

and Britain. Bemberg lost much of its leading market, the hosiery industry, to nylon. Heavy capital costs and patent rights have encouraged international cooperation in the rayon industry almost from the beginning. Western Europe has always been the leading rayon-producing area, except for a temporary dominance by the United States in the immediate postwar period.

Japan is second only to the United States among producing countries, and it is a leader in rayon exports, directed primarily to the tropical markets. Like the European countries, but in contrast to the United States, Japan traditionally has a larger production of staples than of filament.

The American industry was largely developed by European firms that built branch plants behind a high American tariff wall imposed to protect an infant domestic industry. The leading viscose producer was American Viscose Corporation, a subsidiary of Samuel Courtauld, an old Essex silk-weaving firm that held the patents and pioneered the viscose process. When sold during World War II it represented the largest British investment in the United States.[107] American Viscose is still the largest American producer of rayon, followed by Du Pont. Courtaulds also had interests in the German Glanzstoff, the Italian Snia Viscosa, and the Dutch Enka concerns, and these companies in their turn had American subsidiaries. After the war Courtaulds has again established a viscose-producing company in the United States, and retained its investments in and close association with continental concerns. In Britain, Courtaulds has had a virtual monopoly on the production of cellulose fibers since 1957, when it was merged with British Celanese, leading producer of acetate. Courtaulds has long operated an engineering works where much of its machinery is produced. The rayon industry in Japan was initially associated with European companies. In its international links the rayon industry resembles the chemical industry, rather than the textile trades, in which concentration within each country is the rule.

Production of cellulose fibers requires enormous quantities of soft water; large amounts of waste emanate from the process. Selection of plant sites is frequently a problem in industrialized and densely populated areas, where water shortage and river pollution cause increasing concern. In the United States, rayon plants, like synthetic fiber mills, are located in the humid East. The greatest concentration is in Virginia and Tennessee, between the Manufacturing Belt in the north, with its many other claimants of water, and the textile districts in the south. Fuel and chemicals are easily accessible in this part of the United States.

Synthetic fibers. In the 1930's a Du Pont chemist, W. H. Carothers, produced the first synthetic fiber, nylon. Existence of the new fiber was announced in 1938, and commercial production started in 1939. During World War II the U.S. Armed Forces used all nylon produced for parachutes and hundreds of other purposes, but after the war nylon completely replaced silk for hosiery and made inroads in the markets of several other established fibers. Nylon was followed by many synthetic

---

[107] D. W. Fryer, *World Economic Development* (New York: McGraw-Hill, 1965), p. 495.

Table 2.7. Production of Man-made Fibers, 1964
(thousands of short tons)

| | Rayon and Acetate | | Noncellulosic fibers | | |
	Filament	*Staple*	*Filament*	*Staple*	*Total*
United States	389	327	424	280	1,419
Canada	27	27	24	9	87
Brazil	35	13	10	4	62
EEC	309	515	237	173	1,235
Belgium	15	27	7	2	50
France	65	96	58	44	264
West Germany	86	237	88	66	477
Italy	101	135	65	46	346
Netherlands	42	21	20	16	99
Austria	7	64	0	0	71
United Kingdom	106	160	83	57	405
Spain	22	47	7	6	82
India	46	41	1	0	88
Japan	149	378	177	200	904
Communist Bloc	276	457	65	48	846
Soviet Union	168	168	43	20	399
East Germany	30	135	6	13	184
Poland	29	58	7	10	104
Czechoslovakia	25	53	7	2	87
China, Mainland	15	20	1	0	36*
WORLD TOTAL	1.466	2.162	1.077	784	5.489

Source: *Textile Organon,* Vol. 36, No. 6 (June 1965).

* Estimates; included although below minimum limit for inclusion in table.

fibers, including the British terylene (dacron in the U.S.), announced in 1941, and the American orlon in 1950.

Synthetics are often blended with other fibers, natural or man-made, in the textile mills. It is often possible to combine the desirable characteristics of two fibers in one fabric. The polyester fibers (including dacron) are especially used in blends, which means that production of staple exceeds that of filament. The two largest groups of synthetics, the polyamide fibers (including nylon) and the polyacrylic fibers (including orlon), are used mainly unmixed, and chiefly manufactured as filament. Nylon accounts for almost half world production of synthetic fibers.

The synthetic fiber industry is one of the most capital intensive manufacturing industries, highly concentrated in large plants in the most advanced industrial countries. The United States accounts for a declining share—some 40 per cent—of world output, followed by Japan. This country, which dominated the raw silk market in the 1920's, holds a remarkably strong position in man-made fibers. Japan's production of synthetic fibers is on a par with that of the EEC, and far exceeds that of the Communist Bloc.

Production of synthetic fibers is a chemical industry, originated and developed within giant chemical corporations. They have licensees and subsidiaries at home and abroad, thus spreading the heavy research and development costs for new products. In the United States 21 companies produce nylon in 30 plants. The originating company, Du Pont, produces only a small proportion of the total output.

American synthetic fiber plants are concentrated in the eastern states between southern New Hampshire and northern Florida, with a distribution pattern similar to that of the textile industries. The largest concentration of plants is found in Virginia, North and South Carolina, and Tennessee.

SYNTHETIC RUBBER. The first synthetic rubber factory was built during World War I at Leverkusen, Germany. It produced two thousand tons of ersatz rubber which found no peacetime use. In 1936 I. G. Farben put buna rubber on the market. The buna polymer is made from *butadiene*, with sodium (*Na*) as a catalyst. By adding other compounds, alternating with butadiene in the chain, new types of rubber could be made. The most successful was Buna S, to which styrene was added. Buna S is very similar to natural rubber.

The Soviet Union launched an all-out program of synthetic rubber production even earlier than Germany.[108] A pilot plant was built in Leningrad in 1931, and the first industrial plants for production of sovprene were established at Yaroslavl and Voronezh in 1932. In the early Soviet plants butadiene was obtained from ethyl alcohol; plants were located in or near potato-growing districts (I. G. Farben made butadiene from acetylene obtained in its coal chemical works). Almost every organic chemical derivable from coal can also be derived from petroleum, and butadiene is no exception. Germany and the Soviet Union were the only significant producers of synthetic rubber at the outbreak of World War II; neither country suffered any serious rubber shortage during the war.

The Pearl Harbor attack (December, 1941) was a turning point in American synthetic rubber policy. The first American "elastomer" (an abbreviation of "elastic polymer") had been discovered in 1918 by H. L. Fisher, and was named thiokol. It is resistant to the action of oxygen, especially of ozone, making it useful in missiles and rockets, which have to pass through the ozone layer in the upper atmosphere.[109] Du Pont introduced neoprene in 1932, a synthetic preferable to rubber for such uses as gasoline hoses. Shortly before the war Standard Oil developed butyl. These are all special-purpose rubbers. With access to the natural rubber of Southeast Asia, produced at one-third the cost of synthetic rubber, the United States lacked the incentive to develop large-scale production of synthetic general-purpose rubber. Overnight, the Japanese attack made rubber a major strategic raw material. The Federal government initiated a tremendous synthetic rubber program, investing $750 million in new plants, about half of which were located on the Gulf Coast of Texas and Louisiana between Houston and Baton Rouge, the world's leading petrochemical district. The plants, built and operated by leading rubber, chemical, and petroleum companies, pooled patents, personnel, and raw materials. Peak wartime output exceeded 800,000 tons, of which more than

[108] Paul E. Lydolph, *Geography of the U.S.S.R.* (New York: Wiley, 1964), pp. 367 ff.

[109] Thiokol Chemical of Bristol, Pennsylvania, leading producer of this "space-age polymer," ranks among the 250 largest American manufacturing firms.

four-fifths were GR-S (Government Rubber, Styrenetype), the American term for Buna S. When the government decided in 1955 to get out of the rubber business, these plants were sold by "slow auction" to the highest bidders. Many plants are owned jointly by the Big Four rubber companies and leading oil companies. New plants have been added, and production has doubled since the war.

The United States is the world's leading producer of synthetic rubber, followed by the Soviet Union, with less than half the American output. About two-thirds of Soviet rubber is synthetic. Plants are widely scattered; most of the new ones are based on the petrochemical industry (Sumgait, Sterlitamak, Stavropol, Omsk). Canada, also experiencing a synthetic rubber boom during the war, has a larger production than any of the European countries or Japan.

EXPLOSIVES. In 1846 a Swiss chemist, C. F. Schönbein, found by accident that an explosive could be made by treating cellulose with a mixture of nitric acid and sulfuric acid. Schönbein sold his recipe for guncotton, or nitrocellulose, to several governments, but by the early 1860's the guncotton boom was over; guncotton factories blew up as soon as they sprang up. An Italian chemist, A. Sobrero, discovered nitroglycerine in the same year by treating glycerol with the same mixture of acids. The Swedish Nobel brothers made nitroglycerine less dangerous to handle by mixing it with kieselguhr; it could then be hammered or dropped without explosion. Later, nitroglycerine was gelatinized with nitrocellulose. The different types of dynamite tremendously simplified work in mines and in the construction of railroads, highways, subways, tunnels, dams, and canals. When Alfred Nobel died in 1896, he was convinced that war had become impossible because of the destructiveness of dynamite. Peace was one of the five fields in which prizes were to be granted each year out of the fund he left behind.

Modern warfare makes extensive use of other high explosives, including trinitrotoluene (TNT), made by nitrating toluene, a product of the coal tar or petrochemical industry.

The hazard connected with explosive manufacture causes plants to be located well away from built-up areas. The Delaware River has long been the most popular location for manufacture of explosives in the United States, with the center at Wilmington. The great Du Pont chemical empire originated with a powder mill established by a French immigrant family in 1802 on Brandywine Creek, one of the earliest districts of concentrated manufacturing in the country. Wilmington is still the company headquarters, and the Wilmington-Philadelphia area has the world's most pronounced chemical manufacturing landscape. For miles the Delaware River is lined with heavy-chemical plants and oil refineries. In this landscape, however, as well as in the present production program of the Du Pont Company, explosives play a subordinate role. The Newark Bay area in greater New York and the Gulf Coast of Texas also have large plants engaged in production of explosives.

PLASTICS. The term plastics, originally applied to substances that could be formed or shaped by molding (glass, steel, rubber, rosin), is now used in a more restricted sense. Chemists think of plastics as synthetic resins, as distinguished from such natural resins as rosin and shellac. Synthetic fibers, which fit the chemical definition of a plastic, are, for practical purposes, set apart from other branches of the plastic industry. Production of resinous materials is one of the fastest growing chemical industries; in tonnage produced it already exceeds all metals except iron. In cubic footage, the light plastics have an even more impressive position among industrial raw materials. The industry is dominated by chemical giants; in the United States, companies like Allied Chemical, American Cyanamid, Dow, and Du Pont are the leaders. Manufacturing resinous materials into finished products is done mostly by small or medium-sized companies which are widely scattered in the manufacturing regions, much in the way of metal-manufacturing firms. Subcontracting for various engineering industries provides much of the business volume.

In the trade, plastics are grouped into *thermosetting*, which cannot be softened again after cooling, and *thermoplastic*, which may be reshaped by gentle heating. Thermosetting plastics are produced by *condensation* reactions. When the two chemicals used to form the giant molecules unite, water is set free. Thermoplastic resins are *polymerization* products; molecules join other, similar molecules to form a giant molecule or polymer. In addition to synthetic plastics, which derive their carbon atoms from coal or petroleum, there are semi-synthetic plastics, made by modifying vegetable products, like cellulose. The first of these, celluloid, was produced by American inventor J. W. Hyatt in 1869; he was looking for a cheap substitute for ivory in billiard balls. Cellulose acetate, much less apt to burn, came into use just before World War I, and later replaced celluloid in photographic film and many other uses.

Belgian-born American chemist L. H. Baekeland discovered the first thermosetting resin, bakelite, in 1909. This found a ready market in the booming radio industry of the 1920's. British chemists in the 1930's discovered that the gas ethylene, under heat and pressure, would form a long-chain molecule called polythene in England and polyethylene in the United States. This was the first thermoplastic resin. The great breakthrough for synthetic plastics came during World War II, when advanced war technology demanding new materials led to intensified research unparalleled in the history of chemistry. Low specific gravity and salt water resistance were two properties looked for in new substances. Bomber planes soon had some 200 details made in plastics, and battleships had 1,000 details. Research and development has continued in the postwar period. The number of plastics that can be made seems limitless. New products appear daily in the chemical laboratories; only a few reach the production stage.

Output of plastics in the United States, pioneer of large-scale plastic production, has followed a rapidly rising curve, from less than 100,000 tons in 1939, some 300,000 in 1945, 900,000 tons in 1950, to 3.8 million tons in 1963. But the American share of world production has declined as other industrial nations, Japan, West Germany, Britain, and others, have established large plastic industries. The United States now accounts for less than half of world output. The Soviet Union is a latecomer in the plastics industry, but plastics were much emphasized in the seven-year plan. Production data are not known.

World production of plastics will soon exceed ten million tons, and the growth rate is much higher than that of steel, to which plastics are already a serious competitor. For example, automobiles have been constructed in which 80 per cent of the material is synthetic.

CHEMICAL GIANTS OF EUROPE.   Interwar Germany's largest manufacturing corporation, I. G. Farben-industrie, Frankfurt-am-Main, was formed in 1925 through the merger of three large chemical concerns, Badische Anilin- und Soda-Fabrik (BASF), Ludwigshafen, Farbenfabriken Bayer, Leverkusen, and Agfa, Berlin, which had established a "community of interest" (*Interessen Gemeinschaft*, I.G.) in 1904, and other firms that had joined in 1916. In the 1930's I. G. Farben was the world's leading producer of synthetic rubber, synthetic petroleum, nitrates, rayon, aluminum, and magnesium, and a major pillar of Nazi Germany's war potential. After German defeat the Allies resolved to dismantle this industrial empire, but as with the Friedrich Krupp empire, it was not practical politics. In 1952 I. G. Farben was divided into three large corporations, Bayer (including Agfa), Farbwerke Hoechst, Frankfurt-am-Main, and BASF, all of which rank among the 30 largest industrial companies and five largest chemical companies in Europe, with 46,000 to 75,000 employees each.

The chemical empire of I. G. Farben was based largely on coal. It was centered on the Ruhr (coal) and the Rhine (cheap waterway, supplier of industrial water). Major concentrations of chemical manufacturing are found at Ludwigshafen, the Frankfurt area, the Ruhr, and Cologne with Leverkusen. Since the war this industry has increasingly been using petroleum as a basic raw material.

Basel, at the head of barge navigation on the Rhine, is the major center of the Swiss chemical industry. Pharmaceuticals and dyes are major Swiss export items. In France, Alsace is becoming a major area of oil refining and petrochemical industry. The demands made on the Rhine for industrial and municipal water can be met only by re-using the water many times.

The second large complex of chemical industries in prewar Germany, the Bitterfeld-Wittenberg-Leuna area between Berlin and Leipzig, was occupied by Soviet troops and is now part of East Germany. The raw material bases for this area are large deposits of easily mined lignite and the potash of Stassfurt and Mansfeld. The chemical industry is the leading industry in East Germany. In addition to its prewar raw-material base, it now has the oil refinery at Schwedt, the German terminal of the "Friendship line" from the Volga-Ural oilfield.

Imperial Chemical Industries (ICI), the British chemical giant, is the largest in Europe and on a par with America's leading chemical concern, Du Pont. In the interwar years both were surpassed by I. G. Farben. Britain's chemical output is greatly exceeded by that of West Germany.

ICI was formed in 1926 as a response to the I. G. Farben merger the year before. It included four large concerns which were the result of earlier mergers. Some 50 British alkali manufacturers, using the old Leblanc process, had formed United Alkali to meet competition from the cheaper Solvay process, introduced in Britain by Brunner, Mond. The Nobel Dynamite Trust had merged with other explosives manufacturers and formed Explosives Trades. Its monopoly extended throughout the Empire. Like Du Pont, Nobel diversified the company's program to include other chemical products. British Dyestuffs resulted from a government-sponsored merger built around Levinstein, leading British dyestuff manufacturer. The four original concerns, two in alkali and one each in explosives and dyestuffs, later absorbed more than 40 additional companies. ICI has approximately 110 plants in Britain, with large concentrations in the Cheshire-Lancashire area, centered on the Manchester Ship Canal and Merseyside, at Tees-side, in the London and Birmingham regions, and in the Scottish Lowlands, especially Grangemouth.

Three chemical companies rank among the leading French corporations: Rhône-Poulenc, Saint Gobain, and Pechinay. Rhône-Poulenc, formed through a merger in 1928, ranks among the leading chemical groups in Europe, with a multitude of plants in France and abroad. To the public its name is closely associated with drugs (aspirin). Saint Gobain, originally founded as a glass-making company in 1665 during the reign of Louis XIV, became a French pioneer in chemical fertilizers and, later, petrochemicals. Pechiney, of early fame as an aluminum-producing company (since the late 1850's), is now primarily a chemical company.

Postwar expansion has created new manufacturing districts in addition to the old in Paris, Lyon, and the North: the lower Seine, especially the area between Rouen and Le Harve, the Berre district west of Marseille, and Alsace on the Rhine, all closely associated with petroleum refineries, and the Toulouse-Bordeaux area associated with the natural gas of Lacq.

CHAPTER 3 *manufacturing*
in selected regions

The preceding major section had an analytical or thematic approach to the manufacturing geography of the North Atlantic region which has dominated the world's industrial production for so long. The important synthetic or regional dimension of the subject was not emphasized, but the urban-center maps, and selected references in the text, should help throw some light on this aspect of manufactural geography which merges with the field of urban geography.

This short final section is devoted to the manufactural geography of selected regions outside the North Atlantic area: the first non-European nation to achieve the status of a major industrial power, Japan; two large, economically underdeveloped countries, India, and Brazil; and Australia and New Zealand, rich countries of European background, which only recently have emerged as major manufacturing regions and which were long hampered in their industrial development by their small domestic market and by great distances to potential markets for exports.

Japan

Japan, the first major industrial nation of non-European background, has almost 100 million people on a land surface slightly smaller than that of California. Since 1950 the world has witnessed remarkably rapid economic expansion in Japan, which started as a semirural society. Like the Soviet Union, over 40 per cent of Japan's gainfully employed population was in agriculture in the early 1950's. In contrast to the Soviet Union, Japan had an extremely narrow raw-material base for its manufacturing industry. The unprecedented economic growth of Japan in the 15 years after 1950 was boosted by some general conditions (low raw-material prices in the world market after the Suez Crisis, low freight rates, a trend toward coastal location of heavy manufacturing industries, a switch to large bulk carriers) and some specific Japanese conditions (substantial American economic aid, the Korean War, low defense costs, an extremely favorable demographic situation), but basically the postwar developments represent a continuation of prewar trends.

The Industrial Revolution started later in Japan than in the periphery of Europe (e.g., Sweden, Russia, Italy). The Meiji Restoration of 1868 laid the foundation for a modern economy in a nation with strong social organization. First steps on the road to an industrial society were taken with direct government support of large companies, *Zaibatsu.*

In feudal Japan, Edo (now Tokyo) was *de facto* the political capital, Kyoto the cultural and spiritual center, and Osaka the commercial metropolis. To provide access for large ocean liners after the Restoration, an outport for Tokyo was constructed at Yokohama and one for Osaka at Kobe. The first integrated steel plant was completed in 1901 at coastal Yawata, near the large coal fields of northern Kyushu. Japan was in the fortunate position of having an export article, raw silk, much in demand in the world market, especially in the United States. In the 1920's silk accounted for about 40 per cent of Japan's export value. During World War I, a boom period in Japan as in other overseas nations with industrial ambitions, European and American competition was temporarily cut off from the Japanese market and from southern and eastern Asia. After the war Japan had a firm footing in these markets, especially for its cotton textiles. In the 1930's it became obvious that Japan's economic viability was not limited to textiles; postwar economic expansion and exports have been extremely diversified. Steel production exceeded one million tons in the early 1920's, two million in the late 1920's, reached some seven million tons in the early 1940's, and exceeded 40 million tons in 1964, making Japan third largest steel nation in the world (after the United States and the Soviet Union). Japan produced less than one-fourth as much steel as the Soviet union in 1957, but at the end of 1964 produced about one-half as much. Most recent expansion has been in steel made in economically favorable oxygen converters, which should make Japanese steel more competitive in the world market. It should also increase relative demand for iron ore, and lower demand for scrap.

In mountainous Japan, with only 20 per cent of the land surface inhabitable, the coast has been the obvious location for heavy manufacturing plants, most of them located on filled land. No other nation has benefited so from new locational trends in which proximity to markets and tidewater accessibility are dominant. Japan has taken the lead in development and use of mammoth carriers, both for oil and dry cargo. It has led the world in tonnage of ships launched since 1956. Oil tankers of some 275,000 deadweight tons and ore carriers of 100,000 tons are under construction. Economies of scale are substantial in waterborne transport.

Since the beginning of the Industrial Revolution, Japan has had two parallel wage levels, both of which may be represented on the same street. In the 1950's old type labor-intensive shops, employing less than 30 people, paid only 40 per cent of the average wages paid in modern industries with more than 500 employees.[1] This dual wage structure is gradually disap-

[1] Saburo Okita, "Japan's Economic Prospects," *Foreign Affairs,* Vol. 39 (October 1960), 123-31.

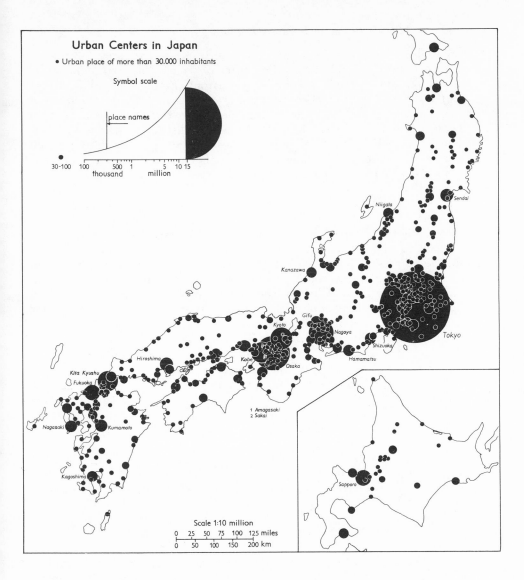

Urban Centers in Japan

• Urban place of more than 30.000 inhabitants

Symbol scale

place names

30-100 100   500 1   5 10 15
      thousand million

Niigata
Sendai
Kanazawa
Gifu
Kyoto
Nagoya
Shizuoka
Hiroshima
Kobe
Hamamatsu
Osaka
Tokyo
Kita Kyushu
Fukuoka
1 Amagasaki
2 Sakai
Nagasaki
Kumamoto
Kagoshima
Sapporo

Scale 1:10 million
0   25   50   75   100 125 miles
0   50   100   150   200 km

pearing as a result of low birth rates and rapid economic expansion.

A duality can also be discerned in Japanese exports. Labor-intensive products, such as ships, cameras, radios, television sets, toys, and clothes are sold to high-income countries, and capital-intensive products, such as steel, chemical fertilizer, and rayon, to low-income markets. Since the rich nations are expanding faster than the poor ones, they are crucial to continued economic expansion in Japan.

The Manufacturing Belt of Japan extends in an 800 mile long zone from Tokyo Bay westward through the Inland Sea to northern Kyushu.[2] The largest area of lowland in Japan, the Kanto plain, contains the largest concentration of manufacturing employment, some 23 per cent, centered

---

[2] Glenn T. Trewartha, *Japan* (Madison: University of Wisconsin, 1965). For a detailed map and an annotated bibliography of Japan's manufacturing industry, see John H. Thompson and Michihiro Miyazaki, "A Map of Japan's Manufacturing," *Geographical Review*, Vol. 49 (January 1959), 1-17.

on Keihin, the contiguous cities of Tokyo, Kawasaki, and Yokohama. Heavy industries tend to hug the shores of Tokyo Bay, particularly the Kawasaki and northern Yokohama waterfront. Filling of land in Tokyo Bay was begun in 1913. It contributed greatly to the later development of heavy industry, but for a long time the Tokyo region was known as a center of light industry. The large industrial district of Kawasaki-Yokohama includes such typical port industries as steel mills, shipyards, oil refineries, thermoelectric power plants, chemical industries, and flour mills. The Tokyo conurbation approaches New York in population, and is larger than London.

The second largest manufacturing zone, Keihanshin, with 20 per cent of Japan's manufacturing employment, has its core in Hanshin, the coastal conurbation encompassing the cities of Osaka and Kobe, each with a population of over one million. Osaka, once the most aggressive commercial center in Japan, took a very active part in the early industrial transformation of the country, and soon became known as the "Manchester of the East." Chukyo, the region around Nagoya, is the third largest manufacturing zone (13 per cent). Manufacturing is of a greater relative importance in Keihanshin and Chukyo than in Kanto.

The shores of the Inland Sea, or Setouchi, account for some 7 per cent of Japan's manufacturing employment, followed by the million conurbation Kita Kyushu, which includes Yawata and four other former coastal cities north of the northern Kyushu coal fields (3 per cent). Unfavorable geological conditions make the Japanese coal industry unprofitable; heavy industry has been attracted by other factors in recent decades, primarily reclaimed land for industrial sites and deep water for vessels carrying raw materials from overseas.

The coastal rims of the five chief manufacturing districts, including the elongated Setouchi industrial area, have attracted, in addition to steel works and heavy engineering works already mentioned, a rapidly increasing capacity of oil refineries, petrochemical works, and large thermoelectric plants. Light manufacturing is being pushed inland, and priority given to heavy industries for the scarce coastal sites that can be created by fill.

Traditionally, Japan has depended on a large number of small run-of-river hydroelectric plants, chiefly located in the mountains of central Honshu, with a relatively large standby capacity of coal-fired thermal plants in the port cities. But tremendous postwar increase in power demand, some 12 per cent a year between 1952 and 1963, could not be met with hydroelectric power alone. Changed cost relations between thermal and hydro in favor of thermal have also contributed to the new Japanese policy of giving priority to large thermoelectric plants. In 1963 thermal plants accounted for 15 million kilowatts and hydro plants for 14 million. The largest thermal plants exceed one million kilowatts, and some 20 plants exceed 400,000 kw.[3] Fuel oil is used increasingly in the new thermal plants located near the market; as in other countries, the thermal plant is often adjacent to an oil refinery, resulting in heat economies.

[3] John D. Eyre, "Japan's Electric-power Supply," *Geographical Review*, Vol. 55 (October 1965), 546-62.

Another effect of Japan's switch to petroleum and electricity is decrease in the demand for fuel and charcoal, which makes available more wood for the pulp industry. Japan already produces more chemical pulp than the world's largest forest nation, the Soviet Union.

Australia and New Zealand

Through their strong economic ties with their antipodian mother country, Australia and New Zealand have long been exceptions to most geographic generalizations about international economic relations. Until the recent reorientation of Australia's foreign trade toward Asia, especially Japan, Britain was Australia's dominant trade partner. A small farm population engaged in extremely extensive farming turned out products that could stand freight costs to Britain and, albeit with some Commonwealth preference, compete on the British market, while British industrial products were imported. Although Australian exports are still derived from ranch and mine more than those of any other industrial nation, the population of Australia is more urbanized and more concentrated in metropolitan cities than that of any other major country.[4]

Manufacturing is not new to Australia and New Zealand. A wide range of manufacturing activity was in operation in these distant lands of European settlement from earliest times, protected by high freight costs from Europe and by tariffs. Plants were small and worked for a local market, centered on a coastal city which had frequent connections with Europe. These areas were independent of each other. Not even small New Zealand forms a national market; there is no national newspaper, but 43 daily papers, each with a small area of circulation.[5] The introduction of refrigerated ships in the early 1880's created export industries, packing plants, and dairies, located with easy access to liner ports.

Modern Australia has a diversified manufacturing industry ranging from basic industries (iron and steel, petroleum refineries, chemicals) to consumer goods industries, many established as branch plants by large European and American concerns. With its rapidly growing population and economy, Australia has become an attractive location for such plants. The government of Australia, like that of Brazil, has used both the carrot and the stick to induce industrial expansion; a foreign assembly plant soon finds it advantageous to manufacture components and parts, or buy them from Australian subcontractors. The basic policy of Australia is to transform the country into a major industrial power.

Australia is a low-cost producer of steel. Production is concentrated in one organization, the vertically integrated Broken Hill Proprietary Com-

[4] Some 80 per cent of the population live in towns of one thousand or more people, and 55 per cent live in the six capital cities. G. J. R. Linge, "The 'Normal' Requirements Method for Analyzing Future Employment Structures, With Special Reference to Australian Towns," *Papers and Proceedings of the First Far Eastern Conference of the Regional Science Association*, Tokyo, 1963.

[5] G. J. R. Linge, "The Concentration and Dispersion of Manufacturing in New Zealand," *Economic Geography*, Vol. 36 (October 1960), 326-343; G. J. Burridge, "The Location of Meat Freezing Works in New Zealand," *New Zealand Geographer*, Vol. 20 (January 1964), 43-59; Alex Hunter, ed., *The Economics of Australian Industry* (Melbourne: Melbourne Univ., 1963).

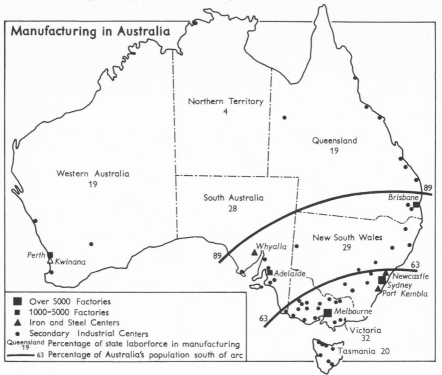

Manufacturing in Australia

Northern Territory
4

Queensland
19

Western Australia
19

South Australia
28

89

Brisbane

New South Wales
29

Whyalla

63

Perth △Kwinana

89

Adelaide

Newcastle
Sydney
Port Kembla

63

Melbourne

Victoria
32

Tasmania 20

■ Over 5000 Factories
■ 1000–5000 Factories
▲ Iron and Steel Centers
• Secondary Industrial Centers
Queensland Percentage of state laborforce in manufacturing
19
——— 63 Percentage of Australia's population south of arc

Australia's population and economic activity are primarily concentrated in its southeastern corner. Sydney and Melbourne each have a population of over two million. Melbourne, Australia's chief financial and corporate headquarters center, is growing faster than Sydney and is expected to become the nation's largest city. The large postwar influx of Europeans, both from Britain and the Continent, has been directed chiefly toward these two metropolitan areas. Large U.S. and European concerns centered in Melbourne include GM-Holden, Ford, Alcoa, American Cyanamide, and Volkswagen. (From Department of National Development, The Structure and Capacity of Australian Manufacturing Industries, *Melbourne, 1952, p. viii.)*

pany (BHP), which, in spite of low domestic steel prices, financed a doubling of its ingot production in the decade before 1965. BHP produces its own iron ore, coal, and limestone, owns a fleet of ore carriers, and operates integrated steel works at the coal fields and at one ore shipping port. BHP was formed in 1885 to develop the rich silver-lead deposit at Broken Hill. A smelter was built at Port Pirie. In 1911 BHP began iron-and-steel production at Newcastle, north of Sydney (coal field near the leading market), shipping iron ore from the Middleback ranges through the port of Whyalla. Newcastle was the leading steel center of Australia until recently surpassed by another coal town, Port Kembla, south of Sydney.[6] Whyalla, the ore shipping port, also has an integrated iron and steel works. A fourth works is projected for the oil refinery suburb of

    [6] Allen K. Philbrick, *This Human World* (New York: Wiley, 1963), pp. 238 ff; John N. H. Britton, "The Transport Functions of the Port of Kembla," *Economic Geography,* Vol. 38 (October 1962), 347-58; Anon., "Australian Iron Ore—Great Prospects and Some Problems," *Steel Review,* 41 (January 1966), 21-29.

Kwinana, south of Perth in Western Australia. The recent discovery of tremendous deposits of rich iron ore in Western Australia, to be developed by, among others, several foreign ore companies which have long-term contracts with Japanese steel corporations, will establish Australia as a major iron ore supplier on the world market. Australia will be supplying its major competitor in the steel markets of Asia with cheap iron ore.

India

The influence of the First Industrial Revolution on daily life in India was limited. Some 70 per cent of the gainfully employed population is still engaged in agriculture and ancillary industries. Some 20 million people are active in manufacturing, but only 4.5 million are in modern factories, including mines (see maps). Most of the people listed under manufacturing are in small-scale industry, but these workshops are different from small factories in industrial nations, where small-scale industry is an integrated part of a highly efficient system.[7] The small Indian workshops, which have their counterparts in all underdeveloped countries, are left over from the pre-industrial period. For instance, Kay's flying shuttle, invented in 1733, is still unknown to a large number of India's 10 million handloom weavers.[8] Caught in the vicious circle of rapidly growing population, poor farming practices, starvation or malnutrition, unemployment, and low purchasing power, India has restricted the production of cotton cloth and some other goods from large factories; other factory-made products, competing with handicraft articles, are being taxed.

Only a minor part of India's factory capacity is the fruit of indigenous enterprise and capital. Factories are still owned and managed to a large extent by foreigners, although the government accounts for an increasing share of manufacturing investments. The modern textile industry, cotton and jute, was first established in the two ports shipping the fiber, Bombay and Calcutta. The cotton industry, largely working for the domestic market, gradually spread into the hinterland of Bombay, while Calcutta and Hooghlyside had a monopoly on jute factories, oriented to an overseas market. The first cotton mill was built at Bombay in 1854; by 1885 there were almost 50 textile factories with over 30,000 workers. In cotton, India's leading manufacturing industry with sizeable net exports, the Bombay-Ahmedabad region is supreme. The first jute factory was established by Scots from Dundee in 1855, and now mills are strung out along the Hooghly, 30 miles upriver and 16 miles downriver from Calcutta.[9] By

[7] Small, highly mechanized, and specialized factories play a greater role in industrial, free market economies than is usually understood in the academic community. The small owner-managed factory is more flexible than the bureaucratic large organization, which usually prefers to buy a sizable part of its components and details from outside, usually from small firms. The small firm also produces consumer goods, sold to wholesale companies. In either case the small firm enjoys all the economies of scale and avoids the diseconomies of bigness.

[8] D. W. Fryer, *World Economic Development* (New York: McGraw-Hill, 1965), p. 258. Also, D. W. Fryer, "The Development of Cottage and Small Scale Industries in Malaya and in South-East Asia," in *Studies in the Geography of South-East Asia* (London: Philip, 1964), pp. 92-98.

[9] William Kirk, "The Cotton and Jute Industries of India," *The Scottish Geographical Magazine* (1956), 38 ff.; W. Kirk, "The Influence of Port-hinterland Controls on the Location of the Cotton and Jute Manufacturing Industries of India," *Proceedings,* Seventeenth International Congress, International Geographical Union (Washington, D.C.: 1952), pp. 633-38.

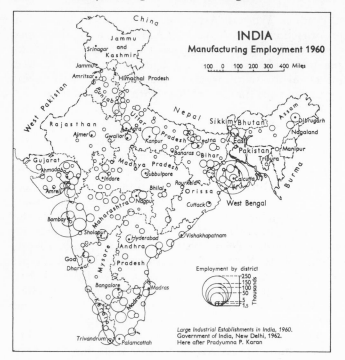

INDIA
Manufacturing Employment 1960

100   0   100 200 300 400 Miles

Employment by district

Large Industrial Establishments in India, 1960.
Government of India, New Delhi, 1962.
Here after Pradyumna P. Karan

1921, a third of India's factory workers were in the tremendous Hooghly-side conurbation. Dundee was outstripped as a jute manufacturing center by 1910. Jute manufactures have long been India's leading export, but the industry is on the decline; in 1960 it was a poor fourth after cotton, food, and engineering. It suffered from partition of the subcontinent in 1947, which left raw jute cultivation in East Pakistan and jute factories in India. The industry has also run into adverse market conditions as products formerly shipped in jute sacks are increasingly shipped in bulk or in competing materials, e.g., kraft paper. The Calcutta-Hooghlyside region, leading manufacturing district of India in 1950, was the only major district registering a decline in factory employment in the 1950's, caused by a loss of 68,000 jobs in the jute industry. The Bombay-Poona district had almost caught up with Calcutta-Hooghlyside factory employment in 1960.[10]

The first successful establishment of a modern iron-and-steel industry in India dates back to the years immediately before World War I, when Jamshedji Tata built an integrated steel works at Jamshedpur, an exceptionally favorable location between the Damodar coking coal and the Orissa haematite ore, and with the largest single market of India, the Calcutta-Hooghlyside area, only 150 miles away. During its first critical years, this works enjoyed a protected market as a result of World War I. With its low assembly costs for raw materials, it exported considerable pig iron in the interwar years, especially to Japan. Tata Iron and Steel is the

[10] P. P. Karan and W. M. Jenkins, Jr., "Geography of Manufacturing in India," *Economic Geography*, Vol. 35 (July 1959), 269-78; P. P. Karan, "Changes in Indian Industrial Location," *Annals*, Association of American Geographers, Vol. 54 (September 1964), 336-54.

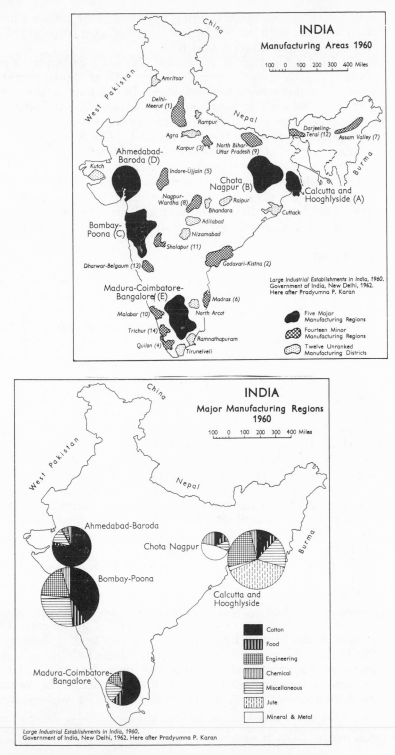

INDIA
Manufacturing Areas 1960

100 0 100 200 300 400 Miles

China
West Pakistan
Nepal
Burma

Amritsar
Delhi-Meerut (1)
Rampur
Agra
Kanpur (3)
North Bihar-Uttar Pradesh (9)
Darjeeling-Terai (12)
Assam Valley (7)
Ahmedabad-Baroda (D)
Kutch
Indore-Ujjain (5)
Chota Nagpur (B)
Calcutta and Hooghlyside (A)
Nagpur-Wardha (8)
Raipur
Bhandara
Bombay-Poona (C)
Adilabad
Cuttack
Nizamabad
Sholapur (11)
Godavari-Kistna (2)
Dharwar-Belgaum (13)
Madura-Coimbatore-Bangalore (E)
Madras (6)
Malabar (10)
North Arcot
Trichur (14)
Ramnathapuram
Quilon (4)
Tirunelveli

Large Industrial Establishments in India, 1960.
Government of India, New Delhi, 1962.
Here after Pradyumna P. Karan

Five Major Manufacturing Regions
Fourteen Minor Manufacturing Regions
Twelve Unranked Manufacturing Districts

INDIA
Major Manufacturing Regions
1960

100 0 100 200 300 400 Miles

China
West Pakistan
Nepal
Burma

Ahmedabad-Baroda
Chota Nagpur
Bombay-Poona
Calcutta and Hooghlyside
Madura-Coimbatore-Bangalore

Cotton
Food
Engineering
Chemical
Miscellaneous
Jute
Mineral & Metal

Large Industrial Establishments in India, 1960.
Government of India, New Delhi, 1962. Here after Pradyumna P. Karan

only autochthonous manufacturing company of the tropics which is comparable in size with the 500 largest manufacturing corporations of Anglo-America, Western Europe, and Japan.[11]

After a long period of stagnation, India's iron-and-steel production climbed rapidly with the completion by 1960 of three integrated works, all of about one million ton capacity: a British-built works at Durgapur, a West German one at Rourkela, and a Soviet plant at Bhilai.

Heavy engineering is highly oriented to the Calcutta-Hooghlyside metropolitan district and the steel-producing Chota Nagpur area of Bihar. Bombay, center of electrical engineering, textile machinery, and automobiles, is a poor second in the engineering industries.

The much needed fertilizer industry is given priority in India's new economic plan; only substantially increased yields can widen the inadequate food basis of India's teeming millions. The other prerequisite for national survival, family planning, is also stressed in the plan.

Brazil

Roughly half of South America and one-third of Latin America by population, Brazil ranks first among Latin American nations in industrial production. Food and textile industries were developed early, and since World War II Brazil has seen a rapid widening of its manufacturing base, including integrated steel mills and a variety of engineering industries, oil refineries, and petrochemical plants.

The modern industry is almost exclusively concentrated in the small economic heartland of Brazil, the São Paulo-Rio de Janeiro-Belo Horizonte triangle. Brazil has vast deposits of iron ore in or near the northern part of the triangle but, like other countries of Latin America, it is poor in coking coal. The small iron works existing before World War II were based on charcoal produced from fast-growing eucalyptus stands. Before World War I, when blast furnaces were economically built near iron ore deposits in many parts of the world, plans were made for large-scale exploitation by European interests of the Minas Gerais ore fields, shipping European coal to Brazil and taking pig iron as return cargo. These plans did not materialize until after World War II, and then in the form of iron ore exports by a government company. The economy of continuous process in steel making and the efficiency of modern bulk transportation had made it uneconomic to separate Europe's blast furnaces from its steel mills.

The government steel mill at Volta Redonda, built with American aid during World War II, has subsequently been enlarged in stages to the present 1.7 million ton capacity, to be doubled in the early 1970's. It is located on the Paraíba River between the two leading domestic markets, São Paulo and Rio de Janeiro. Ore is railed from Lafaiete in Minas Gerais. Imported American coal is mixed with poor domestic coal from Santa Catarina, received by ship through Rio de Janeiro. The location of the plant, contemporary with the Fontana mill at Los Angeles, is influenced

[11] The great Parsee house of Tata has had some share in almost all modern economic development in India. Two-thirds of the Parsees, a small minority group of less than 100,000, live in Bombay, where they occupy a key position in the economy.

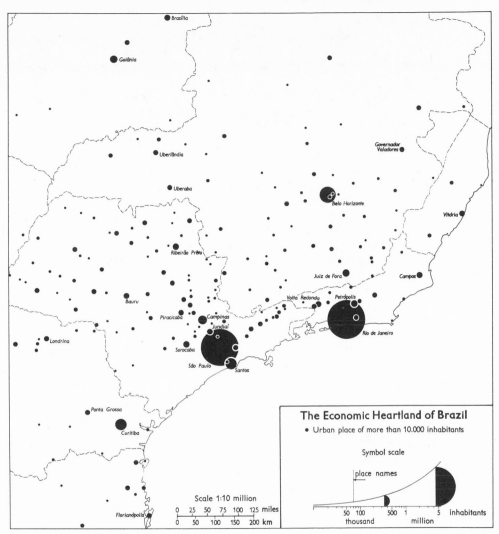

The Economic Heartland of Brazil

• Urban place of more than 10.000 inhabitants

Symbol scale

place names

Scale 1:10 million

by similar strategic thinking. It is unfavorable for exports and for shipping products to other parts of Brazil.

A second large, integrated steel mill was started in 1962 at Ipatinga, near Belo Horizonte. It has a capacity of 0.5 million tons. Plans exist for expansion to 2.0 million tons at the USIMINAS works.

The first stage of Brazil's third large steel mill, located at the foot of the Serra do Mar (Piacaguera) near Cubatão, some ten miles from Santos, was completed in 1963. From 0.5 million tons, the COSIPA works will eventually be expanded to 2.0 million tons. All raw materials will be assembled on millsite by ship. This coastal works enjoys proximity to a huge hydroelectric power plant, a large oil refinery, and Brazil's leading general cargo port. It should have an excellent location for assembling raw materials (including electricity and fuel oil), and for supplying not only São Paulo and other parts of the domestic market but also for exporting steel.

Most Brazilian engineering industry is located in greater São Paulo, turning out cars, trucks, buses, railroad cars, and consumer durables. Many plants were built by European and American firms as assembly plants, later turned into producing units after strong government prodding.

The growth of São Paulo, located on a sparsely populated plateau 2,500 feet above sea level, must be seen against its geographic location. In the seventeenth century and later it was the point of departure of *bandeirantes* in search of Indian slaves, gold, and diamonds over much of southern Brazil, but the city remained small. In 1870 it had only 25,000 inhabitants. Its second birth came with the spread of coffee cultivation into the traffic hinterland of São Paulo and the construction of railways which fanned out from the city. The tremendous cost of constructing a railway from the coastal plain to the plateau gave São Paulo-Santos a monopoly on coffee exports from the leading coffee region of Brazil. São Paulo became the capital of the *fazendeiros*, many of whom made investments in banks, railways, and textile factories and other manufacturing plants.[12] São Paulo became a growth point, one of the world's fastest growing cities, which attracted a diversified manufacturing industry.

Although Brazil is one of the world's leading tropical countries, its economic heartland can hardly be seen as a "typical" growth area in the tropics. São Paulo is located on a plateau under the Tropic of Capricorn, its population is largely Mediterranean, primarily Italian, in origin, and its economy has been sustained by one of the leading commodity flows in world trade.

[12] Pierre Monbeig, *La croissance de la ville de São Paulo* (Grenoble: Institut et revue de géographie alpine, 1953); P. Monbeig, *Pionniers et Planteurs de São Paulo* (Paris: Cahiers de la Fondation Nationale des Sciences Politiques, no. 28, 1952); Richard P. Momsen, Jr., *Routes Over the Serra do Mar* (Muncie, Indiana: Ball State Univ., 1964).

author index

general index